Pittsburgh Series in Composition, Literacy, and Culture

Eating
on the
Street

Teaching Literacy in a
Multicultural Society

David Schaafsma

UNIVERSITY OF PITTSBURGH PRESS

Pittsburgh and London

Published by the University of Pittsburgh Press, Pittsburgh, Pa. 15260
Copyright © 1993, University of Pittsburgh Press
All rights reserved
Manufactured in the United States of America
Printed on acid-free paper

Library of Congress Cataloging-in-Publication Data

Schaafsma, David, 1953–
    Eating on the street : teaching literacy in a multicultural
society / David William Schaafsma.
        p.   cm. — (Pittsburgh series in composition, literacy, and
culture)
    Includes bibliographical references (p.) and index.
    ISBN 0-8229-3758-1
    1. English language—Composition and exercises—Study and teaching
(Elementary)—Michigan—Detroit.   2. Afro-American children—
Education—Michigan—Detroit.   3. Literacy—Michigan—Detroit.
4. Intercultural education—Michigan—Detroit.   I. Title.
II. Series.
LB1576.S316   1993
372.6'23—dc20   93-10230
                                                                              CIP

A CIP catalogue record for this book is available from the British Library.
Eurospan, London

For my parents,
Arnold and Ruth Schaafsma

History is not the past, but a map of the past drawn from a particular point of view to be useful to the modern traveler.

—*Henry Glassie*

CONTENTS

FOREWORD

In his rich book, *Thinking Across the American Grain: Ideology, Intellect, and the New Pragmatism* (Chicago, 1992), a book in search of grounded and native perspectives on experience, Giles Gunn says this about some imperatives for seeing and understanding:

> Unless there is ... reciprocal modification of each category by its opposite, of "self" by "other" and of "other" by "self," there can be no increase in self-knowledge, no challenge to prior conceptions, no opportunity for misunderstanding, no risk of personal confusion and disruption, no possibilities that meaning will be deformed, no danger that understandings will prove incommensurable. (11)

Few of us risk contacts with others that will trouble us, that will unsettle our customary ways of seeing and understanding. Untroubled perspectives on the world, clear and clean ones, comfort us, but they don't help us see much that is there; neither do they help us see ourselves in our relations to others. "Unfortunately," Gunn says, "things aren't that simple."

They aren't on the streets of the Cass Corridor in Detroit; they aren't in the crowded rooms and dangerous hallways of the Jeffries Homes; they aren't in the noisy classrooms of the Dewey Center. David Schaafsma has walked those streets, hand in hand with kids; he has talked with kids and adults in rooms in the "projects," has listened to kids and their teachers in classrooms separated only by courage and commitment from the hazards of the Cass Corridor. Schaafsma has been there, and in this book he takes us there if we have courage to open ourselves to others, to risk confusion and disruption, to deform the meanings that all too often comfort those of us who think we know but do not walk these streets.

For all of the commitment and goodwill of those who employ them, statistics and profiles can blur the vision of those who would see and understand urban problems and urban realities. It does help us to know how many kids are poor, how many come from backgrounds troubled by chemical abuse and domestic violence, how many are marginally housed, maybe homeless. It helps us too to know the characteristics such kids have in common. But educators of urban children need a finer perspective as well, a sharp eye for particularities, if they are to help those children learn. Teachers, and teacher-researchers who work with them in urban classrooms, must have a particularly sharp eye to see what is promising and hopeful in the actions of children who fit less hopeful profiles. Schaafsma has eyes for signs of promise and hope; he has ears attuned to the melodies of single voices singing hopeful songs—the voices of the kids he comes to care about, the voices of teachers whom he comes to admire for their capacity to see, hear, and to act. We meet these children and these teachers, one at a time, in this book.

Because Schaafsma's particular concern is for literacy, we meet these children and their teachers, other adults in the community too, through what they write as well as what he writes about them. This book is rich in its citations for those of us who wish to hear the echoes of real voices as we read—the voices of real people living complicated lives. The pedagogy Schaafsma explores, the one he recommends for urban children, is a pedagogy of voice—one that encourages each student to become, to borrow M. M. Bakhtin's term, a "speaking person." But because Schaafsma knows, as Bakhtin did, that all voices resonate with the echoes of other voices—that each speaking person speaks others' voices, he would have students learn to hear others in what they are saying, learn that they are never alone in speaking out. Dora learns this when she tells a story as Rose Bell might tell it. Struggling to recount a story in this way, Dora sees some of the realities of the lives lived in the Cass Corridor, but she also glimpses possibilities for change of those realities as she speaks Rose Bell's courage. The pedagogy Schaafsma offers us is social in its construction, one worked out in conversations and interactions with other teachers and with students. It is social and communal in its implications as well, and ultimately ethical—ultimately political—in its thrust and aims.

For Schaafsma, the ethical is communal and political, and commitments must always be made subject to revision when encounters with others become unsettling to prior notions of self and community. Schaafsma's is a story of such encounters, and he has learned lessons from them that might be especially useful in this time of strong commitments and monologic discourses when too few people learn to listen to others. This from his own preface:

I hope in the process of telling my story that my own commitments to social and educational change—informed by my colleagues' stories—will be clear. But I also think that our stories may indicate the need to reconsider our unwavering dedication to those commitments in the process of discovering "solutions" to particular problems. Hearing the voices of my colleagues helps me work against the authoritarianism of certain kinds of educational discourse, whether those are "progressive" or otherwise.

So should it help us all, for in some sense all of us, in these times, are eating on the street. We are when we are teachers teaching in neighborhoods in which we do not in all ways live; we are especially so when we are researchers seeking to understand how learners learn and teachers teach in the complex neighborhoods of urban America, for few of us live there. "The stories of eating on the street that Dora and I tell," Schaafsma writes earlier in his preface, "are like the histories of Detroit I encountered, multiple, conflicting, and necessarily limited perspectives on events." As researchers, maybe we should celebrate the fact that our own perspectives are and can only ever be "multiple, conflicting, and necessarily limited." Maybe that awareness is what we need to come to any real understanding of what it is we see or think we see in order to undergo the "reciprocal modification of... 'self' by 'other' and of 'other' by 'self'" that Gunn finds necessary both for self-knowledge and for knowledge of others, as if the two could ever be separated. And just maybe, as Schaafsma urges, narrative is the most valuable means we have, as researchers, to capture the particularities of situated learning and the struggles of kids caught in situations not always of their own making.

Uses of narratives, like Schaafsma's uses, may well be a means toward a modesty of claims of the kind he urges—a way to avoid "unwavering dedication" to unquestioned commitments when we speak as teachers, as researchers, as citizens. Stories can be, as Schaafsma tells us citing Milan Kundera, more than mere, can always reveal "the wisdom of uncertainty." He tells "a story as an experiment in the narrativizing of theory, to illustrate the ways in which story embodies theory in provisional ways." I would urge, in these times, that theory too be seen as always provisional, maybe merely mere. One advantage of American pragmatism as theory, Gunn tells us, is that it modestly claims, that it always "assumes that we can never get beyond stories, narrative, illusions, because the 'analytic' or critical instrumentalities through which we break their spell are no less figurative than the material of which they are composed and the strategies by which they hold us so destructively in their thrall" (15). For other reasons, too, we should not wish to get beyond stories or get beyond them too quickly: In the stories Schaafsma offers us are the particularities of the lived lives of students and of teachers as these lives are lived and have been shaped in the classrooms and on the streets of Detroit; in these stories, if we can read them empathetically and with understanding, there are invitations to us to be something more than "other" to these children and their teachers. But the invitations are complicated ones and far from easy to read.

There is a feast in store for those of us who will eat on the street in Detroit with these children.

Jay Robinson
University of Michigan

PREFACE

The Dewey Center Community Writing Project is a community-based, collaboratively designed summer writing program in Detroit's inner city. During its first summer—three weeks in June and July 1989—thirty fifth-, sixth-, and seventh-grade students from Detroit's Cass Corridor worked with seven teachers from the University of Michigan and the Detroit Public Schools and desktop published their writing in *Corridors: Stories from Inner City Detroit.* I was one of those seven teachers.

Having worked in similar programs for several years, I was interested in the ways students, when given the opportunity, seemed to take "authority" over their own learning. I had been encouraged by such writers as Cy Knoblauch and Lil Brannon to facilitate that process when responding to student texts. Paolo Freire, writing about how dialogue with students is the basis for praxis, similarly encouraged me to explore ways to create conditions so that students might "empower" themselves. Maxine Greene (1978), too, gave me encouragement: "Learning must be a process of discovery and recovery in response to worthwhile questions rising out of conscious life in concrete situations" (19). Armed with "progressive" notions such as these, I sought with teachers and their students to construct a writing program that would focus on students' needs and their ways of learning. In this program, as in others in which I had worked, students explored their community: they visited local sites, interviewed residents, and wrote about their experiences.[1] *Corridors* is available through The Center for Educational Improvement through Collaboration, University of Michigan, 2018 School of Education Building, Ann Arbor, Michigan 48103.

I was not surprised that many students, given the opportunity to choose the content and form of their writing, chose to write stories.[2] I knew from my own experience that composing stories is one of the most fundamental ways we make sense of things. I read what Jerome Bruner wrote, that stories are "a way of exploring possible worlds out of the context of immediate need" (Bruner 1986, 123), with a sense of confirmation. I spent much time thinking about the relationship between stories and learning for students, and I read what others like Bruner had said to know more. I wrote about stories being a means for students' personal inquiry "in response to worthwhile questions arising out of conscious life in concrete situations," because I knew they had been for me. But I also began to think of storytelling as a way we learn from each other. The writings of Mikhail Bakhtin and others helped me recognize the social nature of learning, and Bakhtin in particular helped me to explore the relationship between storytelling and learning. I knew from my own experience that when storytellers tell stories to each other they engage in more than personal exploration: they build a community.

The students in the Dewey Center Community Writing Project seemed to be telling such community-building stories, and I paid close attention to the process, hoping to further examine the relationship between the social processes of storytelling and learning.

In the mornings the teachers met with the students, but in the afternoons the teachers discussed the morning's work and planned the next day. Early on in the program, I noticed that it was not just the students who told stories in order to learn. Each day, during the teachers' meetings, we told stories about students and their writing. There were seven of us: three Detroit public school teachers with extensive experience teaching in Detroit's inner city—Jeanetta Cotman, Debi Goodman, and Toby Curry—and four University of Michigan teachers—Dana Davidson, who had grown up in Detroit and just completed her student teaching there; Susan Harris, who had extensive experience teaching in Southern inner cities; and George Cooper and I, veteran teachers with no experience teaching in Detroit or the inner city. Each day, during the teachers' meetings, we teachers told stories about students and their writing.

On the second Tuesday of the project, I began to consider writing about the storytelling we teachers were doing together. Every day I had been writing to several interested University of Michigan readers via electronic mail about my experiences in the project. Each day I seemed to talk more about my work with teachers and the way we were building our community—*not* into consensus—through the conflicts we negotiated. Some readers of my electronic journal confirmed what I had begun to believe: that I could raise—if not resolve—important social, political, and ethical issues about the teaching of literacy through my writing about the way teachers seemed to learn from each other in the program. In my journal each day I shared what seemed like an explosion of stories about our teaching and learning community from and about community members, students, and teachers. Sometimes my stories chronicled joyful moments, such as the time when Dora first shared her story, "961-BABY," in her writing workshop; sometimes my stories were about conflicts we were having, such as the time when Jeanetta insisted we confront students about eating on the street. I shared the stories I observed or heard from others, accounts of the thrill of seeing our students document their first train trip in their journals, or about the last week, when even the least serious students seemed to be struck with the urgency of book production, and all seemed to be writing with an intensity we had not yet seen from them as a group.

I was struck by the fact that we were learning from each other through the stories we as teachers told each other. How different this was from most education classes or inservice seminars on particular aspects of teaching, which often seem so cut off from what really goes on in public school classrooms and students' lives. Surely issues of authority in the process of learning are no less crucial for teachers than for students. The Dewey Center teachers were engaged in collaborative teaching and learning, and we used that opportunity to focus—through the stories we told each other about the students we cared so much about—on the teaching of literacy. Through the daily stories we told, we were revealing our learning theories, and, upon hearing others' accounts, we reshaped those theories. We seemed to be building a curriculum through storytelling, and I set out to explore this process.

I told stories in my public journal about how we as a group of teachers seemed to be "constructing" our students through the anecdotal sharing we did among ourselves in the afternoons. I noted how variously we each represented Dora, for instance, sometimes as a "misfit" when she disrupted others during free writing time, and sometimes as a "responsible" contributor to our program as a member of the publication committee. One teacher reported her "fooling around outside" near the swings with her cousin when she was supposed to be with a writing workshop group on the same day that another teacher praised her for having written so much in her journal and making great progress on her story. Some were impatient with her, some volunteered to work with her. Some teachers, based on stories about similar students they had worked with, suggested "leaving her alone" to progress at her own pace; others, who knew her and shared stories of working with her in the past, suggested we seriously discuss with her her responsibility as a member of a writing program; others suggested we give her encouragement and guidance.

I saw the other students in the program being talked about in similarly various ways. Our stories about students revealed our learning theories, and we reshaped those theories to some extent as we heard each others' stories. Our daily curriculum—the activities we planned, the ways of working with particular students—was accomplished in terms of our constantly changing stories about our students.

In part because I knew we differed about the best ways to work with our students, I was increasingly aware that the stories I was sharing through my public journal had become *my* stories, or the materials of my story. My story was one of many possible versions of the program, told in my voice, a voice I recognized as echoing other perspectives, other voices. It became apparent to me that my inquiry should also investigate representation itself as a rhetorical issue with political and ethical consequences. For instance, how could I, as a white male university researcher, presume to represent a classroom of inner-city students or teachers, or an individual inner-city girl like Dora, and speak for them, for her? How could I, with comparatively little experience in urban settings, tell the story of collaborative teaching in Detroit's inner city for those public school teachers with whom I had worked? I considered how I could tell a story in such a way that it would preserve various voices in my (our) research process.

In this book I tell a story. The story focuses on one of many conflicts that arose during the program: Should teachers confront poor black children about eating on the street, a conflict related to broader issues of authority and cultural difference?[3] My story proceeds through the successive telling of each teacher's story—and later, some students' stories—told weeks or months after the program was over, in private, informal (though audiotaped) conversations with me. My purpose in telling these stories is, in part, to demonstrate the "constructed understanding of the constructed native's constructed point of view" (Geertz 1973, 8) from many teachers' perspectives. I am celebrating, I hope, the varied voices of teachers—and some students—because their voices in my story help preserve some sense of the complexity of their lives, and the complexity of their experiences with literacy learning in the inner city.

In part I tell a story as an experiment in the narrativizing of theory to illustrate the ways in which story embodies theory in provisional ways, in part to reflect what Milan Kundera says all stories necessarily reveal: "the wisdom of uncertainty" (7). The focus of these stories—a conflict about eating on the street—might at first seem rather peripheral to teaching literacy, but when we listen to teachers tell their stories about the conflict, we can begin to understand what they value as teachers. And because it is generally recognized today that literacy is social action and not simply the encoding of language, it is important for those that are interested in the teaching of literacy to understand how teachers' values shape their instruction. For this reason, teachers' storytelling about everyday conflicts have value—teachers have important stories to share, stories that draw on others' stories and lead to still other stories. We can see the importance of preserving different voices in our discussions about the nature of such conflicts because of their implications for teaching and learning. To silence any of these voices in the effort to find "certain" answers is to deny the complexities of such situations and to risk ignoring important aspects of the process of learning. To tell a story that includes teachers' voices may be one way of working against this tendency.

I begin by telling my own story of our conflict about eating on the street, which led me to relate another one: the history of the Dewey program and other similar programs with which I had been involved. My story also led to one more story about my encounter with interpretive language philosophy and narrative theory which I had begun to explore in an effort to understand the nature of storytelling in the learning process.

In chapters 2, 3, and 4 I tell each teacher's story of eating on the street, and I pair them, two in each chapter, raising issues which I explore from various theorists' and sometimes storytellers' perspectives. Jeanetta's and Toby's stories of eating on the street, and their own brief histories of life and teaching in Detroit's inner city, led me to explore the history of racial discrimination in the city from a variety of scholarly perspectives. I also explore the history of the Couzens School from the perspective of one local historian, Clara Jane Thompson, who had taught in the school since it first opened in 1956. The stories of Debi and Susan led me in still other ways: Debi's to a consideration of Whole Language—the guiding philosophy of the Dewey Center—in light of the work of liberal reformer John Dewey, and Susan's to an exploration of the work of various African American theorists, some of whom question the work of liberal reformers like Dewey. Dana's and George's stories, focused in what I initially thought were similar ways on students' perspectives, led me to document various student versions of our day at the Cultural Center. Taken as a whole, my story is also a history, a kind of "map of the past drawn from a particular point of view to be useful to the modern traveler" (Glassie 329), a history of the Dewey Center Community Writing Project that may be useful for literacy teachers, scholars, and historians.

Historian Hayden White asserts that the only meaning that history can have is the kind that a narrative imagination gives to it. Concerned with the problem of representation in the human sciences in general, and in the making of history in particular, White makes it clear that stories give a necessary but illusory coherence to events. "Real life" is obviously not coherent, not well made. To tell stories, White points out, is to make meaning in a way that annals or chronicles do not. Both history and fiction employ similar processes of chronology and valuing, White observes. He points out that "fact" can only come into being through the use of a language that describes it, language which is selective, perspectival, and necessarily limited. For White, history, to be meaningful, must be a story.

James Boyd White has a similar view: "For history to be true, it must be a fiction" (1985, 161). In history, you are never just reporting, you are creating a world, participating in the construction of a culture, and not just a culture of the past—one of the events you describe—but also the "other," the culture of the present, the one from which you write. There is always a tension between fact and imagination in narrative, whether those narratives are in literature, history, or elsewhere. Stories are one means of representing contrary voices, multiple perspectives in a way that can capture each version's complexity. Perhaps no less than a far-reaching story reflecting the vast complexities of the issues will do for an understanding of the shifting social, cultural, and political world of the multicultural classroom. Easy answers to questions are impossible in a shifting, contradictory, conflictual environment.

Richard Price, in *First-Time: The Historical Vision of an Afro-American People,* explains that the stories of history remain a relevant force against the repetition or continuance of injustices such as slavery—a way of saying "never again," and help to preserve collective identity as well. He pieces together an oral history of the eighteenth-century Saramakas, African American maroons who escaped from slavery and settled in the tropical rain forest of Suriname, documenting how Saramakan historians pass on knowledge of the past in the morning to their younger people: "The knowledge transmitted at cock's crow is deliberately incomplete, masked by a style that is at once elliptical and obscure" (10). Though "all history is a radical selection from the immensely rich swirl of past human activity," (5) most of what the Saramakan teller knows is deliberately left out of the telling, in part for epistemological reasons, because one's knowledge is supposed to grow in increments. This vision of history as a series of fragments works against neat, reductive conceptions of history, against linear presentation, and reflects the messy, incremental process of knowing itself.

The teachers' stories I tell as part of my larger story of the Dewey project are in many ways like the Saramakan histories: with each teacher's story we begin the tale again from another perspective, another point of view, and we see how much richer and more complex the tale becomes, and how much more valuable multiple perspectives can be for capturing the complexity of the classroom. My story of the classroom is an incomplete history of fragments, with each voice, each teacher's story, problematizing and enriching the others.

These fragments, the teachers' stories of the conflict about children eating on the street, provide a backdrop for understanding the stories I share in chapter 5 of Dora Simpson and her story. But the teachers' accounts are more than a simple backdrop; each one's personal history and story of eating on the street is necessary for understanding his or her story of Dora. Our understanding of each story is enriched when we consider it in light of the historical context which shapes it.

The stories that I tell of eating on the street and Dora are like the histories of Detroit I encountered, multiple, conflicting, and necessarily limited perspectives on events which—considered together with other perspectives—provide some indication why collaborative teaching and learning can be so useful in the learning process for both students and teachers. The stories we teachers tell are histories of what was for us an important cultural issue we needed to negotiate as we taught together.

In my exploration of what Denny Taylor and Catherine Dorsey-Gaines insist is "the intimate and necessary relation between processes of actual experience and education" (208), I have come to believe that these issues, these people, these experiences are not in any way completely "knowable." In constructing my fiction of a knowable community, I want to acknowledge the impossibility (and perhaps the danger) of trying to do so with anything like certainty. In my writing I want to illustrate the value and the complexity of bringing lived experience and shared discourse into one's writing, yet I realize that of all the metaphors and allegories I might choose in the process of depicting this world, no synthesizing or totalizing one will do; no literal reduction is possible. Representation, including narrative representation, is always in danger of doing violence to the

Other that is its subject, simply because there are, for every inclusion, many more exclusions.[4] In my own representing of teachers' voices in this depiction of various versions of a history, I necessarily indicate my own ethical and social commitments through what I choose to include and exclude. But, as I see it, one of my chief ethical responsibilities in representing my "research" is to preserve the complexity of what I have seen and heard and to avoid arrogance as much as possible in the claims I make. Telling a story of teachers' stories may be the best way to do that.

I am interested in exploring how to tell my story about a particular instance in teaching literacy and how to preserve the voices—the individual stories I hear—and not drown them out through my own story and analysis. Especially in discussing a collaboratively designed project, a project that was in part an attempt to set up ways to promote talk about the teaching and learning process, my central concern has become how—in any representation that I might compose—to capture the nature of the process, the dialogue, the conversation that took place. In a sense, I see *story* as a metaphor for a kind of representation of research that preserves a diversity of voices in the same way the stories we tell in our everyday lives and the stories we read in imaginative literature preserve different voices, keeping them there to knock against each other, conflict with each other, and change each other.

In spite of my subtitle, *Teaching Literacy in a Multicultural Society,* I do not mean to suggest that I am going to present a coherent or definitive analysis of various approaches to teaching literacy or multiculturalism.[5] My story in this case study is based on teachers' reflections from a three-week writing program about one cultural conflict and one student's writing. I hope in the process of telling my story that my own commitments to social and educational change—informed by my colleagues' stories—will be clear. But I also think that our stories may indicate the need to reconsider our unwavering dedication to those commitments in the process of discovering "solutions" to particular problems. Hearing the voices of my colleagues helps me to work against the authoritarianism of certain kinds of educational discourse, whether those are "progressive" or otherwise.

I was one of a group of teachers in a summer writing program committed to struggling with creating better conditions for teaching and learning, exploring what we felt were progressive approaches in the process of approaching that goal. I see myself and my colleagues as very much "in process" about the difficult concerns of teaching literacy in multicultural settings. In the part of this process that is the present text, I am hoping to do little more than represent my own evolving understanding of a particular conflict that took place during our program. I found that the acts of storytelling—my colleagues', my students', and my own—were useful in negotiating and understanding what a particular conflict meant for our teaching in Detroit.

Finally, I think we have to ask ourselves not which version of "truth" is correct, but how do we negotiate between competing versions in such a way that we might retain the character of experience—and "common" knowledge—as complex and perhaps even conflictual. Story is one key component of the art of conversation which is community making. The issues at stake are important ones for the teaching of literacy in multicultural classrooms everywhere.

ACKNOWLEDGMENTS

My story, like all stories, is one with many voices, and is the work of many readers, writers, and storytellers. For the important stories they have shared with me, and for all I have learned from them, I would like to thank my friends and fellow teachers in the Dewey Center Community Writing Project, 1989: Toby Curry, Debi Goodman, Jeanetta Cotman, Dana Davidson, Susan Harris, and George Cooper. I want to thank, too, all the students in the Dewey program that we teachers learned so much from, but especially Dora, whose work and life become one focus of my story.

For introducing me to generative ideas that are apparent throughout this work or for their careful response to the text in process, I wish to thank many people I worked with or who were my friends at the University of Michigan when I was there: Ross Chambers, Anne Ruggles Gere, Stephen Dunning, Corey Dolgon, Valerie Polakow, David Bloome, George Kamberelis, Carol Winkelman, Stuart Hoffman, Tom Philion, and Colleen Fairbanks. Thanks, too, to those who helped with the transcribing: Shana Langer, Lori Weiselberg, Teresa Mustazza, and Margaret Mullins.

I also give thanks to those who have given me their time, effort, criticism, and encouragement: Michael Apple, Shirley Brice Heath, Alan Luke, Carl Personke, Dawn Perkins, and Michael Smith, Michael Spooner, Pete Stillman, and reviewers Geneva Smitherman and Mike Rose. I'd also like to thank my many graduate students who read and contributed to the text in many ways.

I am indebted to David Bartholomae and Jean Carr, editors of the Pittsburgh Series in Composition, Literacy, and Culture, for their advice and encouragement, to Peter Oresick for his enthusiasm and support, and to editor Kathy McLaughlin for her careful reading and sound advice. To all those at the University of Pittsburgh Press: Thanks.

I am especially indebted to five people who have changed my life in significant ways, and without whom this text would certainly be far different: my close friends and colleagues Cathy Fleischer and

George Cooper, whose teaching and commitment to students have inspired me, and whose friendship continues to mean so much to me; Lori Weiselberg, whose love and support has carried me through these many months of stress and exhilaration, and, finally, Jay Robinson and Patti Stock, whose passionate scholarship and teaching will continue to be an example to me, and whose belief in teachers and the importance of conversation in reshaping curriculum has become my own. Their ideas are present in nearly every page of this text.

EATING
ON THE
STREET

1

IMAGINING EMPOWERMENT: Telling Stories in Writing Programs

Message: 3244767
Posted: 7:45 p.m. EDT, Wed., June 28/89
Subject: Day 3, Wednesday, June 28, 1989. Children's Day!!

A good day, spent mostly at the Cultural Center area in Detroit, near Wayne State University, to which we all walked. I video-taped one of our groups' walking tours out of the rough projects area through the gradually rejuvenating neighborhoods to the very highly developed Cultural Center area. When we got there, it was wild, with thousands of excited kids and a few harried adults escorting them, and many special events. We went in different groups to different places, some to the African American Museum, some to the Science Museum, some to the Detroit Institute of Arts, depending on kids' stated interests. It was a pretty organized day, though, thanks to Debi. The thing we all observed was the traditional African dancers and musicians outside the African American Museum. Very colorful and interesting. There was a children's parade, too. We were stopped by many people who asked us what our T-shirts meant, and asked us where we were from. I was stopped on the street, for instance, by a woman who wanted to know about the project and who offered publication to any student who would write about something to do with plant life, vegetation, or gardening in the area for her Urban Planning State Newsletter! People were really friendly to us all day.

Kids returned to write like mad about what they had experienced about this day, and the outer fringes of "their neighborhood." We have 28 kids as of today, and 2 still coming. We are a

3

little disappointed about having kids come in late, who miss the initial stages of the building of our community, but again, we have to be flexible. I do, anyway. Others already know how, I think, from experience! At any rate, we know all the kids' names now, and are getting to know them. We are all developing "favorite kid" relationships, of course, and there are certain kids each one of us is particularly "watching."

We have our internal struggles as a staff, of course, which is I think interesting in different ways to all of us. We have different concerns about efficiency, noise, organization, freedom/ autonomy; voices have been raised the last couple days in teacher meetings in the afternoons. Some people think the greater experience George and I have merits making most of the decisions for the rest of us, and we deny that right. We are fascinated with what it means to collaborate with each other, which is good (the fascination) because at times it isn't easy. We are teacher-researching this project together, for sure. We all thought it was a good, productive day, but there was some disagreement about just how productive it was. Some tension evident.

Another break-in last night, but our stuff was secure, locked up. We are learning! We are trying to be as careful as possible. It's terrible to have this feeling of "onslaught"; over time I can imagine it gets very tiring and enraging, but it's inevitable, I suppose. It is hard for me to remember that this threat of violence and theft is a way of life for almost all of these kids, and the rule is to be smart and careful and lock things up. I can see why people would just rather not teach in such situations, but for us right now, and for many of us more than just right now, the exciting benefits far outweigh the negative aspects.

I turned off the machine, walked into the kitchen and grabbed a beer. I was tired after another day in Detroit. Hot and tired. I took a long pull on the Labatts, stretched my back and neck and pressed them against the refrigerator, closed my eyes, and waited for the beer to ease into my arms. I kept my eyes closed and waited for the voices to be still.

Relax. Think about something else. Sit in a chair. Read a book. Drink the beer.

I wandered into the living room, spotted Bakhtin on the table where I'd left him the night before. I took another swallow and eased into the familiar comfort of my dark leather chair. I flipped through the text and stopped at a page. I read what he says about language:

I imagine this whole to be something like an immense novel, multi-generic, multi-styled, mercilessly critical, soberly mocking, reflecting in all its fullness the heteroglossia and multiple voices of a given culture, people and epoch (60).

No good. Too much work for right now.

I walked outside and breathed in sweet honeysuckle. I watched the evening creep into the day. Strolling into the garden, a riot of colors and smells swept through me: poppies, roses, peonies, lilies of the valley, bleeding hearts. I sat in a wooden chair in the yard for a few minutes and finished my beer. I was momentarily stilled.

I took a walk down my dead-end street, past the comfortable brick houses and the quiet summer lawns. No one sitting on the porches. I was alone with my thoughts. I returned to my house and sat down to write in my journal. A place to tell myself what I thought. In a way like talking to George Cooper about it. Where I can be more honest, candid. The electronic version had been directed to people in the university, many of whom knew even less than I did about Detroit, most of whom didn't know the individuals and might misconstrue my comments as criticism. I didn't want to tell my story in public in ways I might later regret. I wrote:

Today was a strange day, in many ways exciting, in many ways troubling. I loved parts of the morning. For instance, I filmed Susan and my group's walk from the Dewey Center to the Cultural Center, hoping it would capture the absolute contrasts of the two areas. I liked the African dances and enjoyed filming this, and the kids' reactions, but it was too damned hot, and most things were so badly planned, and so late, that the effect was really sloppy. So much wasted time! We couldn't have known it, but we sat out in the sun for nearly forty-five minutes waiting for the dancers to begin, after waiting for the mask-making demonstration which we finally learned was canceled! I liked the art in the African American Museum. The kids really did very well. On the way back it was so hot that Susan and I let some of the kids go in a water fountain. I wanted to go in myself, but didn't, finally. Kids were tired after the walk and the heat, and though some kids did seem to write a lot, the more I think about it, most of them didn't really write much when we got back. But who could blame them? It just wasn't a great experience. I hope we don't have too many days like this one.

The afternoon was really emotional. Susan and Jeanetta brought up their concern in the teacher meeting, and both of them seemed really upset. Jeanetta and George had been with their group, which included Dora, Tameka, Farrah, Aquileth, and LaShunda. Jeanetta said we all had different standards than she did in the classroom. She reminded us she had a reputation for being a tough teacher, but said she had been trying to "hang back" here in the summer in order to learn. She said she tried to watch and learn, but she had some problems with the way some of us failed to discipline students for certain things; it was sometimes far beyond her tolerance level. Susan reinforced this. She was upset about this, too.

I know Susan thinks things like the planning are too loose but was surprised to see Jeanetta upset. I asked what Jeanetta was specifically upset about, what had triggered this. She said she wasn't upset, really, but "had questions" about some things. She and Susan were sitting close to each other. Dana was sitting between me and Toby on the other side of the room and not talking. Jeanetta got help from Susan, but basically explained how hard it was to see kids not being confronted for "playing around" and not accomplishing much, and "was this normal in this kind of approach to teaching?" More specifically, she said, for example, that she was personally "bothered," and it went beyond her personal "tolerance level" when she saw kids "eating on the street." As a teacher, she would never allow that. George said he hadn't realized it was such a big deal. "I probably eat on the street all the time," he said. I said I did, too. "But you can do that. You are white teachers, and these are black students," Jeanetta explained. Here they were in their white T-shirts, representing the Dewey Center, and they have this food (she mimicked exaggeratedly and comically) dribbling down their chin. "No," she said. "No! Maybe it's just me, but that really bothers me." We all laughed. "No," I said, "You should bring it up, that's what these sessions are for," etc.

Susan I think is really angry about this. She said that black children, and especially poor black children, need to be "guided" to avoid what she called "stereotypical behavior," and she said this was one example of the kind of behavior that stigmatized poor blacks. But who sets these standards? It is repellent to me to have to make these kids follow these standards, if they are essentially racist standards.

"Black students with that food all over, walking on the street, no!" Jeanetta said. We laughed. "I don't let my kids do it, why should I let these students do it?"

Susan said it was important for white teachers to know and be sensitive about "black views for how to raise and educate their children." She told a story about when she had been an administrator of a school in Alabama and there was one white teacher in their school that she and her colleagues really had come to admire because he "upheld the standards all of the black adults had for the black children." She said it was different for black kids than white kids or adults, because blacks have to work against so much prejudice, they have to work twice as hard to succeed, and part of this involved adhering to acceptable forms of behavior for society. She said she and most of her fellow blacks really respected white teachers who did this. (Moral of parable: We clearly were not there yet for her!)

Susan rarely talks in our teacher meetings and usually reserves sharing her concerns for the car ride back to Ann Arbor with George, Dana, and me. She said, "You have to understand! I really love being involved in this project, and I think what you all are doing is wonderful, creating positive learning experiences for these children, but what I'm saying is coming from my perspective as a black educator. I really care about these children! When I think about these children, living in these projects, this gives me pain! This hurts me! Being black, it may be different for Jeanetta and me and Dana, the way we see it. But these are *our* children, and we don't want things to go on this way!"

This pissed off Toby and Debi, and I thought it was troubling, too, in some ways. Toby said she and Debi had devoted all their lives to working with kids of all colors in the inner city, and she felt the kids were "*my* kids, too." Susan was quick to say that we had convinced her, generally, just by the fact that we were there, working with kids and obviously caring to help them. Both she and Jeanetta said they wouldn't even be part of the program if they didn't believe that and trust us, and they loved the opportunity, and were learning a lot, etc., "But you asked us to share our concerns, and this is something we just don't agree with," Susan said.

Both Toby and Debi wondered why it was blacks that got singled out. Toby said she tried to treat all her kids in a way that was "color blind." She didn't like the idea of blacks being treated differently than whites, especially if it meant more restrictions on their behavior. I agreed.

Susan said that blacks are already singled out for negative treatment and are treated differently, so they have to be given special consideration by teachers to overcome obstacles. They just need to be able to fit into mainstream society, to get the same skills that everyone else needs to succeed. She insisted again that blacks need the same education, the same skills that whites get, or they won't succeed. I agreed with this, and am sympathetic to her desire not to create a separate but equal black English vernacular "language apartheid," but after reading the work of Smitherman and Labov, can't fully agree with her. I am mad at some of her assumptions, since her position seems to imply that only blacks can really teach blacks, or that only blacks should decide what blacks need, or that blacks have to "imitate" white standards to survive. Maybe she means none of these things, exactly.

But I like both Jeanetta and Susan very much. We are all getting very close in many respects, and it was an exciting (though tense at times) discussion, which lasted almost three hours altogether. As Debi said, "I have never had a discussion like this with other teachers all the years I have taught. Dave, we have to start taping these talks." This really is a great learning experience!

The learning experience to which Debi Goodman refers is one in which the seven teachers and thirty students who participated in the Dewey Center Community Writing Project in Detroit in the summer of 1989 were engaged. It's an experience with a history and one that makes a history. Its history relies on the personal histories of those of us who participated in it—both the versions of those histories that are written in our memories and the versions of those histories that are inscribed in our cultures. Furthermore, its history is being told in various stories, multiple stories; and in this story, my story—made of all the other stories—it is being written.

I thought about the stories the students were already writing, the stories that they were shaping and the stories they were being shaped by—those they were hearing from each other and from their neighbors in the program.

MISS ROSE BELL
Julia Pointer

Chapter 1
Stepping out of that taxi cab, I finally realized. This was real. This baby inside me is real. The fact that my mama threw me out is real.

"What's wrong with you chile," she screamed when I told her. "Don't you see these five other kids running around me?!"

I glanced about. Mark, Janie and Tony were an inch away from the TV watching a violent show. Millie was in the kitchen eating cookies, again. She never got enough to eat. And little Jimmy, the baby, was tugging at my mother's earrings that hung from her ears. Then, I looked back at my mother just in time to hear her say, "You go find your boyfriend. He got you this far, tell him to take care of you, feed you, and love you. Cause it seems to me you don't appreciate nothing I done for you!" I stood up in alarm.

"Mama you can't do this to me," I pleaded. "I'm only sixteen." (*Corridors* 39)

My Life
Laquida Talbert

I was born in the Phillipines in 1977 because my father was stationed there. When my mother was pregnant with me my dad sent for her and my sister. When I was born I had a disease called sickle cell.

I keep myself from getting depressed about it by not letting it take over my pride. I try to be happy, and not think about how long I have to live with this disease. (*Corridors* 51–52)

I Am a Never Ending Road

I am a never ending road
winding into the darkness
a howling breeze
looming trees
whistling willows
light sprinkles of rain seeping through

I am a vine hanging from the trees
wrapping and twisting through the jungle.
I am James Cook.

(*Corridors* 2)

How important it is, I thought, that these students get the opportunity to share their stories with each other, with those of us who were their teachers, and with their fellow community members, and how important it can be for teachers to have the opportunity to talk together about how to better help students learn to write. I thought about the many students and teachers in other places with whom I had worked in similar writing programs. How different was this world of Detroit's Cass Corridor, this world in which I was still an outsider, eager and impatient to learn.

A Brief History: The Huron Shores Summer Writing Institute, Saginaw Project 98, and Community Writing

During the 1985–86 academic year, Cathy Fleischer, John Lofty, and I were graduate student teaching assistants at the University of Michigan, where we engaged in a collaborative teaching project in Rogers City. Working with Rogers City High School teachers Dan Madigan and Jim Hopp and several Rogers City area students and community members, we developed the Huron Shores Summer Writing Institute. Cathy, John, and I were excited that year about the possibility of putting into action principles of language learning like those Angela Jaggar and Trika Smith-Burke had named:

1. Language learning is a self-generated, creative process.
2. Language learning is holistic. The different components of language—form, function and meaning—are learned simultaneously.
3. Language learning is social and collaborative.
4. Language learning is functional and integrative.
5. Language learning is variable. Because language is inherently variable, the meanings, the forms, and the functions of children's language will depend on their personal, social and cultural experiences. (7)

After months of planning involving teachers, students, and members of the local community, the first year's program took place in Rogers City during three weeks in the summer of 1986. With guidance from five teachers, thirty area high school students drew upon the resources of their experience and their community to investigate their worlds. Students researched in settings as diverse as the Presque Isle County Historical Museum, local libraries, and the Presque Isle Lighthouse; they read primary texts produced in and about their community, observed their surroundings, interviewed their neighbors, and inscribed what they learned from all their research activities. The students' general interest in—and the teachers' consequent emphasis on—interviewing and oral history were apparent in that first year when the students audiotaped interviews with more than seventy community members. Before the summer was over, students desktop published a collection of their writing, *Break-*

wall, explaining the title and their project in its preface: "A breakwall prevents the erosion of the earth. We hope that our *Breakwall* will help to prevent the erosion of our Northern Michigan heritage." In the four summers since its beginning, the Huron Shores Summer Writing Program has expanded, and three more volumes of *Breakwall* have been published. Other area and University of Michigan teachers have become involved in the program, among them George Cooper, lecturer in the English Composition Board of the University of Michigan.

A graduate student in the English and Education doctoral program at the University of Michigan at the time, I had taught at Grand Valley State University for three years, but I had also been a high school teacher for seven years, and I wanted to continue working with high school teachers and students. When I had first returned to school I had worked with the University of Michigan's Center for Educational Improvement through Collaboration (CEIC)[1] in urban Saginaw, Michigan, in a university-school project developed by these teachers from the University of Michigan and teachers from Saginaw's high schools. The project was designed to support the development of innovative approaches to literacy instruction.

In Saginaw, two high schools sit on either side of the Saginaw River: Saginaw High with a 98 percent African American student body, Arthur Hill with 30 percent. In 1987, in one of many projects that formed the larger CEIC-Saginaw Public Schools Collaboration, two high school teachers, one at Arthur Hill, one at Saginaw High, team-taught classes with Patricia Stock. Led by their teachers and other literacy workers from the CEIC, including me, students in these classes produced *The Bridge,* a book of stories about growing up in Saginaw. The texts the students wrote constituted one visible representation of "the bridge" they had begun to form between their two schools, between the cultures in their city. These texts were, as well, an exploration of students' own worlds, shaped in terms of their own interests. While working on this project, I continued to develop my interest in student and teacher collaboration and in community-based approaches to literacy education; moreover, working in Saginaw, I learned more about how teachers might teach and learn better in multicultural settings.

While I was working in Saginaw, my colleague, George Cooper, was also developing an interest in multicultural education through his work in intensive writing tutorials at the University of Michigan. Students, required to take these tutorials as a result of their performance on a university writing assessment, struggle with the demands of adapting to academic discourse and writing generally. Many of these students are minority students, and many from nearby Detroit.

My work in Saginaw and George's with students from Detroit led us to wonder if we could develop a community-based summer writing project in Detroit. Would a similar community-based program, a program emphasizing the collaborative learning and teaching of instructors and students, work in another community? Because of our interest in urban education, and because we had seen some remarkable investment in writing and learning in Rogers City on the part of both teachers and students, we worked to bring a similar community writing project to inner-city Detroit. In Rogers City, we had seen closer ties develop between the community and the school, and we had seen many students become excited about writing and carry that excitement back into school settings.

Detroit: Planning A Community-Based Writing Project

"To study literacy and its uses is to commit oneself to the study of contexts and relations." (J. Robinson, 347)

In several meetings in Ann Arbor beginning in October 1988, several of us from the university, including Jay Robinson, Patti Stock, George Cooper, and I, and two Detroit Public School teachers, Toby Curry, a seventh-grade teacher, and Debra Goodman, a fifth-grade teacher, began to explore the possibilities of developing a community-based summer writing project at the Couzens School in Detroit.

The James P. Couzens School had been scheduled for closing until Toby and Debi proposed developing it into an alternative, "Whole Language" pre-kindergarten through eighth-grade school, which the Detroit Public School Board accepted. In fall 1989, Couzens was renamed the Dewey Center for Urban Education. Located near the Jeffries Homes, a low-cost housing project in the troubled Cass Corridor of Detroit's inner city, the Dewey Center is one of the community schools that serves the "projects." Although it is now an alternative school, a school which students from all over Detroit may attend, fewer than 35 percent of its students come from somewhere other than the immediate area.

Our purpose in developing a community-based summer writing program at the Dewey Center was the same one that led us to develop such a program in Rogers City: to see if, during the summer, we could generate excitement about writing among students and teachers that might move into fall school classrooms. As in Rogers City, we wanted to work with students in Detroit in such a way that they would be able to claim ownership of their writing and have more control over the conditions in which that writing was accomplished. In addition, we wanted to work with teachers researching issues surrounding the teaching of literacy in a multicultural environment— research in literacy consistent with Lather's notion of "research as praxis," or research for reflective change (257).

Together with Detroit students, teachers, and community members, we wanted to develop a language-based approach to learning with one goal of the project also being the publication of a book of students' writing about their community. By developing an alternative to the usually distant relationship between the university and the schools, we knew we might be able to explore possibilities, imagine different ways of teaching and learning, by working with each other. Students, who typically learn in ways that isolate them from their peers and who rarely get the chance to decide what they will learn in an academic setting, were excited about planning a program, about the possibility of seeing themselves as writers, and being published in a book they would shape themselves.

Teachers, who are even more typically isolated than students, were excited to have conversations about teaching writing, about using writing to learn, exploring ways of developing activities for learning consistent with students' ways of knowing that were closely connected with students' lives. Community members and University of Michigan administrators were excited about what they saw as a new commitment to the area, some activity that might link various Detroit and university agencies in thoughtful action.

In the winter 1989 term, Toby and Debi presented a whole-language seminar at the Dewey Center for various area teachers, hoping to use the sessions to introduce the principles of whole language teaching and to promote conversations about better ways to teach inner-city children. Nervous, excited, we got in early for the first session and I took notes on the area as I first experienced it.

A Walk through the Neighborhood

The Dewey Center is located in Detroit's Cass Corridor, on the corner of John C. Lodge and Martin Luther King Boulevard. Standing on the south steps of the school building, glancing to the south, directly across Martin Luther King, I see a row of faded red, two-story apartment complexes called the Jeffries Homes, which most people call "the projects," and behind them, less than two miles away, the towering downtown buildings gleaming high into the sky. These new and newly renovated buildings stand as testimony to Mayor Coleman Young's administration's economic priorities for "urban renewal" in the eighties. Many of the upper stories are clearly visible from the south steps of the school; they grace the skyline, beckoning out-of-state business investors to new financial commitments and possible capital gains.

"Welcome to Jeffries Homes," a large, old sign greets us, across the street from the Dewey Center on the corner of John C. Lodge and Martin Luther King Boulevard, its white paint chipping away. Block after block to the south, rows of red brick, two-story Jeffries Homes extend in the direction of the downtown development. Many more apartment complexes stand, similarly faded, marred with peeling paint and graffiti, with windows boarded over here and there. Consisting of twelve rows of old red brick buildings, the area is circumscribed by Martin Luther King Boulevard to the north, Temple to the south, Fourth Avenue to the east, and John C. Lodge to the west. Women and girls with their babies stroll by; some sit on the concrete steps of the apartments. Two men work on a Buick in the street. The sixty-nine buildings that comprise the projects were built mostly in the fifties; they are home for most of the students who live in the Dewey Center area.

To the east, across the sunken Lodge freeway, there is another section of the Jeffries Homes, more projects, which many people refer to as the "high rises" (to distinguish them from the "low rises" to the south of the Dewey Center), several bleak, mostly ten-story buildings that also stand in stark contrast to the tall buildings downtown. A central location in the late sixties riots, the projects are home twenty years later to retirees unable to do better on dwindling pensions, welfare mothers—many of them teenaged, most with several children—a few struggling longtime residents who have demonstrated their commitment to the area, and some of whom we would meet later—George McMahon, Molly Rubino, and Rose Bell among them. Still bearing the scars from the riots of twenty-three years ago—broken windows, burned wood—the high rises are dark, massive, cold. Encompassing a far greater area than the low rises, from Martin Luther King to the south to Gibson to the north, and from John C. Lodge in the east to Canfield in the west, is more space for grass, but the faded green lawns bear inexplicably large, forbidding signs: "No Ball Playing. Order of Detroit Housing Commission, City of

Detroit." And the rule seems to be obeyed; no children play ball on this grass. Neighborhood advocate Rose Bell would, the next summer, tell us she plants "flowers for peace" on her lawn and encourages her neighbors to do so, too. "Someday," Ms. Bell said to us, looking out the kitchen window past the burned-out apartment to the vacant sidewalks, "kids are going to be playing hopscotch out there. Otherwise, I wouldn't be doing what I'm doing. I'd move out of here right quick."

Other people move from here when they get the chance: statistics indicate clearly that this is an increasingly violent area, and even the most optimistic person, like Rose Bell, recognizes that crack is killing people here. As even Ms. Bell agonizingly admits, even some homeless people prefer the streets to these buildings of despair.

Less than two miles north of the Dewey Center is another area of recent development, the Cultural Center area near Wayne State University, which includes the Detroit Institute of Arts, the Detroit Museum of Science, the Walter Reuther Library of Labor and Urban Affairs, and the African American Museum. Within walking distance of the Dewey Center, the impressive architectural design and powerful, contemporary structures stand testimony to other kinds of commitments: to the arts, to a sense of history, and to an attempt at articulating cultural values that are perhaps—or are presumed to be—shared. Expensive, supported by extensive endowments, they are monuments befitting a great city's accomplishments and are rooted in the past.

Within three or four blocks east of the Dewey Center, in isolated one-block neighborhoods on Cass and Second Avenue, young homeowners purchase affordable old buildings, some of them long abandoned, and restore them to their original condition. Young businesspersons, also attracted to the affordable real estate, have slowly begun to take chances on establishing restaurants in this area, four blocks away from the school. Also to the east on Cass is the Burton International School, a highly successful magnet school where Toby and Debi taught for several years. One business remains from the mid-seventies Cass Corridor Community Business Association: the Cass Corridor Community Food Co-op, one block east and three blocks north of the Dewey Center. Churches, many of them Baptist, are still active in the community. The rubble of demolished apartment buildings and housing projects remains in vacant lots everywhere. Little Cass Park, the only public park in the area, is filled, day and night, primarily with homeless men and occasional crack dealers. Billy Jo Roark writes of this park, in *Corridors:*

CASS PARK

My dad told me not to go in that park, and I said "why?" He told
me that there are drunks and winos there and that they deal
drugs there, too. People who need money sell stuff they've stolen like fans, pin wheels, basketballs and give them to their
friends. They even give them to their relatives. These big teenagers also bust bottles when they throw them at people without
homes who live in the park. (27)

A brief walk down Third Avenue, from Forest to Martin Luther
King, might be useful for understanding the complexity of the world
of the Corridor, especially the immediate area of the Dewey Center,
and the great challenges the area now faces and has always faced. Seeing it, I was reminded of James Spradley's depiction of the world of
the homeless some twenty years earlier: "The streets of America are
convulsed in pain. It is in the streets and alleys, fills the air, crowds
into our living rooms. . . . Can we create a society which recognizes
the dignity of diverse cultural patterns?" (1). But it is more than just
pain, as Spradley would be quick to point out. In the long single block
from Forest to Selden, there are several vacant storefronts, but there
are also many active churches: the Greater King Solomon Baptist
Church, Hale's Tabernacle United Primitive Baptist Church, the Evan-
gelistic Tabernacle of Faith, the Glorious Tabernacle, with the Evan-
gelistic Ministry of Pastor Mary Lou Brown. The City of Detroit Social
Services Building appears long deserted, but I am told that the
churches remain active sources of hope for area residents.

On the corner of Selden and Third, some businesses seem to be
surviving, but on the southeast corner a three-story brick building
stands burned out and gutted, all of its windows broken. "Used to be
a crack house," a man on the corner told me, "but not no more.
Burned out a few times, those people, they all gone, most of them in
jail or shot dead." Many people I would later meet know stories about
various inhabitants of this once elegant building, now destroyed.

Crossing Selden, walking north toward King, I see a large vacant
lot to the west, formerly space for low-income housing buildings,
long torn down. To the east is Jumbo Bar, very busy on payday, slow
but steady on other days. Closer to King, an old brick apartment complex stands, and just east of the Dewey Center, lines form for meals
twice a day at the Detroit Rescue Mission: "The Bible Says Christ
Died for Our Sins," the sign outside it reads. Next door stands Bill's
Recreation: Pocket Billiards. On the street outside a man with one leg

sits on the ground leaning back against the building, looking down the street, not expectantly, clenching and unclenching one fist.

Across the street and north a few yards, in one vacant lot less than 150 yards from the steps of the Dewey Center, a fire burns every day and night, fueled by wood from an abandoned house nearby. Day and night several homeless men and women huddle around this fire, and sometimes when these men and women get very cold they take the fire inside the house; the building bears the scars of several fires which have been set on its floors by a scattering of homeless people, who may seem to the casual observer beyond hope. More than pain here, yes, but still, mostly pain.

After we had attended several sessions in Toby and Debi's whole-language seminar, George Cooper and I conducted a workshop for the seminar in which participants interviewed a woman who was a long-term resident of the Cass Corridor community. We wrote about the interview and explored possibilities for developing closer ties between the school and the community. We were joined in our participation in this workshop by Susan Harris, a former urban school-teacher, administrator, and graduate student, whom we had asked to join us in teaching the summer program.

At this workshop, Jeanetta Cotman, a nineteen-year veteran fifth-grade teacher in the Couzens School, and its teachers' union representative for most of those years, approached George about teaching in the summer program. Characterizing herself as a "traditional" teacher who did not make extensive use of writing in her classes, Jeanetta indicated she was enthusiastic about what she was hearing; she wanted to learn more about what she considered a promising approach to teaching literacy. Several weeks later, we asked Dana Davidson to join us as well. A 1985 graduate of Detroit's Cass Tech High School and 1989 graduate of the University of Michigan in English, Dana had been one of the students in my teacher preparation classes, and I knew her to be committed to teaching in Detroit's inner-city.[2] We also asked Markus Müller, a University of Michigan undergraduate who had worked for many years with Detroit teenagers through his church's youth programs, to assist us with word processing and desktop publishing.

We were seven teachers: four from the University of Michigan (George Cooper, Dana Davidson, Susan Harris, and I), three from the Detroit public schools (Toby Curry, Debi Goodman, and Jeanetta Cotman); four white (George, Toby, Debi, and I) and three black (Susan, Jeanetta, and Dana); three each with more than fifteen years' extensive experience teaching in Detroit's inner city (Toby, Debi, and Jeanetta), and the rest of us new to teaching in Detroit, although Dana had grown up and gone to school in the area and Susan had been an urban school administrator. George and I had ten and fifteen years teaching experience, respectively, in high schools and universities, but not in Detroit.

We began recruiting students from three Jeffries community schools, including Edmonson elementary, where we spoke with fifth graders; Burton International School, the magnet school where Toby and Debi had been teaching; and the Couzens School, soon to be the Dewey Center, where we concentrated our recruiting efforts. We gave special attention to attracting students to our program who were identified by their teachers as "at risk," and who might be struggling in school in various ways. We agreed that the majority of the students should live in or near the Jeffries projects, and we decided to place an emphasis in our recruitment on boys because teachers there felt that boys in particular were less likely to graduate from school than girls. We also defined the fifth through seventh grades as crucial for students if their commitment to learning was to continue into high school and their adult years. Referring to the great numbers of students of color who were dropping out of school in Detroit's inner city, one teacher said, "By ninth grade, they're gone."

Our recruiting efforts in the winter 1989 term involved several visits to the schools and some Saturday planning meetings for students and teachers, where we repeatedly underscored our intent to develop the project in a collaborative fashion with both students and teachers. Understandably, students were not only dubious about our promises and unfamiliar with our way of talking about learning, but also unaccustomed to participating overtly in curriculum planning; however, they were curious, and their interest in the project grew slowly and steadily.

We knew our Saturday meetings would compete with television and other nonschool activities, and we knew the summer program might seem like more school work to students who already feel out of place in school. Why volunteer for more school? What could it do for them? Why should they stay in school, and not simply drop out? Did a high school diploma offer them the prospect of jobs, security, even a sense of well-being and self-confidence? We knew that the possibility of gang membership, for instance, might offer more sense of community and a more immediate sense of power than the classroom for some of these students. These children know, too, that they could earn a lot of money by dealing drugs for these gangs. "What you gonna pay me to come in your program, man?" one sixth grader asked me. Defiantly, he cocked the hat teachers had repeatedly asked him to remove. To be an author, to be a student, would likely look dull compared to other, flashier demonstrations of "success." What could we offer him of any substance to give him hope to change his life? Could we promise him that writing in our program would somehow change the circumstances in his life? Knowing something of the complexity of his and his friends' lives, we weren't at all sure that we could give him any answers he would find acceptable.

The initial enthusiasm for our project came from girls who liked to write and who were generally successful in school. In the end, thirty students signed up: eleven boys, nineteen girls; ten students who actually lived in the Projects, almost all of the others living nearby in the Cass Corridor; twelve from the Dewey Center and other projects area schools, eighteen from Burton International School; many of them current or former students from Toby and Debi's classes. Nineteen of the students were black, eight white, two Latino, one Asian; there were thirteen fifth graders, eleven sixth graders, and six seventh graders. Many joked in ways similar to the way the young man I described joked, and they skipped our planning meetings.

As teachers informed by several discussions with students, we agreed to emphasize several issues in our collaborative planning of the summer project. Although we agreed to encourage students to write at least one piece "about the community," we wanted to encourage writing about topics and in forms that the students would choose themselves and to provide as many occasions as possible for talk to inform students' writing. For instance, by inviting various community members to be interviewed by the students, we hoped this interchange would invite student writing. We planned to take advantage of the ideal four-to-one student-teacher ratio and to give students an opportunity to talk frequently with various teachers about their writing. We planned daily, small-group writers' workshop sessions where students could, if they wished, share and critique each other's writing at every stage of the process. We wanted to break down some usual barriers: between parents and the classroom, between teachers and students, between the school and the community. Most of us dressed informally and agreed to be addressed by our first names, and we wrote every day with the students. Parents and neighbors were invited to drop in and participate at any time of the day; we planned to invite published writers to participate and conduct workshops and readings for us. We agreed to provide as many occasions as possible for writing, including keeping journals. We wanted to involve students in every aspect of the decision-making process, to help them claim ownership of their writing and of the workshop itself. By avoiding presentations or talks about aspects of writing we could instead talk about an individual student's writing in our responses to their writing.

We wanted to get out of the school, too, to visit community sites, to allow for those experiences to provide possibilities for writing. We planned every day to meet with the students; each afternoon, the teachers would meet to discuss the morning's work and plan the next day. Initially, we planned the first two days and "roughed in" some later events that would require transportation; the last week was left free for writing, revision, and desk-top publishing. We agreed to construct a general plan, but also agreed to be flexible, to be willing to abandon any plan for the needs of the particular situation, and the needs of individual students. We also decided to conduct "teacher research" into our own practices by constructing an archive of our work in journals, audiotapes, videotapes, and drafts of student writing. Many of us stated our desire to write about some aspects of the project; there was even some talk of a "teacher book" that we might write (and have subsequently planned) as a companion to the "student book" that would emerge from the project. The planning was filled with excitement and good intentions. Caring as we each did in our different ways about how we should proceed and how we could best teach our particular group of children, we found ourselves daily in passionate intellectual discussions—discussions often characterized by conflict. To understand how our "interpretive community" of teachers got formed in terms of the work we did with our students, it is crucial to realize the creative tension between our good intentions to make the collaborative teaching work and our differences of opinion about how that work should get accomplished.

The Dewey Center Community Writing Project, 1989

The Cass Corridor
James Cook

If I could write about any community in Detroit, it would be the Cass Corridor. Because of drugs and unemployment, many people moved away. But at one time, there were more people on Brainard Street between Second and Third than in most small towns in Michigan. Today the Cass Corridor is mostly a bunch of burned down buildings. There are a lot of drugs and prostitution, but I don't think it is as bad as its reputation. (*Corridors* 1)

The above description of the beginning of the Dewey Project is important for anyone who would like to understand how a particular way of working with students and teachers and communities evolved in practice over time; a brief day-to-day description, or story, of the thirteen days of the workshop, incomplete as this "chronicle" will be, can also be beneficial for understanding the nature of the stories I focus on later in this story. As must already be clear, the months planning the workshop were very much a part of the project itself, but most of the actual decision making on curriculum took place in the thirteen days of the workshop.

Our kick-off luncheon was held Saturday, June 24, 1989, with popular *Detroit Free Press* columnist Susan Watson as our speaker. Watson interacted with the students throughout her presentation, underscoring several things we as teachers were delighted to hear: the importance of local knowledge, community writing, a passionate commitment to the task, hard work coupled with the importance of "having fun" in the process.

On the first day of the workshop, twenty-seven students were present at 8:30 a.m. We began by discussing the program as it was planned as well as the possible directions it might take. We conducted a practice interview session with the teachers role-playing various "attitudes" students might encounter in their interviews with community members. A very lively discussion followed, preparing us for the next day, which focused on how we could ask better questions and deal effectively with problem interviewees. The three-hour afternoon teachers' meeting was filled, as it regularly was, with exhilaration, anxiety, disagreements on how to proceed with various students, stories, various interpretations of events, different representations of students' writing and behavior. For example, we took different stances on what some people termed the "wild" and "unproductive" behavior of two small groups of students, and we differed on how to interpret and respond to this behavior.

On the second day, we discovered that the school had been broken into, glass strewn on the library floor where we met. Some of the materials that we had left out had been stolen, though not our computer equipment, which had been locked away in the ironbound computer room. Those of us from Ann Arbor were struck by the fact that this threat of theft and violence was a fact of life for children in this complex neighborhood. We needed to learn, and learn quickly, how to operate in this world. We resolved to be more careful with storing our supplies, to make them look less tempting to burglars. That day, two longtime residents came to the Dewey Center to be interviewed: George McMahon, who had once gone to jail for protesting the fact that area residents were being evicted from their apartment building, and Rose Bell, who runs a volunteer service for unwed mothers called 961-BABY. Both visitors shared stories which inspired writing by teachers and students alike, including portions of verbatim transcripts, poetry, character sketches, "nonfiction" accounts of what they had talked about, and fictional stories inspired by particular aspects of what teachers and students had heard.

GEORGE MCMAHON: LIFE STEW
Toby Curry

4 cups of hope in the human spirit
3 cups of faith in Christianity
2 quiet summers in Harlem, New York
1 full year of migrant life from Michigan to Texas
3 days in jail, eating green bologna
1 tablespoon of tolerance
A dash of curiosity
21 years of matrimony

Mix thoroughly. Simmer inside
a struggling, inner-city neighborhood
for at least 24 years.
Serves hundreds of troubled, first
fired, last hired people. (*Corridors* 15)

The third day of our program we all attended Children's Day at the Cultural Center near Wayne State. We split up into groups which went to various places, such as the Museum of African American History, the Detroit Science Museum, and the Detroit Institute of Arts, where special events were scheduled. Children were everywhere— several thousand of them. There was a children's parade and traditional African dancing by volunteers from the African American Museum in brightly colored costumes. One student described it this way as part of her published "program diary":

Dear Diary,
Today we went to the Cultural Center Children's Day. It was a lot of fun to see all of the children play and to watch the parade. And the best part about the parade that I saw was the guy on stilts. He was good. He even danced with them. That's all I have to say today,

Billie Jo Roark (5)

But it was a very hot day, some of the events in which we had hoped to participate were canceled or delayed, and students were less enthusiastic than we had hoped. During the teachers' meeting, some conflicts surfaced about the need to collaborate on all decisions: some staff members thought those with the most experience should make the majority of the decisions; others insisted on our being as collaborative as possible in decision making and issues of discipline. For instance, there was some disagreement about whether students should be allowed to eat food on the street. This issue opened up opportunities to discuss the cultural, racial, and class differences among us as well as our individual teaching styles. These were very productive internal struggles; we felt we learned from them. I will deal at length with the story of those struggles through stories of the event as told by each teacher and some students; for now, however, it may be sufficient to note that the conflict took place within our daily schedule as we were dealing with many other issues and details.

On the fourth day, we were visited by storyteller Craig Roney from Wayne State University's Education Department, who told us various culturally derived versions of "Cinderella," including his own personal, "neighborhood" version. Many of us found him engaging, funny, even mesmerizing. Many students were inspired to write sketches or drafts of their own versions of the stories, some of them staying close to their understanding of a "Cinderella" story while others quickly strayed in personal directions. We had discussions about story structure and shared much of our writing with each other. Roney's visit, with its emphasis on storytelling and personal, community-based retellings of stories, was to figure importantly in our work together.[3]

CINDERJULIE
Julia Pointer

"And hurry up," the evil stepbrother said. "I don't have a clean cup to get some milk with!" Cinderjulie just cut up the radio

louder. It was the only thing her evil stepbrother allowed to have
near her when she was working. But that's only because she
likes music, and even if a song came on that she liked and he-
didn't have she changed the station anyway. Just then a commer-
cial about a concert came on: *Tonight! June 30! Al. B. Sure! in
concert at Joe Louis Arena with guests Guy and Vanessa
Williams.* Cinderjulie screamed for joy. She had been waiting for
an Al. B. Sure! concert for months. (*Corridors* 76)

On Thursday we also set up a "family/community celebration day" to be held on the following Wednesday, July 5. Susan
brought in personal and family "artifacts," a plate that had been
handed down through many generations, and a sorority portrait,
and she talked about them, encouraging students to invite their
family members in, to bring their artifacts and tell their stories about
them. On Friday we were visited by four more community members
who were known and respected for their commitment to the community, including Fannie Jones, Manatee Smith, Dorothy Miles, and
Molly Rubino. I helped interview Rubino, a poet who had quit
her teaching job to move to the projects on the day Martin Luther
King, Jr., was killed. She read one of her "political poems," as she referred to it:

> Empty faces
> dirty places
> stumbling,
> humbling
> old
> clinging to life
> $400 a month
>
> Doesn't anybody see?
> Doesn't anybody care?
>
> You'd be surprised
> about the city's
> soul for
> scattered here
> and there
> are people who
> will pay the toll;

fighting,
praying,
living,
to make the city whole

They have heard the anguish,
and are living here to care.

An activist for social justice, Rubino worked in the projects teaching G.E.D. classes three nights a week. Students were industrious, asking questions, talking with all of our guests, and recording their impressions and our guests' answers. We spent an hour after the interviews talking about what we had heard, sometimes sharing ideas on how to shape what we had heard into some form of writing, writing in journals, and writing and revising various pieces.

The long holiday weekend covered four days, but when we returned on the following Wednesday, the much-anticipated family celebration took place, with several parents coming to share their stories. The parents' presentations helped to make the connections between students, parents, teachers, and the community. But there were also conflicts that day about discipline; specifically, trash disposal during break, since some teachers had confronted students with the problem. In the afternoon session, teachers discussed the issue of trash disposal in terms of a broader issue: Should we develop rules for student conduct; should we confront students? What place does discipline have in whole language? What function does telling students to "be responsible" have in a program supposedly intended to increase students' decision-making capacities? What is "student empowerment," and how do you create the conditions for students to possess it?

We discussed related issues as well: Should students focus more on community writing than they initially seemed to be doing? What about the maturity level and developmental differences in the students? To what extent—in a program designed for "student empowerment," where we had asked students to think of themselves as authors—could we as teachers insist on particular content and forms? What was the role of the imagination in community exploration? For instance, was Joe's story about the end of the universe essentially about his world, his community, or was it mostly play, not connected to our investigation of the community?

The Black Knight
Joe Hammer

> The knight weighed 398 tons. All of a sudden he pulled a switch
> and the eyes of the knight were gleaming brightly red and evil.
> So then the knight stood up and said, "YES, I WILL NOW DE-
> STROY THE UNIVERSE." (*Corridors* 123)

None of us were completely satisfied that this was the best work
Joe could do, and some of us were uncomfortable with its violent
theme, but it was important to us that he had written something that
interested him and had completed it. Maybe, some of us argued, his
next piece would pursue what would be for us more productive concepts. Recalling Joe's interest during the interview with George Mc-
Mahon, Debi volunteered to work with Joe and encourage him to try
some writing based more on the community. Though we had seen no
other student writing raising comparable concerns, we agreed that a
confrontation with certain students about their pieces might be necessary and appropriate. We discussed the experiences we had had
helping students "improve" their texts, and we admitted the possibility of and problem with appropriating student texts in the process
of working with students in conferences. We agreed that using a
whole-language approach didn't mean that teachers' personal objections to content couldn't or shouldn't be voiced. Toby noted that
these occasions might be opportunities for productive discussions
with students about sensitive issues.

Thursday, the second day of our second week, was exciting and
exhausting, with a train trip from Detroit to Ann Arbor and a tour of
the University of Michigan campus, including the stadium, sports
arena, natural science museum, the Michigan student union, an "all
you can eat cafeteria," and *college* classrooms. For most of these students and most accompanying parents, this was their first train trip.
Many students wrote a great deal about their experiences on the way
to Ann Arbor, during the tour, and on the way home. Some of us had
been skeptical about the place of a trip to the university in a program
supposedly focused on community writing, but having seen how
much the students enjoyed the experience, and how much they had
written about it, skeptics were generally silenced. The teachers' discussion of this issue circled back to notions of choice as we discussed
Joe Hammer's story. What if students don't want to write about their
homes? One teacher argued: It's fine to get students to write about
and possibly celebrate the good in their world, but you also have to

give them the opportunity to dream of a place and time "beyond their world." Most of us seemed to agree.

The second Friday, like the first, was primarily a "writing day." Students wrote, conferred with teachers, and met in small group writers' workshops. The afternoon teachers' meeting was noteworthy for a fiery discussion about "black English vernacular" (BEV) and its place in schooling, an issue raised in terms of particular students' writing. Again, the debate seemed to focus on the nature of authority, this time directly focusing on issues of language and power: Should we "allow" students to write in BEV, especially considering their writing might be part of a publication? Some of us were initially as much against confronting students about language use as we had been about confronting them about behavioral concerns such as eating on the street. Others emphasized the necessity of conforming to some extent to "majority standards" in order to gain access to power. One teacher argued that outside readers—both black and white—would criticize us as teachers if they read a book of student writing filled with black English. We shared stories and arguments and came to a general agreement to use the standard English/black English vernacular issue as an occasion for discussion with students when the issue could be raised in terms of each student's writing. Certain students, we noticed, demonstrated an understanding of the difference between speech and writing in their use of dialogue, and we agreed that it was useful for students to understand such distinctions, but we couldn't come to an agreement about the place of black English in our student publication. We agreed to raise the issue with the students in a general session. As we negotiated and debated various sensitive, volatile issues, we teachers found how essential conflict was to learning from each others' perspectives. The more we worked together, the better we knew each other, and the better we knew each other, the more comfortable we were with conflict.

On the final Monday, Larry Pike, a local poet, came to read his own and Michigan poet Theodore Roethke's community-based poetry and encouraged all students and teachers to write "I Am" poems, helping to make further connections to our lived worlds through writing. The final Tuesday through Friday were spent frantically writing and revising, as students struggled to finish composing pieces for the book, which we named *Corridors: Stories from Inner City Detroit.* Students entered the text and made changes on the computers themselves, and since there were only four computers, our time with the students began spilling into the afternoons. Tuesday we raised the issue of the use of black English, but most students didn't seem interested in discussing the issue, and we came to no agreement about how we should deal with it in the final editing stages. Most students seemed to agree with student Julia Pointer that all pupils should help edit "the mistakes" in each other's writing "to make it the best possible," but since it was difficult to formulate general rules, others seemed to agree with student Camille Ryan that it should be "left up to the individual student's decision" about their writing. Each piece should be considered individually. Also on Tuesday some students took a trip to the Eastern Market to experience the sights and sounds and smells of the morning sale of fruits, vegetables, and other commodities. Others took a tour of the Cass Corridor Food Co-op to discover how the business is run by its members and to learn about its philosophy of cooperation and environmental commitment. Many wrote about these experiences, others stayed behind to write and revise. On the last day, we had a pizza party and shared our writing with each other and some parents and planned a reunion in the fall to celebrate the publication of our book.

On the actual day of the publication party for *Corridors,* many community members, parents, students, university and Detroit public school teachers and administrators came to speak and participate. Students signed their books for guests. Many students read their texts aloud. Reporters from the *Detroit News* and the *Michigan Chronicle* became the first of many media representatives to write about what we had come to see as a successful project. The first year of the Dewey Center Community Writing Project was in many respects complete. George Cooper and I would continue each week to work with students on their writing in the Dewey Center and follow the progress of the students and teachers with whom we had worked. We were joined gradually by several other University of Michigan teachers in various projects with students.

Those of us who taught in the writing project also agreed to find ways to share our experiences with others. We met in September in Ann Arbor for a long discussion about the program, and this discussion led us to shape a prospectus for a book about the program, *Writing, Teaching, Community Voices: The Dewey Center Community Writing Project,* which focuses on how and why students wrote their texts and collaborative learning and teaching.[4]

I was compelled by several issues during the three weeks of the program. Abstract terms like "collaborative learning and teaching" and "community-based" came to life in our program in complex ways and in a seeming cacophony of voices and perspectives. Teachers—some of them black, some of them white, some of them public school teachers, some of them university teachers—struggled to negotiate differences—some of them cultural—in their efforts to work with students in a particular multicultural setting. Students wrote versions of "Cinderella" and teachers told stories about these students' writing. I was fascinated at the ways teachers shaped curriculum and developed theories together, each day struggling with conflicting "versions" of events and issues. Student stories were written about community stories, and teachers' stories were told about those students and their writing; each story led to other stories. Every story, whether about Rose Bell, trash disposal, or eating on the street, led me to explore ways to understand the nature of stories themselves and to understand particular issues that the stories raised for me about teaching.

TELLING STORIES AND LEARNING

I was interested in the way in which the Dewey program, in its focus on the students' community, drew on the stories of community members, which in turn engendered stories from students. I heard these students' stories form the basis of the teachers' daily discussions about the classroom, which also took shape as stories. The teachers began telling each other stories early in our collaboration, sharing stories not only about our experiences and professional interests, but also about our lives outside teaching: stories of our families, stories of our hopes and fears. Through these stories we came to understand each other and learned from one another how to be teachers of the children we were meeting each day. With each story, we knew each other better, working toward a language through which we could talk about the world we were coming to share.

Before we began planning and working with students, our stories came necessarily and exclusively from our various backgrounds, but as we began to meet with students, our shared experiences changed the nature of the stories we told together. Each day of the program, after working with the students from 8:30 a.m. to 12:30 p.m., we met for several hours together, planning the next day, swapping tales about our teaching. We interpreted our ways of working with the students and interpreted our students' stories. The "retellings" of events and stories emerged from our various perspectives, and, like all conflicting histories, they did not neatly mesh. We disagreed about the progress of particular students; we disagreed about what activities to plan for the next day—whether, for instance, to visit the Eastern Market during the last week or remain at the Dewey Center to devote more time to revision; we differed on how much control a teacher should have over a particular student's writing, about trash disposal and eating on the street; we argued about political and ethical issues. Through listening to each other's varied perspectives on the students, we found ourselves reshaping our own perspectives, learning from each other. Although at times we didn't feel as if we were getting anywhere in our talk together, eventually we came to appreciate the usefulness of each other's differing perspectives.

Conversations were often exhilarating as we celebrated the progress of Dora, for example, or the overall success of a trip to the Eastern Market, but they were also sometimes volatile as we disagreed about how to "deal with" the twins Walter and Dale, the place of black English in the classroom, or the general shape and direction of the program, and as we tried over a short thirteen days time to develop a language for talking about thirty individual students and how we might best teach them. The four of us from Ann Arbor continued our talk in the car on the way home each day and later sometimes via electronic mail or on the phone, and we renewed our talk together each morning in the car at 7:00 a.m. We had dinner together two evenings during the program and shared stories on those occasions as well. As we worked together, it became increasingly clear to us that our talk was one of the most important—if not the most important—aspects of the program. Over time we began to ask each other why the stories so significantly informed our planning and our understanding?

I found the kind of knowledge that the students and teachers created through storytelling to be similar to the "personal" knowledge that biologist Michael Polanyi describes, a way of knowing that is invested with intentionality—passionate, experiential knowing. Polanyi begins his inquiry into the nature and justification of scientific knowledge with a rejection of the ideal of scientific detachment. For him, knowing is an "active comprehension of the things known" (viii), requiring the personal participation of the knower in all acts of understanding. Polanyi rejects any approach to research or learning that separates thought and feeling in its attempt to be "objective." He establishes a view of knowing that is inescapably bound to human commitment: "The personal participation of the knower in the knowledge he believes himself to possess takes place within a flow of passion" (300). All knowledge is fundamentally personal, involving purpose and passion.

Contrary to the traditional scientific goal, Polanyi suggests that, "in order to describe experience more fully, language must be less precise" and at the same time "more complete," saturated with "experiential content" (86). As he sees it, "Only words of indeterminate meaning can have a bearing on reality" (251). He notes the centrality of language in the process of knowing: "To modify our idiom is to modify the frame of reference within which we shall henceforth interpret our experience; it is to modify ourselves" (105). And it is precisely the passion in language which is "heuristic" for Polanyi; it makes things valuable through "intrinsic interest" (136).

Although Polanyi didn't privilege a particular genre in his discussion of personal knowledge—essays are experiential, too, though usually less obviously so—narrative seems to me to be the genre best suited to allow individuals to capture, to shape this personal knowledge Polanyi describes, saturated as stories are with "experiential content" and the passions of the lived world. The nature of story is to heighten the indeterminacy, the possibility of change in reality by demonstrating through the interplay of voices the shifting nature of experience. Wasn't this what Dora was trying to accomplish when she wrote "961-BABY"?[5] Wasn't Dora constructing for herself experiential "personal knowledge" through her story? What drove her to write if it's not a passionate commitment to concerns that matter to her? In a similar vein, when we teachers argued and told our stories about social and cultural "standards," weren't we doing something similar? We certainly weren't "detached" or "objective" in our research. I wondered: How, then, does knowledge get constructed? What is the role of language in learning?

LANGUAGE AND REALITY

In order to fully understand the value of narrative in learning, I felt the need to ground myself in a perspective on language that was consistent with Polanyi's view of knowing, a perspective that is meaning-centered, one that emphasizes the interpretive functions of language in the construction of self and other.[6] When Dewey Center students and teachers were writing and talking with one another and with community members, they seemed to be constructing something new together through their language use. Language is constitutive of reality, not reflective of it. It is constitutive of objects and experience, and not just about objects and experience: "Where there are no sentences there is no truth" (Rorty 5). Languages are human creations, as is "truth" itself. Rorty speaks of language's central place in self-creation: "The human self is created by use of a vocabulary rather than being adequately or inadequately expressed in a vocabulary"

(7). This constructivist view of language made sense of the process of storytelling I observed in the Dewey program.

The later work of Wittgenstein is useful for thinking about language in this way. For Wittgenstein, words in use complicate the issues of reference and signification. Language use requires rules, as any game requires rules, but the conditions for these rules change constantly according to the contexts in which they are used: "Word meanings change to fit every instance of use" (140). Conditionality, which is central to intentionality, is at the heart of language. Language is therefore "imprecise," a game of sorts, rule governed but not fixed, "logical" but not in such a way that requires a set of rules to govern all situations. Thinking of Wittgenstein's view in terms of the conflict we had had about black English vernacular during the program, I was inclined to agree with student Camille Ryan that decisions about language use might best be made in terms of each writer's individual texts. It would be difficult to formulate rules for all situations, given the very conditionality of language use. The concept of "standard" English itself took on a more provisional status in a framework such as the one Wittgenstein described.

In Wittgenstein's perspective on language, as with Polanyi's work, there is a close connection between knowledge claims and belief. As Wittgenstein, and other language philosophers such as Heidegger, Cassirer, and Langer point out, language is not a neutral mirror to the world; it is an active force in shaping our lives, our selves. Language is complex and partisan, Wittgenstein reminds us. He emphasizes, too, the imagination and the creative forces in language use. He speaks of the mythical basis of language, based in willing, feeling, and belief. As I saw it, our students were using language to shape their world, themselves, through the stories and poems that they were writing.

Wittgenstein, like Polanyi after him, was responding to positivist claims for knowledge, claims he had done much to advance in his earlier works. Michael Shapiro summarizes this effort: "There is more to the understanding of human phenomena than can be developed within the bounds of scientific, causally oriented explanations" (2). What does it mean to *understand* human phenomena? Shapiro sees the positivist separation of normative, or advocacy-oriented, and empirical, or explanation-oriented approaches, as not viable. Language, he points out, is an expression of human experience, not just a tool or symbolic structure. Whereas positivist language philosophers, and the epistemological position on which their philosophy depends, emphasize the importance of verification in knowing, philosophers in the tradition of Wittgenstein's later work question whether verification, or certainty, is even possible. Wittgenstein helps one to realize that there is always an interpretive element in any descriptively oriented statement. We have to reject the notion that we can radically separate the empirical and normative functions of language.

In accepting this perspective on language, one can begin to see that meaning itself is *metaphorical*. Human beings, within such a conception of language and knowing or learning, are essentially networks of beliefs and desires. Within such a perspective on language, the intellectual history that humans tell is essentially a history of metaphors, or fictions, about these beliefs and desires. Theories, concepts, and ideas—including the things our students learn in school—are metaphors, not facts, as Wittgenstein points out. If language is constitutive of reality, then one can easily see the degree to which these language "constructions" (essays, poems, stories, or blurred genres) are fictional representations of reality. I began to see the importance of seeing the world as constitutive—as provisionally constructed and endlessly open to reconstruction through language—for those of us teaching and learning in the Dewey Center. What part might students' and teachers' texts about their communities possibly play in the process of changing their world?

NARRATIVE AS SELF-CONSTRUCTION

Polanyi's emphasis on the autonomy and commitment of the individual knower seems consistent with what many others have written about narrative as a primarily "personal" or individual act or process.[7] Most writers who concentrate on narrative emphasize the psychological or intrasubjective aspects of the form; Barbara Hardy, for instance, emphasizes individual psychological functions when she identifies narrative as a "primary act of mind" (73). Teacher Betty Rosen sees stories as "a way of dealing with matters of deep concern in people's lives" (17) and emphasizes the "therapeutic" value of stories. As in journal writing, it may be "good" for you to talk through your problems and difficult experiences and make sense of them. Others highlight the use of the imagination, of metaphor and fantasy in storytelling, or the way it can help students develop an "authentic voice." As Gordon Wells puts it,

> The education of the whole person, which is the declared aim of probably every school system, can only be achieved if there are opportunities to explore feelings and values in specific real or

imagined situations as well as lessons devoted to the considerations of general principles." (203)

For Wells, these opportunities primarily include engagement in storytelling as readers and writers of stories. Many composition theorists, such as Peter Elbow and Ken Macrorie, champion the story for
similar reasons. Viewing much student writing as stilted and artificial
"Engfish," Macrorie sees stories as a kind of writing based in personal
experience for readers and writers, which is to be valued particularly
for its demonstration of "voice." Voice in this tradition is often
closely related to the emotions, presumably "repressed" in most academic writing.

   When Camille Ryan writes in this excerpt from her poem,

> I am a painting,
> complex and interpreted in so many
> different ways, yet cherished and valuable.
> I am a vine,
> growing
> growing
> growing so recklessly
> and then suddenly blooming
> with white flowers,   (*Corridors* 26)

she is constructing for herself "personal" knowledge of the kind that
Polanyi was discussing, with a "voice" that Elbow, Macrorie, or any
teacher might admire. But what about her fictional story, "The Other
Side of the Projects"? In imagining a character who had left the
projects, graduated from college, and considered returning to work
in the community, Camille writes about herself, but she also writes
about her community:

> All of a sudden something dawned on me. What about those
> people who had no hope? What about those who are trapped
> such as we were? Who will open doors of opportunity for them?
> When I was a school kid I remember thinking, "No one cares
> about a poor black kid. No one wants to help us out." So now I
> have the opportunity to help them out myself. (*Corridors* 20)

Taking a look at this excerpt from her story, I felt that, as in her poem,
Camille was engaging in personal knowledge. But content, and the
extent to which it was "personal," wasn't the primary issue. All

knowledge, all language use is, to a certain extent, "personal," as Polanyi points out. Looking again at her poem, I could see that she was doing much more than writing about herself; she was inscribing a possible world in which she might live. In other words, in each of her texts Camille constructs a self and Other. Through her writing, she creates an imaginary world out of which her present one might be considered.

Though I found various psychological considerations regarding the study of narrative writing useful in helping me value stories in learning, I felt it important to develop a view of narrative that went beyond the merely personal, such as what Gordon Wells touches on here:

> Through stories, the child is beginning to discover the symbolic potential of language: its power to create possible or imaginary worlds through words—by representing experiences in symbols that are independent of the objects, events and relationships symbolized and that can be interpreted in contexts other than those in which the experience originally occurred, if indeed it occurred at all. (156)

"Storying," as Wells calls it, "encountering the world, and understanding it contextually, by shaping ideas, facts, experience itself into stories, is one of the most fundamental means of making meaning; as such, it is an activity that pervades all learning" (194). To learn, to understand, often means to frame new information in terms of experience, to "make sense" of it in terms of a "story." Camille and Dora, in similar ways, tell stories to make sense of their worlds, reconceiving them in terms of the possibilities they are exploring.

Structuralists such as Tzvetan Todorov and Gerard Genette identify distinguishing features of narrative texts—either the features of whole texts or of those embedded in other forms, such as the anecdote used as a supporting example—and focus primarily on the use of sequencing and the reporting of experiences from another space and time. Clearly, the study of narrative texts for more than their literary or aesthetic value, as particular ways of representing and ordering the world to the exclusion of others, should and does yield some important information about the role of narrative in the representation of reality. And as anthropologists such as James Clifford and Clifford Geertz point out, a study of narrative structure can help us think about the political and ethical problems of representation itself. But was it identifying and describing the limits of a particular genre that was important to me in understanding Camille's texts? It didn't seem useful to me at the time to study the structural aspects of genre in general, or narrative in particular. Defining terms seemed to me a less interesting activity than analyzing the uses of storytelling within the particular circumstances of the Dewey project.

What became increasingly clear for me in my study of the nature of storytelling was that the most important aspects of story are those generally, and surprisingly, ignored by narrative theorists—its social aspects. One way I began to appreciate the virtue of this kind of analysis was to take a broader view of the text as a process of negotiation between writers and readers. This certainly seemed to be the case among those of us in the Dewey program, each day changing our stories and interpretations of students in terms of one another's stories. As Harold Rosen sees it, a story "is always a collaborative process between storyteller and listener (or reader), and other stories" (25). The notion of text itself as an "object" or product for study begins to expand if we focus on the collaborative nature of text making. As psychologist Jerome Bruner points out, in the process of sharing their particular human concerns through their stories, students become members of a "culture-creating community" (1986, 132). A "text" is clearly something far more than marks on a printed page. As Bruner says, "It is not just that the child must make his knowledge his own, but that he must make it his own in a community of those who share his sense of belonging to a culture" (127).

Psychoanalyst Roy Schafer would seem to agree. As he sees it, the telling and reshaping of stories is the way we see and make sense of the world: "We are forever telling stories about ourselves and others" (31). Psychoanalysis for Schafer is itself a storytelling event, where "reality" is mediated by narration, an exchange of telling and retelling until a kind of useful (never perfect) understanding or interpretive "version" is constructed between patient and therapist, who exchange places periodically as tellers and listeners. The relationship between teller and listener is a central consideration of the texts created through therapeutic storytelling sessions. Schafer, like many others, helped me see that language is fundamentally social and essentially constitutive of reality. In his view, narrative is a key dialogic instance of that social construction.

If we were to follow Bruner's and Schafer's perspectives on storytelling, Camille's story might be studied in terms of her community and the part the community and story have played in each other's formation. The stories that we as teachers told each other about our students evolved collaboratively, through dialogue, as I discussed briefly in the preface. We always shaped the stories we told in terms of each other's stories and in terms of our daily, changing experiences with each student. In shaping our stories together, it seems to me, we were creating a community of learners, learning what we needed to know for our particular circumstances. Understanding those stories could only take place through a consideration of their function in those circumstances.

The social perspective on language and storytelling advanced by writers such as Polanyi, Wittgenstein, Bruner, and Wells is helpful as I think of stories that were shared in the Dewey Program about Rose Bell or eating on the street, but it doesn't fully address a fundamental dimension regarding work in a multicultural setting—the political dimension. In our teacher conversation about eating on the street, for instance, choices—political choices—had to be made about whether we would confront students for certain kinds of public behavior. How would we decide the issue, and on what basis would we decide? The stories that shaped our curriculum were stories told from differing political perspectives, with political consequences. In addition, the language of the "discourse community" with which we were forming ourselves and our students seemed very much tied to issues of power. I knew that all schools and classroom communities within schools limit and constrain in certain ways what students learn in school, and I was critical of these practices. My hope was to find ways in our program to do away with those usual constraints, but I needed to know more, so I turned to the work of Michel Foucault for an understanding of the political nature of discourse in our teaching community.

FOUCAULT AND DISCURSIVE PRACTICES

Foucault's work stands in many ways in the tradition of Heidegger's with regard to language, but focuses on the political dimensions of a social perspective on discourse. Like Heidegger, he illustrates the provisional and constitutive nature of language but highlights the social and political nature of this constitution. I find Foucault's work useful for developing the necessary critique that some social constructivist theorists lack, and though I find his perspective finally inadequate for the task, I see it nevertheless as a critical component in developing a view of narrative as a language of possibility. For Foucault, as with Heidegger and others before him, language and speech practices are more than tools for "discovering" some underlying Truth. But his analysis differs from his predecessors in some important ways:

Truth is a thing of this world: it is produced only by virtue of
multiple forms of constraint. And it induces regular effects of
power. Each society had its regime of truth, its "general politics"
of truth: that is, the type of discourse which it accepts and makes
function as true; the mechanisms and instances which enable
one to distinguish true and false statements, the means by which
each is sanctioned; the techniques and procedures accorded
value in the acquisition of truth; the status of those who are
charged with saying what counts as true. (1980, 131)

Foucault's "archaeologies" of discursive practices in various disciplines explore the nature of truth making in those disciplines, demonstrating that ideology and the structures of power that construct it
are inseparable from knowledge. Extending Heidegger's perspective
on knowledge, Foucault attacks structures of domination through a
radical rejection of the prevailing positivist epistemology, but he goes
on to examine the various ways particular discourse systems within
a positivist framework create certain kinds of persons by excluding
certain kinds of language. For Foucault, discourses are domains
within which power and authority are conferred on some and denied
to others. Language operates within certain rules of exclusion, providing boundaries invested with institutional support and correlated
with social, political, and administrative practices. Language has us,
as Heidegger says, but for Foucault this linguistic subservience represents a central means of social and political constraint.

Foucault, in *Madness and Civilization,* for instance, makes it
clear that people *create* madness in each age.[8] Madness, for Foucault,
far from being a medical fact, is a myth the discursive practices of
cultures throughout history create for the purpose of exclusion and
control of certain kinds of behavior. His work explores the "merciless
language of non-madness" in each age and renounces "the conve-
nience of terminal truths" which this language entails (1965, ix).

With Heidegger and Wittgenstein, Foucault decries the notion of
"certainty"; he opposes the "exclusionary monologue of reason." At
the heart of this grand narrative of reason is "the hidden perfection
of a language" (95) which only Reason itself can discover. Foucault is
interested in exploring the nature of "the forbidden limits of knowledge" (22) and language to help critique the discursive practices of
reason. Madness, as Other, as cultural difference, is perceived as er-
ror, wrong, deficient in right reason. As Foucault points out, "The asylum is a religious domain without a religion, a domain of pure
morality. . . . The asylum reduces differences, represses vice, elimi-

nates irregularities" (257–58). His work helped me see the ways in which all discourse systems, including educational ones, have the potential to control, repress, limit, and, ultimately, do bodily harm. He illustrates in his work that what we call madness—or illiteracy—in each age and society is a way of knowing very different—but, importantly, no less useful for understanding the world—than ways of knowing commonly associated with reason.

Foucault's work is useful for understanding the ways that most schools limit student ways of knowing. Standards for acceptable linguistic behavior are imposed by teachers in terms of the "regimes of truth" of district language arts requirements, state departments of instruction mandates, and mainstream expectations for linguistic performance. A range of constraints provided by mechanisms such as in-school ability grouping or tracking shape and limit student performance in school: students are assigned to classes on the basis of their apparent inability to master particular forms of English, are drilled in terms of these forms but are rarely allowed to move out of their assigned track. Most of the students with whom we were working in the Dewey program would likely be the victims of such practices, where language use becomes a primary tool for maintaining and reproducing the social order. Accepted and unquestioned rules of exclusion operate as "truths." As Jeannie Oakes makes clear, tracking is one of the fundamental means within which power and authority are conferred on some and denied to others. These mechanisms are tied to ideological bases inseparable from structures of power. I had come to understand the politics of standard English as very much tied to regimes of truth and domination advanced by tracking practices, and early in the program was concerned that some of us might be too uncritically accepting of the usual practices of schooling. I felt and still feel that those of us who are committed to equitable schooling and society have to question such practices, and I was grateful to Foucault for providing a framework for addressing them.[9]

I wondered how we in the Dewey Center program, in spite of our best intentions, with all of our progressive emphasis on collaboration and student empowerment, were helping to reinforce existing social relations through our practices. On the other hand, how were some of our strategies useful in working for change? Was change even possible within Foucault's perspective? His study of prisons in *Discipline and Punish* is useful in analyzing the way schools shape students into particular kinds of persons, and it helped me consider as well some of our teachers' approaches to "disciplinary" practices. I felt sure at times during the program that some of the early calls from certain teachers for more "structure" and explicit rules for students were a way for us to reproduce relations with students as they usually are in schools. I and others argued against restricting students according to perceived notions—fictions—of "societal expectations" in language use or other kinds of social behavior. Those of us who felt this way argued for creating conditions where students could make choices for themselves and where they could learn as well about the political and cultural implications for such choices.

Foucault, by calling attention to social injustice, speaks in some sense for the dispossessed, the excluded, those on the margins, such as those in prison or in psychiatric hospitals; I felt he could help us speak for those who taught and learned in the Dewey program. Yet something troubled me, too: Foucault's "heroes" were aesthetic and intellectual ones, those on the artistic and literary margins. Scorning liberal pretensions to revolutionary change, he championed icono-clasts—artists such as Artaud, Magritte, Nietzsche, Roussel, those who rejected all traditions, who denounced the rationality that drives contemporary technocratic and militaristic societies. In any discussion about developing a language of possibility, Foucault seems to side with the voices of surrealism, dadaism, and the absurd. This direction is ultimately inadequate for developing an agenda for social change and can be demonstrated by examining the work of one artist Foucault applauds, Antonin Artaud.

Artaud, dramatist and author of *The Theater and Its Double,* devised his "theater of cruelty" in response to what he calls the "positivist theater" (12). In "the spirit of anarchy" which he says is the spirit of poetry, he rages against the theater of "fixed texts" and "logical, discursive language" (54). Since "all true feeling is in reality untranslatable," (71) and because speech distorts and hides "the poetry in thought" (73), Artaud says he "distrusts language" and instead advocates "the intuitive language of symbolization" (73) exemplified in Noh and Balinese drama, a theater of gesture, music, and poetry. Like Foucault and Heidegger, and reminiscent of many French feminist critics, Artaud sees the way language limits—and thus invents—new words, new ways of speaking, and exalts the languages of music and dance. While he usefully calls attention to the limits of written language, Artaud, like Foucault, ultimately fails to acknowledge the emancipatory possibilities in the social construction of knowledge, possibilities that are already there, and in many ways "drops out" of any conversation which might point to praxis, to change. Although Foucault cannot be held responsible for Artaud's views, the fact that he champions Artaud and shares his ultimately paralogic perspective helps us to see why Foucault's work is more useful for developing a language of critique rather than a language of possibility.

By examining recent work in this tradition by rhetorician Thomas Kent (who also works within the perspective of Jacques Derrida), we can further see the limitations of Foucault's perspective on language. Kent argues that "discourse production and perception are paralogic acts that cannot be systematized and then talked about in any meaningful way" (25). The sophistic tradition provides a historical foundation for this perspective, which illustrates that discourse refutes codification. Thus, as Kent believes, neither reading nor writing can be taught as a systematic process; rather, discourse production is open-ended dialogic activity, the most fundamental activity of which is the hermeneutic act, or what he calls "the interpretive guess." Kent finds the work of Derrida, who emphasizes the "essential drift of the sign" (Kent 28), as most useful in understanding the "arbitrary" nature of language and stresses (in many respects like Artaud and Foucault) the nature of intuition, luck, sympathy, and "taste" as central to theory-building in rhetoric.

Stressing the paralogic and contradictory dimensions of language, Kent calls attention to assumptions we have about objectivity and which we might assume some forms or genres embody. Like others, he points out "the impossibility of teaching writing and critical thinking as an epistemologically centered body-of-knowledge" (19). While Kent does advocate "dialogic writing, and forms of writing which capitalize on or seem to emphasize the dialogic capacities in language itself" (31)—such as narrative—he, like Foucault and Derrida, ultimately seems limited by his ability to see beyond a "lack of center" in discourse when he could emphasize the emancipatory possibilities in rhetoric seen as a function of dialogue.

As useful as some of their ideas might be in identifying much of what's wrong in our schools, what possibilities for change could thinkers like Foucault help us see in Detroit and situations like it? How could Julia and Dora expect to work against the systems apparently determining their futures? Are their voices alone howling in the darkness, or can they contribute together to changing the world? And what place might teachers occupy there other than as unwitting agents in ceaseless domination? Is teaching for change even possible within such a perspective?

James Boyd White replies, "One response to the world is to make a text about it, a reorganization of its resources of meaning tentatively achieved in a relation, newly constituted, between reader and writer" (1984, 4). In other words, individual text making to some extent reconstitutes language in the very act of its making. Polanyi agrees: "Every time we use a word in speaking and writing we both comply with usage and at the same time somewhat modify the existing usage" (208). In his social perspective on language, Foucault, with Kent, ignores the necessarily historical contributions of individual subjects like Julia and Dora and public school teachers like Toby Curry and Jeanetta Cotman who are working with others to make changes. Agency, born of the intentionality of particular commitments, largely ignored by Foucault, is an important function of knowledge construction that rescues it from mere relativism and chaos. For Foucault, philosophy surrenders to poetry because he denies the active, intersubjective possibilities in language.

For those of us who are committed to change, like the teachers in the Dewey program, issues of language and discursive practices are crucial. Some of the central questions that need to be addressed become clear: does language evolve blindly simply because there may be no facts or divine truths "behind" or "beneath" language, or is language created in terms of culture? And if it is indeed created by culture, is it "sheer contingency" that directs language, without the contributions of individual actors (or groups within those cultures), or can that contingency be characterized in any way that can illustrate how change might take place, as for example, through dialogic interaction? Our answers to these questions ultimately point to ethical stances, moral commitments such as whether we believe in praxis, the possibility for social change, and the extent to which we see humans as historically (or otherwise) determined.

Foucault has said that his work was meant to have people rethink and question certain commonplace notions about institutions and "contribute to changing certain things in people's ways of perceiving and doing things, to participate in this difficult displacement of forms of sensibility and thresholds of tolerance" (1981, 8). Though he does not provide a theory of social and political change, his "archaelogies" of knowledge help us to understand the ways particular kinds of discourse, and perhaps different rhetorical styles, might serve discursive practices that have power and control as their primary ends. To realize that discursive practices are inescapably political practices is crucial to developing what could become an emancipatory perspective on language learning.

Foucault's work is useful in demonstrating how all discourse has its basis, in some important respects, in poesis, how all culture is in flux, changing, provisional, a constructed entity. He illustrates that the world cannot usefully be reduced to paraphrase, to formula, to logical system and helps us avoid the arrogance and ethnocentrism that usually accompany our certainty about what we know and what we institutionally sanction as worthwhile ways and things to know. Foucault helps us question the usual practices of schooling and helps us avoid a similarly repressive regime in our efforts to be more "progressive."

In questioning widely accepted and largely unquestioned discursive practices, Foucault paves the way for a reconsideration of story as a means of inquiry, as a valid means of learning, within and working against the often oppressive grand narratives that, in part, shape culture; he points the way for imagining a broader perspective on texts and a broader, more inclusive perspective on literacy. Although he is usually perceived as a nihilist against any system, any theory, any form which he assumes will ultimately prove to be cruel to some of its members, Foucault nevertheless resists the dominant discursive practices and reshapes (or reinvents) them in terms of the possibilities for social justice:

> I am fully aware that I have never written anything other than fictions. For all that, I would not want to say that they were outside of the truth. It seems plausible to me to make fictions work within truth, to introduce truth-effects within a fictional discourse, and in some way to make discourse arouse, "fabricate," something which does not yet exist, thus to fiction something. (1979, 75)

This kind of critical reflection, this "fictioning" (or what others call "storying"), is necessary as we think of students' and teachers' stories of the Dewey program as a particular means of fictioning the world in order to change it. As Jay Robinson has pointed out, language is an activity, a means for that socially and culturally specific fiction—consciousness. Language may "have us" to some extent, as Heidegger says, in the sense that there are limits to what language can express and very real limits with respect to particular discourse systems where individual voices have been effectively silenced; but meaning in discourse systems is always variable, always open to change, and individual expression in the dialogic acts of interpretation contributes to those changes. Building on Foucault's critical notion of language as power and ideology, we need to look beyond critique to possibility. The work of V. N. Volisinov helps one to construct a theory of narrative learning consistent with the work of Mikhail Bakhtin, which is an attempt to be both critical and emancipatory. I felt the need for both in trying to understand the nature of our work in Detroit.

BAKHTIN'S HETEROGLOSSIA: STORYTELLING AS
THE LANGUAGE OF POSSIBILITY

V. N. Volisinov, in *Marxism and the Philosophy of Language,* focuses on language as a continuous generative process implemented in the social-verbal interaction of speakers. He, like others, is opposed to merely descriptive or mechanistic categorization in language study. Interested in examining the concrete utterances of individuals in particular contexts, he emphasizes social and political factors. For him, as with Foucault, the word is an ideological sign. And, like Foucault, he emphasizes language as function rather than essence, but unlike Foucault he stresses process more than system. While Foucault's archaelogies account for structural properties in language, properties that are consistent in all discursive systems, Volisinov emphasizes a view of language as active, open to change: "A word in the mouth of a particular individual person is a product of the living interaction of social forces" (40). Verbal utterances, then, are social interaction; language itself *is* social intercourse. Thinking of the active, social interaction within the Dewey program, I was convinced that Volisinov might be used as an explanatory tool for how change might take place. His view of language seemed to make a place for students' and teachers' voices as change agents.

Primarily sociological, Volisinov's view insists that language study cannot be detached from social existence. He resists individual psychological subjectivism, with its focus on individual acts of expression, as if they existed in isolation—he would reject the notion of a "personal voice," as we discussed earlier—and abstract objectivism, with its linguistic positivism and its ahistorical focus on mere form. The sign, he says, "is socially constructed, intersubjective" (21). Moreover, Volisinov sees that the "psyche" itself is a sociological fact, and introspection, that aspect of the making of the self that we might deem the most "private," is a kind of social understanding. Inner speech is dialogic, worked out through continuous conflict. In other words, language is somebody talking with somebody else, even when that someone else is one's own inner voice.

Was the kind of social learning that Volisinov describes a better depiction of what was taking place in the Dewey program than the one Foucault offered? I felt it was. In many respects, our program fostered interaction—writing groups, conferences with students, large group sharing with peer comments—and we tried to provide opportunities for students to write about their world, the social world of their community. Students wrote and published their writing for community members as well as those beyond the community. Students made use of regular and frequent opportunities to talk and write with each other. When we made time for teachers to get together to discuss how we would work with students and plan a curriculum, we were attempting to build on the social possibilities of language and learning.

Storytelling is particularly useful for helping us to understand this social nature of language and learning, as Mikhail Bakhtin makes clear in his pioneering work on the novel, *The Dialogic Imagination.* He was certainly a colleague of Volisinov, and many think *Marxism and the Philosophy of Language* was actually written by Bakhtin. At any rate, his work is based on a similar philosophy of language: "Form and content in discourse are one, once we understand that verbal discourse is a social phenomenon—social throughout its entire range and in each and every one of its factors, from the sound image to the furthest reaches of abstract meaning" (259). The study of language for Bakhtin is also consistent with Volisinov's work: "Language is not an abstract system of normative forms but rather a concrete heteroglot conception of the world" (293).

Bakhtin, like Volisinov and Vygotsky, sees utterances as fundamentally dialogic and, as he points out, this "speech diversity within language has primary importance for the novel" (68). The novel itself may be viewed as a "system of languages that mutually and ideologically interanimate each other" (47), the very image of the way language functions in learning. Represented speech and thought, in which it is often difficult to know where the characters' words end and the narrator's words begin, is a good example for Bakhtin of how different kinds of discourse interact.

Bakhtin's view of language is that it is like the novel itself, not systematic or formalized, but a clashing; struggle and conflict is at the heart of language. Language, for him, is a diverse field characterized by ideological contention and conflict; in fact, language for Bakhtin is ideology. We speak with our ideologies, which are constituted in polyphony. A novel, reflecting the way the voices of the world interact with each other, is a representation of that polyphony, and primarily a forum for cultural discourse. And it is struggle that is at the heart of discourse in process—in the novel, in culture, nature, human relationships, the nature of interpretation, individual consciousness, and individual utterances.

The novel "best of all reflects the tendency of a new world still in the making" (7), Bakhtin points out. The world becomes "polyglot" in the novel. There is no inevitability in it; all is possible. There is no "final answer" but instead, as novelist Milan Kundera puts it, "a constant redefinition of the world as problems" (27). As an image of the language of possibility, novelistic discourse is "always criticizing itself," never fixed, or "there," but always in process, the very image of change and critical reflection. The novel for Bakhtin is a kind of "process approach" to being, a world always criticizing itself, a struggle of voices "stamped with the seal of inconclusiveness" (30).

In the work of Bakhtin I thought I had found a description of the talk and writing of the Dewey program. The teachers' meetings, from which we all seemed to learn, was filled with useful conflict, with stories of struggle and possibility. Our teacher session stories were like the best of novels where different ideological voices are present, preserved to knock against each other and to some extent change each other. The Dewey program teacher stories were a local, cultural forums on literacy.

Novelistic discourse, similar to the our exchange of stories, is heteroglossic, a webbing or interweaving of voices, a carnival of irony, parody, and resistance. Bakhtin helps us recall that most stories seem to resist systematization and reject in various ways the rules characteristic of most other forms. Novelists also generally work against societal and textual conventions developed in previous historical periods. Historically, each novel is a conversation with other texts, a response to other ways of representing. In our program, I felt we were engaging in such a conversation with each other and with competing conceptions of language and its role in the shaping of culture.

The novel, Bakhtin contends, is the best example of the way language works, and each novel is a conversation between various voices within itself, with other novels, and with the social world in which it is located. For example, as Bakhtin points out, the author Pushkin is

> in dialogical relationship with his character Evgenij Onegin's language; the author is actually conversing with Onegin and such a conversation is the fundamental constitutive element of all novelistic style as well as the controlling image of Onegin's language. The author represents this language, carries on a con-

versation with it, and the conversation penetrates into the interior of this language image and dialogizes it from within. And all essentially novelistic images share this quality: they are internally dialogized images—of the languages, styles, world views of another. (46)

The novel can be seen as a series of languages connected with each other and with the author via their own characteristic dialogic relationships. The novel indicates potential in language because the representation of many voices interacting is similar to how student and teacher voices interact in the collaborative acts of reading and writing. As Bakhtin makes clear to us, the novel demonstrates always new ways to mean and the ways we learn. The novel gives us some indication about how useful it might be for voices to interact in order for learning to best take place. Bakhtin seems to give both justification for providing more social circumstances for learning as well as a means of describing those circumstances. In many ways, he seemed to be talking about the Dewey Center Community Writing Project.

Stories exhibit "resistance," through which we can observe the interactive struggle of the "voices" in the text. Stories represent a struggle against the discourse of authority because they call attention to the interpretive, unstable character of understanding; they indicate by their very nature the importance of displaying this image of understanding-as-struggle in texts instead of eliminating it as one might be encouraged to do by the conventions of other forms. Kundera calls this the "wisdom of uncertainty" (7) inherent in stories, which calls attention to the complexity of knowing itself. Telling stories confutes our zeal for closure, for regularity. It celebrates the rich wholeness of experience, the relational character of experience, and works against solo, one-dimensional conceptions of learning. In this sense, stories exhibit more than mere resistance. This openness to contexts which storytelling seems to embrace is a paradigm of a kind of learning that might invite learners' exploration of what Jerome Bruner calls "possible worlds." This experience with storytelling can occur for us in all acts of reading, writing, and speaking, including those acts that take place in the classroom, such as in Dora's writing her story, and in the teachers' discussions about ways of teaching writing or issues such as eating on the street.

I looked for answers to my questions about the nature of stories such as those told by students and teachers in our program and thought I had found some, answers more complicated than I expected, answers that lead me to affirm several things, one of which is that stories are representations of a negotiable reality. Told as they always are, from particular perspectives, they are interpretations of reality, or what Foucault would call "fictions," particular ways of shaping experience in terms of particular values and concerns. When we teachers in the Dewey Center told our fictions to each other about our students and their fictions, they were not frivolous tales. Told with an urgency and a conviction we all shared, we hoped to affect students' writing and students' lives with them.

Stories, as an important potentially empowering form of speaking and writing, are more than just tools for individual imagination and self-discovery. As Bruner says, "narrative provides a map of possible roles and possible worlds in which action, thought, and self-definition are permissible (or desirable)" (1986, 66). The storyteller creates possible worlds "through the metaphoric transformation of the ordinary and the conventionally 'given'" (1986, 49). Students and teachers telling stories in talk and writing explore both personal "roles" and cultural "possible worlds" through their writing. In some respects, stories may be seen as selves, provisional representations of our struggle to define ourselves and the world. But in the process of shaping those selves, stories may also become one means of shaping relationships with others in community: "possible worlds."

One's own language then, within this kind of world making, is never a single language. The voices in the stories the teachers tell about their lives and about eating on the street are voices that each have a history. Shared in the afternoon teacher meetings or in the car or on the phone or in a postprogram conversation, they also forge a history—possible worlds—out of which certain understandings are gained and curriculum is designed. These stories are provisional, stories for the moment, but we must take them no less seriously for being so; they also indicate passionate commitments and have real consequences for students' lives. Shared in the process of talk about teaching, they may also be a means for us to learn from each other.

In this book, this story, I hope to demonstrate that for teachers and students stories are at the heart of the social and political transaction that constitutes teaching and learning. The stories that we as teachers told each other, and continue to tell each other, are rooted in our separate and common experiences. To examine these stories in terms of our personal backgrounds, in each other's terms, and in terms of the students who are the stories' primary subjects is to reveal the unfolding of a larger story. As I understand it, this larger "story" or narrative we constructed in our daily, shifting interpretations of our teaching experiences became our curriculum, our plan for teaching.

In order to illustrate the ways in which our larger story or narrative functioned to realize the particular teaching-learning community that the Dewey Center Project became, I need to demonstrate how our individual stories confirmed one another, denied one another, appreciated one another, tolerated one another. In my telling of our larger story, I emphasize the importance of seeing stories as one kind of socially constructed, interpretive representation, and I highlight how some of the teachers' stories are themselves usefully different interpretations of students' stories of the stories of their communities. As I do so, I argue implicitly that the teachers' storytelling built not only the curriculum at the Dewey Center but also our theories of teaching.

In the chapters which follow, I will pay particular attention to the way our "interpretive community" of teachers in the Dewey project was formed through these spoken stories, particularly the stories that individual teachers told me when I asked them questions about the conflict of "eating on the street" and about the writing of Dora, one student in the program. My decision to present and discuss transcriptions of teachers' stories about these two subjects was in many respects arbitrary, for, to be sure, we had conflicts on numerous issues and we were interested in all of our students. I chose to explore the issue of eating on the street because initially it seemed so unique to me and made me feel very much an outsider when we first talked about it. I chose to discuss Dora because all my colleagues and I were interested in the way her writing had developed. The stories we told about eating on the street and Dora and her writing exemplify the storytelling we shared daily as we designed curriculum and built theories.

In each of the following four chapters, I share a conversation, which took place weeks or months after the program was over, with another teacher at the Dewey Center. Stories embedded in these conversations, stories that the teachers tell, led me to other voices, other storytellers and theorists who speak to the particular issues that particular story raises for me. As in this chapter, where a story has led me to explore the nature of story and language, each teacher's story has resulted in an exploration of issues I felt needed to be addressed in order to learn about teaching together in that environment. In other words, stories have led me to other stories and ways to understand the stories. I begin with the story told to me by Jeanetta Cotman, who, with George Cooper and seven girls, walked to and from the Cultural Center on Children's Day, and who first raised the issue about whether on such occasions teachers should confront students about eating on the street. That story, told in terms of Jeanetta's own history, led me to explore, from a variety of perspectives, another history, the history of race relations in Detroit. The story that Toby Curry tells follows those stories and in many respects extends and expands on them. Toby, who in many ways seemed to agree with Jeanetta's perspective on eating on the street, led me to examine various perspectives on the ways people are trying to change literacy and history in Detroit, beginning with her own role in changing the James Couzens School to the Dewey Center for Urban Education. I pair these conversations somewhat arbitrarily since each teacher talked with me at separate times and in separate places, but they also echo similar concerns and passions though their tellers are in many ways very different people.

Kenneth Zeichner points out that most curriculum and theory building in education is "concerned with procedures and organizational arrangements for the purpose of efficiently helping students realize tacit and often unexamined ends" (114). The discourse community of storytelling teachers is a very different one, concerned with continually problematizing teaching and learning for particular students in particular times and places and concerned with continually articulating and evolving understandings. Theirs is provisional inquiry, shaped conditionally in forms that allow understandings to be continually revised and reshaped. Furthermore, their provisional inquiry, molded as it is in stories, allows them to tender names for not just their practical understandings but also their passionate commitments.

The stories we Dewey Center teachers told each other constitute a form of inquiry into teaching and learning that is consistent with the critical pedagogy we tried to establish in our practice. This research as storytelling was inseparable from our pedagogy; it characterized our conflicts, our negotiations, and it ultimately shaped our actions. It was local, provisional, and narrative, serving to build knowledge and curriculum and yet performing another purpose as well: Research as storytelling is a critique of the dominant practice of educational research which reduces the worlds of teaching and learning to paraphrase, to formula, to a set of neatly boxed variables.

It is important that our storytelling-as-action research took place in one of the "margins" of our society, in the inner city of Detroit, in a program designed to help us all begin to redefine for ourselves the best ways to teach literacy. Patricia Stock and Jay Robinson identify a *margin* "for what it is—a generative site for making meaning, a generative site for building knowledge with the potential to benefit all of us wherever we reside" (273). As the margins in our nation shift with rapidly changing demographics, we need as many stories as possible from the margins to inform our thinking and planning. For the challenges ahead, we need a complex view of culture rather than lists of discrete traits or similar rationalistic means of battering and flattening culture into comparability. Perhaps this complex perspective can best be reached through the stories we tell about it.

2

JEANETTA AND TOBY:
Literacy and History in
Detroit

THE REAL ME
Billie Jo Roark

When I was brod I was dead because I got stabbed in my
mommy stomache. Outside of my house my dad another man
were fighting my mommy jumped in ti. The man stabbed she in
the stomach in went my lag that's why I don't walk the same as
other people.

But I'm doing ok. I like to cook but my Dad won't let me
cook. I like candy bout I don't eat it a lot because I will be a
diabetic for the rest of my life.

I like to play games and puzzles. I like shcool, writing. I like
some sports like basketball, Hocky, or baseball, football, I like
danceing a lot the eacsiccily thang in my live in my club house
a lond time. (Unpublished classroom essay, 1989)

MY PLACE
Billie Jo Roark

My name is Billie Jo and this is my place. One time we had to
move from our house. We were just driving around our block and
we seen an apartment building. We stopped. My dad said, "Let's
live there." Then we went to the manager. We asked, "Is there an
apartment? A cheap one?" She said, "Yes. In the basement." Then
we moved there. It is my place now forever. But I did not like to
live in the basement because it is spooky. But I like my house
during the day. (Unpublished classroom essay, 1989)

I live with my step-mom and dad. I have a sister named Florence, and a new baby sister named Mary. I also have a step-brother named Bobby. My grandma lives with us sometimes.

I will tell you about my cat. Fellamena is her name. She is about 2 years old. I do not like her at all, because she ate my mice and hamsters. (Unpublished classroom essay, 1989)

I AM A HORSE

I am a horse. I am brown and white
I gallop through the field with
the sun so sunny and bright

I am a rose so tall and thorny
and I am harmless and red and
lonely as I don't know what

I am a motorcycle so fast
and clean when people look
at me I shine

I am Billie Jo Roark
The Best I think
I am special and sunny Your Famous Poet,
Billie Jo Roark (*Corridors* 8)

"All truths being multiple, it is not surprising that the true version of any story is also multiple." (O'Flaherty 64)

"Teacher talk matters." (Himley 1)

JEANETTA: HARD-NOSED

Jeanetta Cotman radiates strength in her voice, in her firm stance in the classroom, and in the strong opinions she freely shares. For many years a tough union negotiator, she is also admittedly proud of her reputation as a tough teacher. In an interview with Jeanetta in late August 1989, six weeks after the summer program, I asked her why she had volunteered to join us on the staff. I even expressed my surprise about this since she had seemed very skeptical about issues of whole language and using writing to learn. She had told me she didn't write often herself and in recent years had not had students writing as much as she wished.

David Schaafsma: At the beginning, you said, "I'm a traditional teacher, I have a reputation in this school as a tough person." I think you said something like, "I don't know if you want me in here, I'm..."

Jeanetta Cotman: I'd call it hard-nosed.

DS: Yeah, hard-nosed. And other teachers have said that about you, that you had that reputation. And you were right up front with us. You said, "These kids, they know where I've been coming from."

JC: But isn't it a poor person that sees change coming and then doesn't change with it? You see, I'd be fighting against myself if I tried to remain the traditional teacher and decided to stay in that way of working, because if you read the papers, alternative schools are the things that have come to pass, although it is going to be tough getting these teachers in the Dewey Center together in terms of alternative school teaching. Because it's going to be a long time before a lot of us will really be doing things like that, so individualized, having "centers." That's a lot of work. It's not easy. You have to go to work early, stay late. You have to have some time to give.

DS: It's more work, but it could be more satisfying.

JC: Well it would be more satisfying if I could see some difference in the children, because this year my children almost drove me to the brink. This was the worst year of my teaching career. It seemed like there wasn't anything I could do to motivate them. You know, they just ... like April ?

DS: She can be hard to work with.

JC: Whew! But she's smart. See, that's the problem. That's what upsets me, when you have children that are really good, but there's no way you can talk to them. They were so busy fighting me. You see, they spent this year fighting me. [Jeanetta imitates students]: "Well, you're supposed to be higher. You think you're *bad.*" They were so busy testing me, until they lost track of the real reason for being there. You see, they were all busy fighting me. They were sitting there rolling their eyes. [Again Jeanetta imitating]: "I can't stand you. You make me sick." "Okay," I would say, "But now what are you going to do with the lesson?" Oh, it was terrible.

DS: It's hard. And then to see some of those same kids in the program.

JC: But I encouraged them to come into the program. I thought that if they saw someone different—and I wanted them to work with other teachers. And it was for me, too, you know. I was ready for a change, and I thought if I tried a different way. But then I saw the same thing with other teachers. There's still some of the same pulling and tugging. So that's when I realized it wasn't just me. Because sometimes you do start to think, and you hurt in here.

DS: I know. I've felt that myself.

JC: But I have been here since 1971. And now the custodian has changed my room around for me. He brought in tables. And I have my centers, and I am going to try it. I am going to be a whole language teacher, or at least try some of it out in my own room after our experience this past summer.

DS: Do you find that the kids are different than those you had years ago?

JC: Oh! Are you for real? Not so long ago, it seemed like I could motivate the students, and it didn't take a whole lot of effort.

DS: Years ago.

JC: Yes. But I think with all the things that are going on with television and all the different things now, the violence, the drugs, the gangs, all the babies having babies, children are very, very different.

DS: They are less inclined to work because of all they have to contend with.

JC: Yes.

DS: And less parental support at home for school work? Or is that about the same?

JC: There's less parental support than even five years ago. But it depends on the area that you go into. When we went into the projects years ago, there were more true families—more father-and-mother families.

DS: Now it's mostly just mothers.

JC: It's all mothers. But then, both would come in and they'd sit down and talk with you.

DS: This year no one came in for conferences?

JC: No. And there used to be corporal punishment.

DS: And that's been outlawed now.

JC: Yes. You see, I had never had children tell me to shut up and call me a "B" until this year. I never had a child run into me like one did.

DS: It was a hard year. You think teachers should be able to spank children again.

JC: I don't see anything wrong with it. I don't say a teacher should be allowed to beat a child over the head. On their bottoms, not on their backs. No. You see, if I was too angry, I wouldn't spank. I'd take the student right to the office. I sent a student home this year. I could not take him. I told the parents I could not take this kid in my room. I keep a running journal on some of my kids: "On this day he called me a bitch." "On this day he threw a paper ball at my head."

DS: So you, like other teachers, feel held back because you cannot use the punishment and feel you have less control over your classroom than years ago.

JC: Yes, very much. Parents tell me to do that. Parents say they will give me written permission to spank their child, but I will not do that. Because the board said, and the union has asked us not to. And I believe in the union wholeheartedly.

Jeanetta first spoke to George Cooper about the issue of children's eating on the street when they accompanied their group of children to the Cultural Center. When they returned to the Dewey Center, she discussed the issue with Susan Harris, and the two of them decided to raise the issue at the teachers' meeting. I asked her to talk about how she viewed the incident and the issue.

Jeanetta Cotman: You know where that comes from? When we were little children growing up and going uptown, that was a thing that mother knew. We would buy candy and she would not let us eat the candy until we were on the way home. And if she ever saw us eating on the street, she'd say, "I hate that. I detest that. You look like . . . whatever."

David Schaafsma: And Susan agreed with that. That matched with her past, the way she had been brought up.

JC: That's right. We've been taught that, taught that by my grandmother. She lived in Monticello at the time. And, by the way, my grandmother was a teacher. She graduated from Kentucky State University when it was a "normal school." And then my mother and father studied at Kentucky State University and then I studied there. So we're from a family of educated people. All of my

sisters and brother have been to college. That's part of our tradition. Some things you just do, and eating on the street is not it.
And my boys weren't allowed to eat on the street.

DS: At first I thought it was a race thing, something that black kids
can't do, but now I think it's more of a class thing of sorts.

JC: I think it's more of a class thing. Well, it's both. The way our parents raised us, eating on the street and in cars, all of that was a
no-no. You eat out when you're on a picnic. That's the rule we
had, so I like to stick with that.

DS: And those kids did it on Children's Day, but I really didn't see
much of that.

JC: Because you didn't walk with that group that bought a bag of
goodies on the way.

DS: That was the group with you and George?

JC: Yes. Afterwards we talked about it. We were laughing. It was com-
ical, because I'm upset and he's not.

DS: But he learned a bit from that, and so did I, thanks to you and
Susan. See, now, Susan ordinarily wouldn't have said anything, but
might have exploded later in the car.

JC: I'm not one to explode. Like that day, I embarrassed myself. I felt
like I was talking too much. That day I said, in reference to white
teachers, how they just let children whoop and holler and carry
on. And Toby turned beet red and was angry. Then I said, "Oh,
Jeanetta, you have to watch what you say." I've got to really work
on it, but what comes up comes out.

DS: Toby and Debi have been teaching in the city for a long time.
Toby had heard from Susan that day a couple of references like,
"These are our children." As if somehow it's, "I have a different
stake here because I'm black and those are black children and
then they're mine." But Toby and Debi have been teaching black
kids, and they've paid their dues.

JC: Well, George isn't the only one who learned something, you
know. We all learned something from that discussion. That's the
value of team teaching. You learn from each other, right? You talk
about team teaching as negotiating, like power struggles, and I
never thought of it that way. I never thought about it as negotiating. "Team teaching" is just my term, my name for it. To me it
means the meeting of the minds, coming together with one specific goal that's workable. That's my idea of what it means. But I
hadn't looked at it that way before. You see, when I think of ne-

gotiating, I think in terms of union negotiating or negotiating with the principal. You see, I look at it more like that. "Collaboration" to me is a team teaching sort of thing, where you sit down and discuss your plans and everyone comes to an agreement. But that day we were definitely not in agreement, and then we had to learn from each other's disagreements.

I asked her if it was difficult for her to think of teaching as involving negotiation. In her experience, she had always made the plans herself, and there was no negotiation necessary.

Jeanetta Cotman: At first I said no, but then I felt like I was a part of it.

David Schaafsma: If you have to make a decision, then it's yours.

JC: And that made me feel more a part of the team. At first, I had not been to any of the meetings, like Toby and Debi, because I joined a little later. I had never been up to Ann Arbor like they had. And I really didn't start feeling a part of it until I came to a meeting in Ann Arbor, too. But then more and more I started making suggestions and telling things from my experience, and you all seemed to like what I had to suggest, so I knew I had something to offer.

DS: And you're not normally shy.

JC [smiles]: No, I'm not shy. You'll know what I think.

Jeanetta said that when she and Susan spoke during our discussion about eating on the street, they were principally talking to white teachers, and particularly George and me, white males with what I admitted were "looser" or more "liberal" disciplinary styles. She said they were also talking about teaching and discipline, generally. She thought Susan was also talking specifically to Dana Davidson, to some extent. I asked her how she felt about the fact that Dana wore different clothes, different hair styles than she and Susan, noting that Susan had expressed her frustration to me about it:

David Schaafsma: This points to the larger issue of how anyone, black or white, deals with people of color, whether it is black teachers dealing with white kids, or white teachers dealing with Hispanic kids, or whatever. But now we are talking about the issue of how anyone deals with black kids specifically.

Jeanetta Cotman: Well, with Dana, I didn't like it, but I wasn't upset about it, really. I just didn't like that hairstyle. Do you follow me? But not to the point that I would say anything to her. But you have got to remember that I have children of my own Dana's age. I didn't like it. Not around those children. You see, when Toby came in in shorts, I was, "My god." But then children seemed to accept it OK, and then I wore mine. But Dana was also a good model as a student, I don't care what her grade point average was. She made it at the University of Michigan, which is not an easy place for anyone to survive, I don't care what your color is.

DS: But Susan would never have worn shorts, and you did.

JC: No, and I never have ever before in my life. I am kind of prudish when it comes to certain things, and I think there are certain standards when you are around children, just like I didn't want to be called Jeanetta by them, I just don't want to. I think I can be as warm and friendly and motherly to the children without their calling me by my first name.

DS: I'm glad you stuck with that. It was useful. And Toby didn't, either, finally.

JC: That's right.

DS: But Dana changed. Not because I talked with her. I would never do that. I thought Susan should talk with her herself. But no one did. I thought she might have picked up on something from Susan's discussion about role models when we were talking about eating on the street.

JC: That's a wise person to me, she didn't ignore it. And you are right, I think. Susan was talking to Dana and not just you and George about this business of helping set standards for these children. You better believe it. But you know, when you're in a room, it's hard to tell people they're wrong. But sometimes it's best to do that, bring up the conflict out in the open like that and give your reasons or make it clear somehow why.

I asked Jeanetta to tell me about what she felt had shaped her views as a teacher.

JC: My parents were educators. My mother was a schoolteacher. Daddy was the principal of the school, and when they stopped having segregated schools and integration came, they put her out of a job, so she took the test to be a social worker. She became the first black social worker in Montgomery County, and I think there hasn't been another one in that county since she got the job. So some feelings are hard to talk about. It's just hard. Then they burned the school down where my daddy was principal.

DS: Where was that?

JC: In Mount Sterling, Kentucky. They burned the black school down. This was during the time of integration, in the sixties. But when you live through something like that, that affects you, believe me. In other districts they let other black principals be assistant principals of white schools, but not in Mount Sterling, Kentucky. And my father had his master's degree in administration. But they put him back in the classroom as a history teacher. For a year they let him do nothing, just kind of filing files, working with records. So you get a little uptight. But the black-white relations with our family in Mount Sterling were good, generally. We didn't have many problems. Both my father and mother were involved in everything, like the chamber of commerce, everything. My family was very involved in the community, you know, visible. I mean, I haven't had a lot of ugliness.

Jeanetta graduated with a B.A. from Kentucky State University, where she was active in a sorority, and earned her M.A. in Reading from Marygrove College in Detroit. She began teaching in Kentucky, married, moved to Detroit, and has taught for more than twenty years. She and her husband have three children. I asked her to tell me about her teaching career.

JC: It is really crazy. I came here from Kentucky and was married in '64, but I worked in Kentucky a year because I signed my contract to teach there for a year. Then when I came to Detroit I started teaching in November of '65 at Parke School, over on the east side. And there I taught for two years, second- and third-grade classes. So Couzens was not my first school. You see, I graduated in April, and I taught in the school where my Daddy was the principal, and finished out the year there.

DS: When was that school burned down? Was that after you left?

JC: Well, see, I finished school in April '64, and I went home and finished out the term. And then it burned, in August of '64, so it has been twenty-five years this month that it was burned.

DS: So that school wasn't started again?

JC: Well, the building burned down, except the gymnasium, and they made that into a recreation center. And they took the land and built houses. [She smiles, shakes her head, and shrugs.]

DS: Those things happened, right? You can't erase that.

JC: That's right. You can't erase history.

To hear Jeanetta's story, her history, is to begin to understand what a constructivist perspective on the social nature of self and Other might mean. Jeanetta Cotman's story, and every other teacher's story I tell in this and the following chapters, is one voice in a story—my story—without an absolute, without an essence or a center, just as her own story contains echoes, voices, from many sites or historical moments in her own history as a teacher. Jeanetta's story helps us exchange a view of the self as "a tissue of contingent relations, a web which stretches backward and forward through past and future time, for one as formed, unified, present, self-contained substance, something capable of being seen steadily and whole" (Rorty 41). Bakhtin says "an individual cannot be completely incarnated into the flesh of existing sociohistorical categories" (37). In other words, we can't reduce Jeanetta—or anyone else—to a "type," or fixed category. Learning, development, is a kind of conversation between competing, conflicting voices from her past. In Jeanetta's brief story, we get a glimpse of a "process approach" to being contained within it, a world always criticizing itself, a struggle of voices "stamped with the seal of inconclusiveness" (30).

Jeanetta's stories reinforce what she calls a "traditional" perspective on teaching and learning, but they also indicate a desire to change, a move to rethink her approach to the classroom. Her talk here helps me better understand the complexity of her confrontation in the teacher's meeting on the issue of poor black children eating on the street. Her stories in this conversation help explain her "toughness"; the school in which her father worked was burned down, and both of her parents—Kentucky-educated African Americans—were victims of job discrimination, but they not only survived, they succeeded. Though she says they haven't had "a lot of ugliness," the world she came from was a world of struggle with conflict, and some of that struggle was with racism. "So you get a little uptight," Jeanetta says almost matter-of-factly. She and her family were prepared to struggle for power when they moved north to Detroit, and she continues to fight for it today. She struggles for power in teaching too many kids for nineteen years in a classroom short on supplies; in an area where drugs, violence, teenage pregnancy, single-family homes, and poverty exist daily in the classroom, she finds the students increasingly difficult to deal with. She also struggles for power in her role as union representative where she has to negotiate for her fellow teachers in a financially burdened school system.

In many ways, Jeanetta resists a sudden embrace of whole language and similar progressive approaches to the classroom. I needed to look at situations from her perspective in order to understand eating on the street, to construct my own story about how to teach better in multicultural settings. I need her story to introduce some skepticism into what I was firmly committed to accomplishing with our students: She helped me put quotation marks around the word "progressive" when it was attached to actions I had unquestioningly viewed as such. Jeanetta helped me to see that the realities of the inner city and the possibilities for change within the context of those realities are complex and conflicting issues. She also helped me to realize that changing the story of schooling in very fundamental ways is a complex task that may not be separated from the necessary task of changing society.

After many years of teaching, Jeanetta doubts, even after what she agreed was a successful summer program, whether a whole language approach will necessarily be successful with poor black children. But she is determined to try to change her classroom because she sees the need to change, and because she saw successes in the summer program she would like to see occur in her own classroom. She taught in the program's second summer, and in her own classroom she has students writing often. More than ever before, she makes use of individualized instruction in her classroom and has begun to organize her students into writing workshop groups.

Hers is a testimony to the usefulness of collaborative teaching, but it is also a tale of ambivalence, of contradiction, of doubt, of the difficulty of adapting to new concepts about teaching after a lifetime of teaching another way. It is no fairy tale of change through collaboration, but an indication of the need for support in teacher change and for continued dialogue that does not silence contradiction but welcomes it, as narrative conceptions of learning must surely do. The self is a "web of relations to be rewoven" (Rorty 43), and Jeanetta can be seen as struggling through her stories to reweave a self out of the stuff of the past and future—her past experiences with and understanding of the forces of discrimination and successful struggle of herself and her parents against it; her resistance to writing and teaching writing and her willingness to explore a whole language approach to the classroom that would depend on writing; her belief in the uses of corporal punishment and her sense of loyalty to the decisions of the teachers' union; her disapproval of Dana's appearance and her sense of humor and playfulness; her "hard-nosed" commitment to being a role model with certain standards for young African American children in her personal and professional lives.

Jeanetta's story of eating on the street, within the context of the story of her life as she tells it in this brief, informal conversation, relates a history, one in part shaped by incidents of racial discrimination, and dealing with them in particular ways. In talking with her, I began to realize that to understand her story is to understand the history that gives it shape. To begin to understand the nature of literacy instruction in the inner city of Detroit is to understand the history of race relations that gives it shape.

By reading into the history of Detroit, I become a historian of it, too—a storyteller and a historian, and in the process begin to make links to Jeanetta's history and the history of teachers like her. The history of Detroit which I tell is a story told by an outsider taken from many different written versions of Detroit history. It is a story of discrimination against African Americans and native Americans by white people like myself, and it is a story of the struggle for self-determination, too. The racial discrimination that Jeanetta documents in her own Kentucky family history is also a part of the history of Detroit; her history leads me to its history.

DETROIT AND RACE RELATIONS: HISTORICAL VERSIONS

For centuries, various native American tribes inhabited the area now known as Detroit. Ottawa, Chippewa, Potawatomi, Huron, Iroquois, and other tribes found it good hunting ground. In 1628, slaves came to Canada with French "settlers," and it was the French explorer Adrien Jolliet who soon after that settled in the Detroit area, recognizing it as an ideal location for trade, situated strategically along the Great Lakes waterway. From Teuch-a-Grondic, for "good hunting ground," or Wa-we-a-tunog, for "bend-in-the-river," the Chippewa came to call it Yon-do-tega, for "great village," as the settlement steadily grew. The French eventually began to call the settlement Ville de Troit, for "village on the strait," or Detroit.[1] Hearing from his fellow countrymen about the rich economic possibilities for the area, Antoine de la Mothe Cadillac arrived in 1701 with fifty French soldiers and fifty fur traders and helped "develop" the area as a center for commerce. In 1760, the British took over control of the settlement in spite of Chief Pontiac's objections; many reports identify this point as the "beginning" of harsh relations between native Americans and the new settlers. The British were, it seems, even more insensitive than the French about the native Americans' ways of life and their culture.

In 1796, the American flag was raised in Detroit, but this was no more advantageous for native Americans than French or British control. "Economic expansion" continued to attract increasing numbers of white easterners hoping to better their lives. The city grew rapidly over the next several years. In 1805, a great fire spread through the city, and Father Gabriel Richard gained fame by organizing the people of Detroit to rally for recovery, which was swift. Within two years, nearly all the original buildings were replaced and new growth continued.

Although both native Americans and African Americans were enslaved during these early years, by 1750 there were only thirty-three black slaves in the town and no native American slaves. By 1830, all the slaves had reportedly left or had died, and there were numerous free blacks in the area.

David Katzman provides an informative historical perspective on black-white relations in Detroit, and one that for me had a surprising emphasis. Katzman documents a century of struggle to achieve equality by blacks in Detroit and notes the stand of resistance many whites took to the black struggle. In 1827, the Michigan Black Code was signed into law. Ostensibly intended to protect free blacks, it was in fact an attempt to discourage many fugitive slaves from settling in the area by requiring them to register. Katzman illustrates, in a century of what he calls "Negrophobia," that discriminatory practices were a result of whites fearing that escaped slaves were primarily of "the criminal element." Michigan Governor Lewis Cass established his early reputation as an abolitionist in a fiery speech against slavery, but the majority of the population supported the fugitive slave law which would return slaves to their "rightful owners."

Katzman's version of the Blackburn Riot of 1833 demonstrates how it came about as a response to the Detroit circuit court's decision to return black community leaders Thornton and Ruth Blackburn to Alabama slaveowners. Though the Blackburns eventually escaped to Canada where they became once again successful civic and business leaders, whites and blacks were again embroiled in a bitter fight over the issues. With much property destroyed, and fears that a repetition of the 1805 fire might result, the mayor requested U.S. troops to be dispatched to the city "to restore tranquility" (12), an action that would be repeated periodically over the next 140 years. An all-white citizens' commission of ten people, the first of many similar "race riot commissions" in the history of Detroit, placed the blame for the riot, not surprisingly, on the blacks themselves.

While slavery was indeed legally abolished in 1837, racial distinctions, which blacks had to fight the rest of the century to overcome, remained in the law. In spite of these disadvantages, as Katzman's history reveals, the first black school was established in 1836, and in

1843 at the Michigan State Colored Convention blacks charged that as a people they were being discriminated against in terms of opportunities for education and segregation. William Lambert and William Monroe, both black men, were politically active in the struggle for the right to vote for blacks in the 1840s and in the fight to end segregation in the schools.

In 1863 there was another riot, which Katzman tells us began with white violence against blacks after a black man was convicted of raping two white girls. Blacks were outraged at the verdict, which they felt was false. The violence that erupted stemmed from this verdict, but was also in part the black community's response to housing inequities in the growing city. The conflict left deep divisions in black-white relations, ironically during a time when Frederick Douglas was successfully recruiting blacks for the First Michigan Colored Volunteers. During the time when Douglas singled out Detroit as the worst city in the north with regard to racism against blacks, many Detroit blacks left the city to enlist in the North's fight against the South.

In spite of prevailing conditions, Detroit blacks successfully fought to end segregation in the Detroit schools, and in 1867 the first black student was admitted to a "white school." Robert Pelham (one of the inner-city schools is named for him) was one leading black politician who led this fight, and with other black men such as D. A. Straker took a central position in Michigan politics in the last quarter of the nineteenth century.

Katzman illustrates the ways in which Detroit's poor "black bottom" gradually became a city within a city, a situation that continues to exist today, where poor blacks are separated in various ways from whites, but also from a wealthier middle-to-upper-class black population, as Jeanetta Cotman similarly relates in her own story of nearly a century later. What Katzman calls a "caste system" prevented poor blacks from making fundamental changes for themselves within Detroit's economy, but there was room in this system even in the late nineteenth century for a few blacks to "move up." Straker was noted for stating that he had never been a victim of racial discrimination by whites in the upper class, a class he inhabited himself.

Katzman points out the central position of the black churches in providing emotional strength and moral leadership and in reinforcing the hierarchy that existed in the black community and continues to exist today. For instance, black leaders who were invited to join white (predominantly Episcopalian) churches occupied a higher social position in the black community, whereas the majority of poorer blacks were members of various Baptist churches. Katzman persuasively documents a history of race and class discrimination in Detroit, one which is complicated by black class relations, too. He also documents a history of possibility, not just failure, in naming the African American heroes and heroines who struggled at specific times and places to act against injustice. The history of discrimination that Jeanetta tells is echoed in these stories from Detroit history. The legal struggle for an end to school segregation that Robert Pelham and others fought, for instance, bears similarity to Jeanetta's parents' struggle with these issues in the 1960s—but the stories she tells of her father as a leading Kentucky educator and her mother as her county's first social worker are also echoed here, as is Jeanetta's own story of leadership in her school.

THE POLITICS OF NAMING STREETS AND BUILDINGS

"Naming is an art, a transformation of our intellectual life." (Polanyi 106)

"We only realize concepts by means of language, through the very act of naming them." (Cassirer 24)

In spite of the obvious accomplishments of Detroit blacks for more than two centuries, the specter of wealthy white males looms large in the inner city, it seems to me, their troubling legacy all too obvious. That legacy exists, for instance, in the naming of streets and public places in the area where the Dewey students live: Lewis Cass, James Couzens, John Christian Lodge, and Edward Jeffries. These names intersect with a few more recent names such as Martin Luther King, Jr., and Rosa Parks, an intersection of often conflicting and sometimes troubled perspectives on race relations, on the question of the institutional response to cultural diversity, and in particular on black cultural life in Detroit. The names are everywhere, of course, names that represent traditions and particular kinds of commitments.[2]

Cass Corridor and Cass Avenue

One of the key figures in Detroit history is Lewis Cass, who was born in Exeter, New Hampshire, in 1782. The first "Indian Superintendent of the Michigan Territory," he was also Michigan's first governor. In a life spanning from 1782 to 1866, he was known as an able explorer and a skilled mapmaker. A statesman, he was a noted minister to France, negotiated an important treaty with Mexico, and was an ardent and outspoken abolitionist. He was a general for the North during the Civil War when Detroit became a key (and not entirely uncontroversial, as Katzman indicates) part of the Underground Railroad. He ran for president in 1848 but was not a popular candidate outside Michigan and was finally defeated after being lampooned in a popular and funny speech by Abraham Lincoln. The speech called attention to certain of his well-known and obvious physical and personal characteristics; he was large, was viewed as emotionally cold, and was widely known for having amassed considerable wealth in office. Reportedly, a central reason for Cass's coming to the Detroit area was, like most easterners, to exploit the area's economic opportunities: He used his power and position while in office to purchase millions of acres of land for himself in the Michigan territory.

Cass was also criticized by many people, including Lincoln, for what was perceived at the time as "weakness" with regard to his actions with the Michigan native American tribes. He was responsible for what is regarded to this day as the most sensitive and thorough study of the day of the North American populations in the Detroit area, a pamphlet he produced in 1823 entitled "The History, Traditions, Languages, Manners, Customs and Religions of Indians Living Within the United States," based on extensive interviews with the chiefs of various tribes on a wide range of social and cultural issues. This report was intended as a preliminary study in response to increased conflicts between white Michigan citizens and native Americans over area land use.

On the basis of this study, Cass drafted the controversial Western Indian Colonization Policy, a plan for the "humane removal" of native Americans to reservations west of the Mississippi, a plan criticized for its impractical nature and, ironically as well, for its tolerance of native American needs. Even though he often expressed personal repugnance for many native American customs, and though he clearly and not surprisingly played a role in the white man's steady destruction of native American culture, Cass can be credited at the very least for being one of the sole voices speaking for cultural understanding in American political leadership. Justly praised for his abolitionism, yet appropriately criticized for his "Indian removal" policy and accumulation of great wealth at the expense of his constituents, Cass occupies an uneasy place in the history of respect for cultural difference, one of the first of many major Detroit figures to occupy such an ambiguous and unsettling position. In a sense, his story sets the ambivalent tone of the troubled racial history of Detroit.

John C. Lodge Freeway

John Christian Lodge lived from 1862 to 1950 and was Detroit mayor from 1928 to 1930. Like Cass, an easterner who came west to make his fortune, Lodge occupies a far less central position in the history of race relations in Detroit. In many ways, however, he was typical, a wealthy white male like Cass whom the dominant power structure could trust to help maintain its position. He is not noted for having accomplished anything more illustrious than helping to maintain close relations to prominent Detroit businessmen and encouraging downtown development, but he did invest much of his considerable wealth in the Detroit area. When the freeway that passes between the high rises and low rises of the Jeffries projects was built in the early fifties, the Lodge name stood for development and as such was a natural name to attach to it. As celebrated as the Lodge Freeway was in the business community, it maintains a troubled reputation for those older inner-city residents whose lives were considerably disrupted by its construction since thousands of residents occupying low-income housing were evicted and several older (and needed) apartment complexes were torn down and not replaced.

James P. Couzens Community School

James Couzens, for whom the elementary school that now houses the Dewey Center was named, was born in Chatham, Ontario, on August 26, 1872. Lending his prominent name to the Detroit community, Couzens was one of the top executives of the Ford Motor Company from its organization in 1903 until his resignation in 1915 during a quarrel with Henry Ford. He played a major role in the history of the firm, helping to propel it and Detroit into international prominence. Among his contributions were the creation of a nationally recognized sales force and the supervision of the purchasing of materials. Credited with conceiving of the $5.00 minimum wage, and also having suffered a widely publicized personal tragedy when his son drowned under an overturned boat, he managed to garner a rather positive reputation within the larger Detroit community.

Volatile, forceful, Couzens was the police commissioner from 1916 to 1918, resigning after numerous conflicts with officers due to his unyielding management style. He had a reputation as a tyrant, and it was said that he tried to run the force in his short tenure there like a Ford production division. In 1919, he sold his remaining stock at Ford for twenty million dollars and with the money established the Children's Fund of Michigan for handicapped children. By doing so he established his reputation as a philanthropist, increasing his already solid popularity. That same year he was elected mayor of Detroit, having defeated his former colleague, Ford. Couzens served in that office from 1919 to 1922 when he was elected to the U.S. Senate and served there from 1922 to 1936. Longtime *Detroit News* journalist Malcolm Bingay, who claims to have known him "as well as anyone, and not well," describes him as "a man of contradictions" (115), not happy, not likeable, almost inscrutable in his raging. Yet Bingay saw him as "tireless" in his commitment to Detroit and clearly generous; Bingay points out that Couzens saw to it that much of his twenty-million-dollar gift for children went to Detroit organizations.

The Couzens name in Detroit stands primarily for certain commitments, some of them positive, but he is primarily associated with money and power, and his name on a community school in an inner-city neighborhood is rather ironic. Part of the legacy of the still rich and powerful automobile industry through which he gained his fame and wealth is everywhere in the inner city—the last downtown plant closed in December 1989. Unemployment in Detroit's inner city in 1989 was 37 percent.

The Jeffries Homes and Jeffries Projects

Malcolm Bingay describes Couzens as a man of contradictions. He depicts Edward Jeffries, Jr., and Edward Jeffries, Sr., who both became mayors of Detroit, as political and personal opposites. Edward Jeffries, Sr., for instance, was a defender of labor while his son was vehemently antiunion. Seeing the police as the "tool of capital," Jeffries, Sr., was a defender of the poor in his long tenure as circuit court judge. In 1894, he marched with Arthur Coxey's army of poor people to Washington, D.C. His son, on the other hand, was decidedly a friend of business in his long tenure as mayor.

Bingay's description of Detroit's devastating 1943 riot when the younger Jeffries was mayor, is typical of various accounts written almost exclusively by white males after that terrible event: "The riot was not made in Detroit. It was brought here" (43). In his view, the riots were caused by "outside elements," southern blacks and whites who had come north to fight for wartime jobs and who simply couldn't get along as northern whites and blacks had learned to do. Bingay notes briefly the then widely held white view that Jeffries himself was in part responsible for the loss of life (thirty-four people died) and the severity of the damage that occurred during the riot, because of "his failure to respond quickly to the violence." But Bingay does not mention the then widely held black view that Jeffries had repeatedly failed to respond to the needs of blacks in his community, particularly with regard to housing and education. B. J. Widick agrees that Jeffries indeed handled the situation badly, up to and including the time of the riot, yet afterwards was widely praised by whites for blaming blacks and the "Negro Press." In the early fifties, so soon after the 1943 riots, naming much-needed low-income housing *Jeffries,* housing intended principally for blacks, was again, at the very least, ironic.

Bingay fails to address the inequities in the social and economic conditions of Detroit, choosing, like Mayor Jeffries, to put principal blame for the 1943 riot on the blacks themselves, adding a footnote about several blacks he has admired, such as Joe Louis, for their "patience," "quiet forbearance," and constructive actions on behalf of his race. His "history" of Detroit is admittedly "personal," but it is useful for getting at the "mainstream" or conservative white view of twentieth century Detroit history. Bingay is fond of humorous anecdotes and shows the "fun" side of Detroit politics: "Politics is funny" (329), he says, and "hard as we have fought and labored, we never forgot how to laugh" (360). His book is filled with anecdotes about the social world of Detroit's wealthy and famous, but he almost completely ignores mainstream Detroit, for instance, its often violent working-class struggle to unionize.

B. J. Widick documents a twentieth century of discrimination against the poor, including primarily blacks but also other minorities in Detroit. He carefully illustrates the central and often seemingly unchallenged place of Ku Klux Klan activity in helping to shape public policy in the three decades before the 1943 riot, with its very visible presence in the struggle for wartime jobs and low-income housing in the early forties just preceding the riot.

Widick, like Bingay, tells his history from a particular political perspective, one with very different social implications. While Bingay, Republican and popular conservative spokesman, supported big business leaders like Couzens in his *Detroit News* columns, Widick was very involved in the labor movement, was a close friend of union leader Walter Reuther, and writes his history in ways that clearly betray his sympathy for the struggles of the disenfranchised. His reputation in Detroit as a liberal historian is obvious from his text; he passionately denounces the leaders of the automobile industry in a way few others have done.

University of Michigan historian Sidney Fine's *Violence in the Model City* (1989) is a good example of what might be described as a more "moderate" version of a historical event and is easily the most thorough account of the Detroit riot of 1967.[3] The *Washington Post* reported that the riot was "the greatest tragedy of all the long succession of Negro ghetto outbursts" (Fine 1). Part of the reason for this judgment was Detroit's designation in March 1967 as an "All-American City," largely for its efforts with regard to civil rights. Fine, a member of the Civil Rights Commission at the time in Detroit, examines the riot in the context of the development of race relations in the city during the years 1962–69, when Jerome P. Cavanaugh was Detroit's mayor.

In his effort to understand the late sixties riots, Fine takes a close look at the 1943 riot and some of its social and economic causes, noting the astonishing inequities in housing, education, and employment. From 1943 to 1963, fifty-seven local agencies were developed for the purpose of improving human relations in the city, but Fine questions their effectiveness. In 1960, 67 percent of sixteen-to-nineteen-year-old youths were unemployed, and though legal desegregation was occurring in some schools, there was more segregation in housing in 1960 than in 1930 (Fine 10). Blacks were paying more for poorer quality housing from significantly lower salaries. The *Detroit News* noted that 65 percent of the 1960 crimes were committed by blacks, leading to a crackdown and increasing the tension in already strained police–inner-city relations (15).

According to Fine, an important turning point in Detroit seemed to have occurred when Jerome Cavanaugh was elected mayor in fall 1960. Cavanaugh quickly gained a national reputation for his commitment to reversing the trends in Detroit's inner city. By 1963 the city's books were balanced, and he had procured 230 million dollars in federal funds for urban programs (Fine 17). In 1963, Cavanaugh joined Martin Luther King, Jr., with 125,000 people in the Walk to Freedom (27). In Fine's view, the city seemed to be leading the nation in the area of civil rights under Cavanaugh's capable direction.

Fine's account makes it clear that school desegregation was a priority in the early sixties. Detroit had seventy-three all-white schools in 1961, but had only twenty-two in 1966 (Fine 53). In that year, Detroit had the highest percentage of black teachers and administrators of any major city in the United States, and Detroit Public Schools led the nation in the early sixties in getting textbooks to portray racial diversity (51). The Shared Experiences Project of 1965, which enabled students attending schools of different racial composition to join together in a variety of extracurricular activities, was one of many projects designed to promote understanding between races (51). There were several programs underway such as preschool (Head Start) and parent-school education programs, as well as continuing education programs for pregnant teenagers (52).

According to Fine's account, though, change was slow, and the inequities were great. Blacks felt compelled by inadequate conditions to act for immediate changes, and, as had occurred in the past, they made their feelings known. Public recreational facilities were lacking in low-income neighborhoods, especially in the Twelfth Street-Dexter area which became the center of the riot. In summer 1967, forty-four inner-city playgrounds had to be closed down for lack of funding (56). Blacks expressed their outrage, but their cries were ignored. Black newspapers called attention to the blacks' general dissatisfaction with the quality of inner-city schooling and the rising dissatisfaction with "ghetto merchandizing," which meant higher prices in poor black areas. There was a boycott at Northern High School on April 20, 1966, and as a result a separate "Freedom School" was temporarily set up and students were taught for a time by sympathetic teachers (54–55). As Fine makes clear, conditions were bleak in the schools. The dropout rate was 50 to 62 percent in all inner-city Detroit high schools, and only 6 to 7 percent had good employment prospects if they did in fact graduate (55). According to Fine, there was a general recognition that young people especially needed (and were not being provided) activities both in school and out that called for responsibility and dignity and were relevant to their lives.

Still, discrimination in housing was, to Detroit blacks, a more crucial problem than the discrimination in education from 1965 to 1967 (Fine 58). There were plans for low-cost housing in 1967, but these were to be built in white, middle-class neighborhoods. Most whites were increasingly resentful about "forced integration" and opposed open housing ordinances. The housing code was out of date and poorly enforced (59). Police-community relations were also poor, which Fine points to as a central consideration in the riots, as indeed they had been in the 1943 riot; he documents as important factors rampant racism in the police system, few blacks on the force, understaffing, and an unpopular "blue flu" police strike for better conditions and higher wages that was taking place in summer 1967 (62–65).

The riot that erupted on July 23, 1967, stemmed from conditions that were inadequately addressed. What Fine calls the "worst civil disorder in American history" (291), resulting in forty-three deaths and forty to forty-five million dollars worth of damage, obviously demands close scrutiny if we are to understand the background of present circumstances in the Dewey Center neighborhood. These circumstances in part give rise to interpretations such as Jeanetta's about issues like eating on the streets.

At the time, as now, there were many conflicting perspectives, many different "versions" of the nature and causes of the violence. The "middle-class view" (both black and white) at the time was generally that there was little or no connection between the riots and civil rights; they viewed most of the looters, for instance, as criminals (Fine 376). The NAACP, which espoused a generally moderate-to-conservative interpretive position during the sixties, saw the riots as impeding, rather than advancing, the black cause. Its members were afraid of disrupting what they saw as steady progress for blacks in Detroit (409). Fine notes that many people saw the riots as a rebellion of the poor, involving many poor whites in addition to blacks, against the white power structure. Widick saw it as "not blacks versus whites, as in 1943, but poor blacks and some whites against the power structure, the landlord, the merchant, and the hated police" (xxi). This very interesting perspective on the riots as at least in part a class struggle is supported by the arrest statistics, which show poor blacks but also many poor whites booked as looters. Twelve percent of those arrested were white (352). Representative John Conyers called it a "war of the haves versus have nots," and consistently objected to its being characterized as exclusively a race war (352).

Contrary to the view of many whites at the time who thought the riot had been the cause of "outside agitation" by black radicals, Fine's research shows how little "revolutionary ideology" influenced the actions of rioters. The majority of the "rioters" were fifteen- to twenty-four-year-old black males (330), mostly high school dropouts who in postriot interviews expressed hostility toward whites and talked about "black pride" but did not speak out of ideological convictions, such as black militancy. Thirty-seven percent of the rioters said they had "no major complaint about living conditions in Detroit" (Fine 366), according to the interviewers. Sixty-five percent of those who characterized themselves during the interview process as "non-involved" in the riots themselves agreed with the statement that it was "lazy, greedy bums" who were responsible for the majority of the looting and damage (349). Of course, many saw the riot primarily as a form of protest against the conditions of poor blacks in the city, but others referred to it as a "monster without a head" (366), an example of mob violence out of control.

In the twenty-two years following the riot, during what has been primarily Coleman Young's long tenure as mayor, many changes have occurred. Initially there was some violence in the years immediately following the riot, such as in 1968 after the murder of Martin Luther King, Jr., and also in that year after a highly controversial shooting of blacks at the New Bethel Church.[4] "White flight" dominated Detroit in the seventies and eighties; blacks gained political control of the city but still lack economic control. Detroit's economy was far worse in 1990 than it was in 1967. Fine offers a litany of statistics to support this assertion. For instance, he reports that 195,000 jobs were lost between 1967 and 1985 and many more since as a result of the continued closing of automobile plants (Fine 458). In 1967, 8 percent of Detroit's residents were on welfare; in 1987, 34 percent (459). Detroit has the highest infant mortality rate of any major city in the nation, and 65 percent of its households consist of single-parent families (459). From 1967 to 1987 the homicide rate tripled, maintaining Detroit's dubious distinction as the "murder capital" of the nation (461). More teenagers died violent deaths in 1986 than in the 1967 riots, almost all of them poor blacks whose deaths were at the hands of other blacks. Inner-city residents express increased fear due to the crack trade and the easy availability of guns. The dropout rate is steady at nearly 50 percent in city schools (461). While community relations with the now almost half-black police force were in 1989 far improved, compared to the late sixties, the quality of housing and education remain as two central complaints for city residents (460). In Fine's view, the quality of life in Detroit for most blacks, which was poor in 1967, was considerably worse in 1987 (458–63).

In 1960, the Detroit High School Study Commission reported: "Our high schools are appallingly inadequate, a disgrace to the community and a tragedy to the thousands of young men and women whom we compel and cajole to sit in them" (Fine 215). They were "outmoded and overcrowded" and in financial disaster. Recent reports echo the same complaints about the schools, and the financial situation for the Detroit Public Schools is far worse today than it was thirty years ago.

Widick, like Fine, identifies social and economic forces "that victimize its shrinking population and make living a nightmare and the future bleak" (231). He notes the persistence of racism and, like Fine, an increase in gun violence, homicide, and crime in general. Widick also shares ominous statistics: In 1967 there were 281 deaths from violent crimes, 43 in the riots; in 1986 there were 646, with 500,000 fewer residents. In 1986, 237 youths under the age of 16 were wounded from gunfire, 343 in 1987. The unemployment for area youths is generally high, but in the inner city it is well over 80 percent. Widick notes the consequent "get-tough-on-crime" approach and the drive to build more jails, particularly "juvenile delinquent facilities, rather than fund projects directed to education and social needs." He also notes "declining neighborhoods, white flight, crime and economic problems and ever present feelings of racism" (237). He observes: "Visible everywhere are burned or dilapidated houses, gutted apartment dwellings, hundreds of boarded-up small stores—all testimony to the plight of the city" (236); the metropolitan area's resurgence "is primarily a white community gain, whereas the blacks are still on the periphery" (238). As Widick sees it, Trapper's Alley, Harbortown, River Place, an expanded Cobo Hall, the Renaissance Center, all developments which Mayor Young and his administration point to as "progress" downtown, have little or nothing to do with Detroit's majority population, the poor blacks; they are, as Widick says, the "illusions of a successful city.... Detroit is a city of angry, anxious, and concerned citizens, outraged at the youth killings, the homicide rate, and joblessness" (246, 265). He notes a widening gap in education, employment, income, health, longevity and other basic measures of individual and social being between members of minority and majority populations.

Widick speaks of today's "anger" and "outrage," born of citizens' "concern"; Fine tells it a little differently. Perhaps his most damning commentary on the current situation occurs when he compares the "psychological climate" of blacks in the sixties to the attitude of blacks today. In Fine's view, the riots of the late sixties, as destructive as they were, were at least in part engendered by hope, through action by poor people for themselves. Why are there no riots today? He characterizes Detroit's present attitude "as one of despair, not hope.... The riot goes on, in slow motion. Instead of a single, stupendous explosion, there is a steady, relentless corrosion" (459).

Hugh Scott shares Fine's harsh view of the situation in the inner city and echoes how Jeanetta feels about the worsening conditions in her city. Scott isn't optimistic about the prospects for change in Detroit or in inner cities elsewhere:

> Oh, things are much worse now. There are fewer jobs, more drugs. Oh, there are more black kids graduating from high

school than in the thirties and the forties—you see, there never were any good old days for blacks in this country with regard to education—but what's frightening is that even fewer are going to college. It's far more, five times more, likely that a black male will go to jail than to college in Detroit.

He sees no significant improvements in urban education nationwide:

Over the past twenty years I have seen no real change, and I foresee none, either, in the next twenty years. It's social change that needs to take place and significant change involved: economic, political, educational. The system itself is as it always has been: racist, classist, filled with inequities that need to be addressed before fundamental change will ever take place in the schools in Detroit.

Narrative and History: What Happened and What Does It Mean?

A historical background of race and class relations in Detroit, even a brief one such as this, can be very useful for understanding the present situation of the Dewey Center and its neighborhood, both for examining what events helped shape the present conditions and why fundamental changes need to take place. When we examine the stories Jeanetta tells about eating on the street—told in terms of other stories in her life—in light of this complex and sometimes disturbing history of race and class relations we can understand more. However, whose history of Detroit will help shape the policies of the present? In my exploration of Detroit history, I discovered widely divergent interpretations of events. What do these various conflicting portrayals and apparent contradictions mean for our understanding of the vast complexities of urban Detroit in the nineties? Even if we can agree that social and economic inequities need to be addressed, and even if we were to agree with the general view that a historical reading of events is useful (or even necessary) for understanding how to go about making social change, a single version of what happened simply doesn't exist. Recognizing the glaring differences between, for instance, Katzman's and Bingay's versions of the history of Detroit, how do we choose between competing versions? We must acknowledge that there are arguable, contested social and personal purposes in the making of history; it is important to recognize that the various historical interpretations in each politically derived "story" of the riots, for example, have political consequences for the possible ways in which these inequities are (or are not) addressed.

Orlando Patterson points to three basic ways of viewing black history, three different stories: as *catastrophe* (emphasizing social injustices), as *contribution* (not only to American, but also to world culture), and as *survival* (focusing on the ways blacks have survived and triumphed, a focus on the culture of slaves rather than on slavery). Jeanetta Cotman's stories, her history, include accounts of social injustice; the stories remind us of the sometimes overwhelming conditions people living in the inner city of Detroit and elsewhere face. However, her stories also clearly point to ways of coping and, more than survival, to academic and economic success.

Jeanetta's stories of history remind me of yet another historian of discrimination, poet and G.E.D. teacher Molly Rubino, who was asked by a student during the summer program why she continues to live and work in the Cass Corridor. She replied, "One day last year a crack addict placed a newborn baby on my desk, wrapped in dirty rags, two days after the baby was born." Realizing that she intended this story as her answer to his question, the student asked her to elaborate. She said, "Socially, spiritually, anyway you want to look at it, this area is being killed, by the economic priorities of the government, by the desertion of this area in a variety of ways, by the increasing homelessness and poverty, by all the drugs and violence. People can't turn their backs on these problems because, well, mainly because it is right to do something about it, but also because if they do turn their backs they just might get stabbed, eventually." Jeanetta, like Molly Rubino, by continuing to teach in the Cass Corridor and making changes in her classroom, faces some of those problems instead of turning her back on them.

Jeanetta's history, and the various histories of Detroit I explored as a result of hearing her stories, led me to consider some of the uses of history for reflecting on both problems and solutions from a variety of perspectives in order to make social change. These histories make me realize too the complexity of making those changes, considering the shifting nature of self, history, and culture as viewed in terms of competing interests and perspectives. The Detroit Public Schools is one public institution among many in Detroit. Its administrators, teachers, students, parents, and community members live and work within—among other things—what Foucault would call the "discursive practices" of racism and classism and economic forces that increasingly widen the gap between the very rich and a growing underclass. Still, seeing individual teachers like Jeanetta, programs like the Dewey Center Community Writing Project, and schools like the Dewey Center for Urban Education as functioning within that larger system, one can begin to see the basis for possibility and change. With Bakhtin, I can see that there are no inevitabilities, and that the possibilities for change are conceivable through our exchange of diverse stories in dialogue.

Toby: Mother Curry

Born and raised in Detroit and having taught for more than twenty years exclusively in inner-city Detroit, Toby Curry was a highly successful teacher at Burton International School for more than ten years before fulfilling a dream with her friend and colleague Debi Goodman to establish an alternative whole language school in the inner city. Having heard her and Debi speak at the National Council of Teachers of English in Los Angeles in November 1987 on the use of family histories and community ethnographies in their classrooms, and talking with them about their work afterwards, I felt they shared many of my assumptions about language learning and students. When they heard me speak at the same conference about the Huron Shores Summer Writing Institute and were enthusiastic about it, I was even more confident of our shared beliefs. When George Cooper and I began discussing the possibility of developing a writing program in Detroit, they were the first people we talked with.

Toby is an exciting teacher, energetic, highly committed to students learning in meaningful contexts. I talked with her about the program in late November 1989, focusing for some time on the issue of eating on the street:

David Schaafsma: What happened on that day at the Cultural Center?

Toby Curry: As you recall, I was the "snack person" that day, so I didn't walk over with the kids. I stayed at the school for awhile with Markus [Markus Müller, computer assistant, a student at the University of Michigan], and then we took my van to pick up the snacks. I got as close as we could to where we had agreed to meet, in front of the Detroit Institute of Arts, or the library, wherever it was. I dropped Markus and the cooler and all this stuff off, right? And then I went to park somewhere. Where I parked I don't know. But everybody got there, and everybody had snacks, and they said they'd had a great time so far, and then they cleaned up, everybody cleaned up great, and then they all took off, and then Markus and I got all the garbage and leftovers and went back to my van. And then it was in the afternoon staff discussion that these issues started coming out, because we were talking about going to other places. You want me to talk about just what I remember from that conversation?

DS: Uh huh.

TC: I don't even know who brought it up. My memory says it was Susan or Jeanetta, but it may not have been. But somebody brought up about not letting the children bring food on this field trip, this walking trip. And Dana agreed. So it was like the three black staff members were focused, that this is inappropriate behavior for young black kids. For black kids anywhere, but especially young black kids. Young black kids are not taught like this. And the kids that behaved like this haven't been taught properly. They tried to elaborate on how this was culturally unacceptable in black families, that you don't teach your children to do that. And that we shouldn't contribute to this as a staff. And that's when I think I said, "You mean that pulling out an apple is a problem?" Because to me, walking down the street eating an apple just seems like a very informal but friendly thing to do. I didn't know what the food was.

And then Susan or Jeanetta or whoever was talking got real detailed about how the kids were pulling out bags of snacks and junk food and pop and juice bottles, and they had food all over their face, and they were walking. And then they got into a description of black families, that that was something the kids were taught not to do; in an affluent black family or in a middle-class black family, you don't walk around with food on the street. You sit down and eat your food.

I couldn't get the historical reference. You know, even though I read lots of black authors and historical fiction, and other texts about blacks, I still didn't know what the allusion was because I'm not black. It's about the way you carry yourself out in public in a basically white world, and how you're perceived. And you don't want to be perceived as slovenly or sloppy. I think that was the general thrust or worry, of how these black kids were perceived out on the street. And then I think someone said something about white teachers not being able to understand black standards, or black kids, and I remember I got defensive about it.

DS: It was Jeanetta, I think.

TC: Was it? OK, I couldn't remember. Am I pretty on target with all this? But I can't remember how I responded, exactly—

DS: Susan talked about a white teacher in her otherwise predominantly black school who was respected by the black teachers because she respected the black families' wishes to have order and a certain kind of manners maintained—

TC: Oh, I remember. Well, this is my view: I do what I do for every kid. I don't care if they're black. I just came out of teaching with this multicultural, multiethnic, multilingual population at Burton, and I hadn't focused just on the black kids. There's appropriate and inappropriate behavior, like on a field trip or anything. You know, if somebody had pulled out a lot of food to eat, I probably would have said something. But I didn't understand what they were talking about until they described it.

DS: They admitted that they were more concerned about the black kids than the white kids. Because black kids have to try harder—that sort of perspective—have to do more. Whites can get away with it, but black kids can't get away with it. They'll be stereotyped—

TC: Criticized and stereotyped, right. They do have a point there, though it personally doesn't make me scream to see kids eating on the street, as a rule. But when I go on field trips, and I've been doing this for years with my kids, I tell them it's like being out with Mother Curry, it's like being out with your parents in public, and I have certain perceptions or expectations of how people are going to behave. We've been to plays and been the quietest group in the audience, next to raucous white suburban schools that are active and obnoxious, like calling out to the actors and doing other inappropriate things. I make it clear to my kids that if they don't like the performance they can just sit quietly and we'll discuss it later; they can criticize it in a paper or something. But I've taken numerous groups to Orchestra Hall, and everywhere, and though I don't ask the kids to dress a certain way—I think that violates their civil rights—I expect them to maintain a certain level of behavior.

DS: These standards you have, Mother Curry, they have nothing to do with race or class—

TC: No. It has to do with how you should behave when you're out in public, in an audience. You shouldn't be talking when you're watching a movie, for instance. So I don't do anything differently for black kids or white kids. At Burton, I didn't have a majority black population—well, gradually we got to be about fifty percent black there—but this is the way I've been doing things for years.

DS: Sometimes I feel that the fact that Susan and Jeanetta have come from upper-middle-class black backgrounds has something to do with how they are when they work with poor blacks.

TC: Like they're more rigid or more controlling?

DS: They're maybe more controlling than they would be with white kids. This is a theory that I have. For instance, Jeanetta really liked working with Thadd and Jason quite a bit, maybe because she didn't feel that same kind of pressure that she did with some of the other kids.[5] She liked them, she didn't have to worry about this constant pressure of authority that she had with her black kids—

TC: You think she liked working with Jason and Thadd because they were white?

DS: Yeah. I've never said that aloud; it's just a private feeling I have, somehow, that she feels a lot of pressure about that and liked being more relaxed with some of the white kids and some of the middle-class kids like Camille.

TC: She feels pressure for how black kids behave because she's black.

DS: Because she knows the stereotypes. It's just a theory, now.

TC: Maybe. Let me give you a horrible example, of something that happened to me once. A black teacher I knew told her black kids that she was going to videotape their class and send it to the suburbs. Can you imagine making a threat like that? Like what is that saying? Do you know what a loaded statement that is to tell your kids? But that kind of feeds into that whole idea of how you're perceived, and worrying about the stereotypes. It can backfire on you. Jeanetta's not that extreme. She is just going one way to get her kids power.

DS: It's an issue, it's a real issue, and I think it's very interesting, about how you get power. What does it mean to empower a kid in terms of language? It's a tough one.

TC: Yeah, I haven't come to grips with that myself.

DS: I haven't either, I've told you that.

TC: I feel the need to help kids edit for publication. And I think that's a real consideration. I don't care if they're black or white or Hispanic, I want them to be able to succeed in the broader world, which is a white standard English world. And I don't want them not to be able to get a job, or apply to a college, because they can't speak standard English. And 98 percent of the time when I ask a kid to rephrase something in standard English, and I do it frequently in the classroom, they do it. So it's not an issue of not being able to do it, it's like, it's OK to talk a certain way with your friends when you're hanging out, and I encourage that a lot. I've had kids who have written plays in dialect. I had two girls that wrote a play about two old slave women after Reconstruction; they were sitting on their rockers, these two eighty-year-old women, and they were talking all in dialect. And that was really appropriate for the setting.

DS: I wonder if there isn't a connection between the insistence on manners for black kids and the insistence on—

TC: Standard English. Maybe. But you know what it is with me: I've had so many different ethnic groups in the last ten years. I mean, lots of kids have lousy manners. It has nothing to do with whether they're black, white, or Asian. I've had to chastise kids out in public for acting like morons, because you're not supposed to act like that in public. If you're with your friend in the mall, that's one thing, but if you've got an adult with you, then I expect a certain kind of behavior. In fact, I have had a lot of excellent black kids, and many of them were the strongest and best-behaved in our program, so it wasn't generally the black kids who were the problem; it was the Cass Corridor white population that was acting the flakiest on my field trips at Burton, and in our summer program, too.

You know, I see it as a class issue for Jeanetta and Susan, not in socioeconomic terms, or not in terms of race. I'm not sure, but that's what I think. But I would imagine there's a real connection, a strong connection between their perception of language and their perception of behavior, you know, the social graces and all.

DS: Yeah. So what was going on in the tension that took place about eating in the street? There was tension among staff members suddenly about how we look, how differently we're looking at kids, particularly black kids.

TC: Well, obviously somebody didn't respond to some things. I wasn't there. You know, did Jeanetta or Susan talk to the kids to put the food away?

DS: I thought it was George and Jeanetta walking together, and Jeanetta thinking that George would take over, as the codirector of the program. At this point she still thought it was a U of M program, and not hers. So there's this conflict on this day about how black kids should act, and it's partly because we have different individual tolerance levels, and it's partly because we see teaching differently, and it's partly because we see teaching inner-city kids differently. And it might be like you said, more a class thing. But on that day Jeanetta and Susan took ownership in a way they hadn't before.

TC: I think it's partly because we have black staff members who are always thinking of black issues first, and they're more sensitive to that. You know, I take food away from my kids when they come in with it in their mouths, but I would do that for every kid. As blacks, though, it's like they're sensitive to perceptions of black kids. That makes sense. But I try to treat everybody the same, with the same standards. Maybe that's wrong.

DS: I don't know.

Toby was complimented by Susan Harris during the program for upholding strict standards for the behavior of black children. Susan praised Toby specifically for "being tough" with students with regard to trash disposal on the day following Children's Day at the Cultural Center, and though Toby said she had responded "defensively" to Jeanetta's statement about white teachers who let their students "whoop and holler and carry on," Toby also made it clear she is not one of those teachers. Though she is supportive of individual students' needs and is personally "not bothered" with eating on the street specifically, Toby makes it clear that her standards for students' behavior in certain situations, with adults on class trips in particular, are exacting. She consistently broadens the issue of cultural conventions to multiple cultures due to her experience teaching in a multicultural setting at Burton, but she makes it clear that in teaching students from different cultural backgrounds she will consistently reinforce what she perceives to be "appropriate and inappropriate" student behavior. She tells students that on class outings she will take to some extent what she perceives to be the position of their parents, as their "Mother Curry."

Toby's interpretation, while not insensitive to black cultural conventions, helps us to think about how teachers might respond to cultural difference in terms of a continuum. Her story of the teacher who would videotape her students for the suburbs in order to frighten them into conformity might describe one extreme end of that continuum; on the other end might be those teachers who would never confront student behavior for fear of being racist and intolerant. Her approach, in some respects similar to Jeanetta's, asserts the need for teachers to help students of all cultures to an understanding of the expectations of a "standard English world." She also makes it clear, however, that even her many years as an inner-city teacher have not given her "all the answers" to the issues; many remain unresolved, and she demonstrates her eagerness to learn more from others. Her story, and her history of commitment to literacy work in the inner city, reminds us that in Detroit's history there have been both whites and blacks working together who are committed to social change for people of color.

In spite of her giving the impression in this conversation of a "tough" stance with regard to her students' behavior in public, Toby did not have the reputation as a traditional teacher in the Detroit Public Schools system. She, like others, had been increasingly dissatisfied with the language arts and social studies curricula that the Detroit Public Schools had to offer students. With Debi, she began to investigate other possibilities, other ways of teaching that the schools in which they had taught couldn't seem to accommodate, ways consistent with the whole language approach to learning they had been developing in their own classrooms and through conversations with each other about teaching, ways which led to the proposal for the Dewey Center. The story that Toby tells of eating on the street, embedded in the story of her and Debi's commitment to this inner-city neighborhood and particular ways of teaching, echo yet another story. This story, told by a woman who had long taught in the Couzens school, contains a brief history of that school as she recalls it, and provides a different perspective on literacy and history in Detroit, a perspective that continually looks to the future.

The James P. Couzens Community School: Working with Hope in Detroit

The James P. Couzens Community School opened March 19, 1956, with Ralph Carpenter as principal and Karl Marburger as assistant principal. Clara Jane Thompson was one of the teachers and was still teaching thirty-three years later in the 1989–90 school year, in the same building, now known as the Dewey Center. She speaks of the school when it was first built:

> The school got under way with a partial but enthusiastic staff. There was a great need for the school in the area, because the children were being bussed out to other schools. Although parts of the building such as the gymnasium were not quite completed, there was a need! The Jeffries Homes were filled to burst-

ing! These low-cost housing units were built in the early fifties and would quickly fill up just as fast as they were completed. They were totally occupied by 1956. So in 1956 there were a thousand kids in self-contained classes in the Couzens School, and 1,670 kids by the next fall, September 5, 1956. I was one of the first-grade teachers, though I've been teaching the third grade for the past ten years. In 1956 we had to have a split for awhile in the first grade because there were so many children. I had thirty-eight in the morning, thirty-nine in the afternoon. There was a pre-K in the high rises. We all felt this tremendous commitment that just propelled us. We were proud, and there seemed to be room to make the kind of changes that needed to be made.

Mr. Carpenter, the principal, was a wonderful man for the job; he was sensitive, intuitive, and wanted to help students and teachers understand black people and culture. He really made an effort himself, which is something you have to do if you are going to work in an inner-city school. He got a dental program going when we saw the terrible need for dental care. There was a hot lunch program instituted that first year that remains today. We were all excited about this new school. And we were all activists then, as teachers. In 1959 we helped to get the millage passed, and also that same year we were selected as one of the Great Cities School Improvement Project sites.

Walter Banks, the school-community coordinator, was very successful in organizing a cooperative nursery for preschool children, story-hour classes for all grades, and several special interest clubs. He also organized adult evening classes such as sewing and millinery. As Thompson says, recalling the work that was accomplished during the time Banks was in the building, "We organized and put into operation the Couzens Summer Program for approximately two hundred children. We held regular language arts classes in the morning and activities and field trips in the afternoon." During the 1960–61 school year the school inaugurated a program for selling low-cost books to parents and children, which lasted several years. "For years, we had a wonderful celebration every March 19 for the school and the community, to express our joy that this school was here." Thompson went on to say,

Of course, things change, and funding has been cut for so many inner-city schools and special programs. The commitment is the same, but it gets hard for some teachers. I know I think about retiring, but then I think of how these kids need me, and somehow I just keep coming back. I don't know what it is; just stubborn, I guess.

She told of one principal who followed Carpenter whom she felt didn't really understand the community or black culture as Carpenter had. As an example, she said,

> He wanted to get kids interested in the drive to restore the Statue of Liberty in the late seventies, but it didn't catch, and he couldn't understand why. You need to be sensitive to these things. I mean, our people didn't come in waving, hearts thrilled, sailing into the harbor in New York. They were down in the stronghold, starving. It's that kind of understanding, that knowledge of history that is necessary if you want to work in these schools, if you want to understand these children.

Marshall's words reinforced my belief that it was important to develop community-based literacy programs—and classrooms—in Detroit. When Martin Luther King, Jr., was asked why he had come to Birmingham, he replied, "Because injustice is here, and injustice anywhere is a threat to justice everywhere." As Thompson makes clear, you can't teach literacy in Detroit without addressing broader social, cultural, and political questions, questions that too often get ignored. The Dewey Center stands in the area where the 1967 riots took place and where, in 1992, the highest concentration of crime and unemployment exist. To commit to literacy work in Detroit is to commit oneself to addressing the inequities that are there.

One resident of the area near the Dewey Center, whose story is recorded in Raphael Ezekiel's *Voices from the Corner,* said: "What's it like to live here? It's a motherfucker living in this kind of neighborhood, living in this environment, I can tell you. People don't want to live like this, but there ain't nothing else they can do, no jobs. Nowhere to turn, no way to see out of it" (24). This sounds like a view of the cultural history of this area as catastrophe, yet the collective tone of the stories Ezekiel retells from this area of Detroit is one of survival and not despair: "We realized we had expected a world of shattered souls rather than bright, struggling human beings" (4). He documents the often heroic struggle for survival of the poor residents during the late sixties and early seventies in the Dewey Center area, a struggle that continues no less heroically today. His story of this environment is consistent with the emphasis on survival in the work of writers such as David Katzman and Molly Rubino, and the commitment of teachers such as Clara Jane Thompson, Toby Curry, and Jeanetta Cotman.

I asked Thompson why she still remains teaching in the inner city after a quarter century, and she replied:

> I know it's bad, with all the drugs and the guns. I know it's ter-
> rible, worse than it ever was before. After all is said and done,
> though, they're just kids. They're the same, year after year. They
> have the same needs, and they respond in the same way if you
> give them the kind of attention, the kind of treatment they de-
> serve. You can't give up on these kids. There have been many
> times when I have been inclined to give up, but then these kids
> keep bringing me back. They need me, and people like me, to
> show them ways out, or at least help them get better, feel some-
> what hopeful about their lives.

Henry Glassie points out: "History is not the past, but a map of the past drawn from a particular point of view to be useful to the modern traveler" (621). We need to draw our map of literacy in a multicultural world with many pens. My own brief history of Detroit in this chapter is drawn from the diverse voices of such well-known historians as Sidney Fine, B. J. Widick, David Katzman, and Malcolm Bingay, and some lesser known historians such as Jeanetta Cotman, Toby Curry, Molly Rubino, and Clara Jane Thompson.[6] All histories value particular voices over others; this one is a kind of map, a map drawn from a particular social and political perspective.

As I construct my history of eating on the street, the value of multiple perspectives in developing an understanding of complex cultural issues—such as the teachers' daily storytelling about collab-orative teaching in the summer program—becomes apparent. In the light of the stories, we learned from each other; through my telling their stories here, the ways diverse voices problematize and enrich each other and lead to explorations of still other relevant issues, be-comes evident.

I turn in the next chapter to two more voices, storytellers, his-torians of every day events: Susan Harris, who helped reinforce Jean-etta Cotman's perspective on the issue of eating on the street at our teachers' meeting, and Debi Goodman, who was quiet at that meeting but in basic agreement with their perspective. In order to better un-derstand and appreciate Susan's story, I was led to explore writing about issues of black culture and language; from Debi's story, I reflected on an area of scholarship with which I was more familiar—the liberal educational tradition of John Dewey—scholarship that in part shaped her and Toby's proposal for the Dewey Center, but which also informed the perspective that I had first brought to Detroit.

3

DEBI AND SUSAN:
Changing Schooling,
Changing Lives

THE DEATH PENALTY
Hayat M. Ali

Suddenly Brian jumped on his back and the man and Brian began to fight. As they were fighting, Brian grabbed a chain that was around the man's neck and it fell to the ground. Brian fell on the ground and the man stabbed him, then the man turned and stabbed Tere also. The man sailed away with Brian's sailboat. Tere and Brian were left to die. (*Corridors* 110)

THE OTHER SIDE OF THE PROJECTS
Camille Ryan

Things will work out, Ms. Bell said. "Trust in the Lord." The lady's eyes still seemed to hold a tiny sparkle of hope even through all she's faced.

Nine days later Shaunda called to tell us she was going to try to get help with her problem but that she needed our support. We told her we were behind her all the way and that if she needed any help to call us. She also told us she named her daughter Rose. That same day I decided I wanted to spend my weekends and summers helping Ms. Bell. Anybody who has such a wonderful power to help people's lives in such positive ways, I would be honored to work for. Maybe together we can help show people the other side of the projects. (*Corridors* 25)

"Present in good conversations are always the pasts that they presuppose and the futures that they inevitably prefigure."
(J. Robinson 7)

"Stories can't be spoken of as things apart from their tellers."
(Glassie 37)

DEBI: COLLABORATIVE TEACHING AS WONDERFUL DISCUSSIONS

Though she was born in Los Angeles, Debi Goodman, like Toby Curry, grew up in Detroit. The daughter of noted whole-language theorists Ken and Yetta Goodman, she was one of five white students who graduated in 1972 from Detroit Mumford High School. At Mumford she says she was "politically active," especially in the Free Angela Davis campaign. She explains her relationship with her fellow students: "Because of my somewhat dark skin color," and "because I grew up speaking black English" in school, "many people in high school actually thought I was mixed. I was very active in many black, as well as Jewish, and other causes." She continued her political activism at the University of Michigan, where she received her degree in Creative Writing and later at Oakland University, where she received her M.A. in Reading.

At Navajo Community College in Arizona, under her parents' tutelage, she worked on a "cultural study of reading" using "miscue analysis" and soon after became an elementary school teacher and reading specialist in various inner-city Detroit schools, though she worked for several years as a fifth-grade teacher and reading specialist at Burton International School.

An articulate and enthusiastic spokesperson for whole-language teaching, having run seminars and workshops, made presentations at assorted national conferences, and published various articles on her classroom teaching, she is always eager to share the work her students are doing. I interviewed Debi on several occasions about the program, Dora, and eating on the street, but the latter subject was particularly the focus of an interview which took place November 14, 1989:

Debi Goodman: I believe it was Jeanetta and Susan who first raised the cultural issues. I think it was Jeanetta who brought it up and Susan who articulated it. As I recall, Jeanetta began with an apology because she said she felt like a fish out of water with different teaching styles, but was still uncomfortable holding back and not being hard on kids as she was in the classroom. But anyway, she starts out, "I'm sorry, but I don't like the kids eating on the street." And I think she might have said, "Especially the black kids." But she didn't say that immediately. And Susan agreed, but the interesting thing was that Dana also immediately agreed.

David Schaafsma: You and Toby both mention that. I didn't recall that. I thought Dana had a different perspective.

DG: Yes, Dana immediately agreed, which is interesting because Dana is younger. But Dana nodded her head. And the rest of us said "Why?" picturing ourselves eating on the street. I think we're street eaters. But it was very interesting. The immediate reaction was that the three black people in the room immediately understood the issue and felt the same way about it. So, it was definitely a cultural thing. And the four white people in the room, it wasn't so much that we disagreed, it was like we hadn't ever thought about it. It would never have occurred to us to think about it.

And that's the interesting thing about cultural differences, that the three black people who were there reacted identically, and the white people would have been so culturally insensitive that we would have kids eating on the street and not even be aware that it might upset a black teacher to do it. It wouldn't occur to us.

Sometimes you can say to yourself, "OK, if I do this, it might upset this person culturally," and then you decide whether you will do it. And sometimes you decide not to do it because you might offend that person. But this didn't even occur to us because we're ignorant of this cultural bias, or standard. That's the first intriguing thing about it. And that speaks to one, having black teachers in the program, for the importance of considering cultural identity, cultural mindset. For example, Jews tend to be sarcastic, and Jewish children think nothing about sarcasm. But if I go out and talk sarcastically to kids who are not Jewish, they might be offended.

DS: Yeah, it reminds me of David Bloome,[1] and what he said his family and friends were like in New York and how different it was for him living in the midwest. When he first came to U of M, he said he had lower teaching evaluations because people thought he was somewhat caustic, just for being the way he was at home with his family. He said, "If you really care about someone in my family, you argue with that person."

DG: Yeah.

DS: And you don't let him up, you grab him and don't let go, and if it comes to screaming, that means you really care. If you don't care about people, you don't argue, it just doesn't matter.

DG: And you expect other people to argue with you. My friend Cheryl has a book for therapists about different cultural groups. These authors had a person from each culture write about their families so that other therapists could read about a culture. Specifically what they might be like in therapy. To be sensitive to that. Those are some things I find important to be aware of when working in this community—for instance, when we are interviewing people, especially when they talk about church and their belief in God. I, as a Jew and an atheist, have a very different perspective. But it's important for working with the children, too, and particularly Mianne, who's a Jehovah's Witness. Church is really important in black families and in black culture. Church has been the political and social institution that has sustained black culture since slavery.

DS: That was why we were very excited about Susan, because she was interested in connecting with some of the black churches. Susan's moral framework is guided by the church and her faith. And Jeanetta's to some extent. It's important to understand that if you're going to work with people.

DG: And the church plays a very important role. Whether the kids are tied into some sort of community institution is significant in whether or not the kids will do all right. For me, when I was in high school, I felt that politics served the same role. It gives kids a way of explaining to themselves the plight that they are in, instead of just "the world is dumping on me." When you see these criminal things going on, that kids hate society so much, that they have no regard for a person: we should pour our money into schools, not in jails. School can be one of those institutions that can play a significant role in kids' lives. The discrepancy between our kids and kids in the suburbs is a couple thousand dollars per kid. You have these kids with every disadvantage, more kids in every classroom and less attention given to those disadvantages. I have more kids in my classroom every day than we had in the summer writing program.

Anyway, back to the sidewalk. Susan said something that was very familiar to me because I grew up in a black, middle-class area in Detroit, and I'd heard the speeches of the black teachers: "You're going to go out there and you've got to be better, twice as good to succeed." And it's true, you can't deny the truth in it. So Susan's immediate point was that "We don't want to take black children out on the street looking like stereotypical black ghetto kids. We want them to look good, make a good impression, act right. The image of the ghetto kid with the food on the face, we don't want that. It's fine for the white kids, they don't have to make impressions on the world. But we don't want it for the black kids." And in that sense I understand completely what she's saying.

But on the other hand, and I said this to her, I said, "It's a tremendous burden to put on a child. Why should the child have to carry the culture on her back?" That child, everywhere she goes, has to represent her culture. They have to be superhuman all the time. And I wonder if it doesn't backfire, because it creates some of these egotistical black men who come to the university and are real full of themselves. And I don't say that in a derogatory way; they have to be full of themselves, because no one else will say it for them. But I feel it is a burden to put on a child. I felt that way a little bit being Jewish. I know how I used to feel when we had a horrible substitute teacher and she was wearing a Jewish star, and I wanted to rip the star off her neck. I didn't want a Jewish person to act like that. I know that feeling. But you are asking children to be more than children, to be better than themselves.

I asked Debi how she felt about black English vernacular, which she said she had spoken in high school:

DG: I think I'm the farthest to the left of the teachers in terms of dialect. I believe that it's purely political, that it's status, that there is no such thing as poor speech, or ungrammatical sentences, except within a dialect. But the only reason a dialect is low status is because of the status of the speaker using the dialect. And I think, about the dialect related to the writing, we talked back and forth about standardize, don't standardize, and it's funny that Toby and Jeanetta complained about it at all, because they were comfortable about it if it was Camille [Ryan] and recognized that in dialogue it had a place, doesn't it? But to them, it was that *Camille* could use it in dialogue because she knows what she's doing.

DS: But when April from the projects does it, it's *wrong*.

DG: Yes. And I know that the percentage of dialect miscues we anticipated was wrong. When we first discussed it in March or April we thought it was going to be a real point of contention between us. But I'll bet anything that it never became a big issue because it never really happened very much. In the writing it didn't really occur that much. I think we saw that children do change registers and they weren't writing in black dialect.

DS: There's a number of agreement problems that happened in some of the kids' writing, actually, in terms of standard English conventions. But fewer than we expected, I think. It is true that we didn't have the knock-down fight that we should have. I would still like to have that discussion. But the issues change when they're no longer abstract.

Debi pointed out that some of us expected Burton students to do far better than Couzens students, but we gradually learned from three students how to overcome our apparently limited expectations of them:[2]

DG: We all started out with a certain notion about the Couzens' kids, and let me frame that by remembering the first meeting with them. There were nine kids there, including Allen, April, Aquileth, Farrah, Eboney, and Lashunda. And they were really reluctant about writing anything. They crumpled their papers up and said they would stop, remember? And they didn't want to read out loud. But many of them weren't writing. What did I say to them? Oh, I said, "Sometimes when I have trouble writing it's because I don't know how to start, so I skip the beginning, write the story, and then go back to the beginning later." And that got some of them going. I think I talked to Aquileth about how the subject of not wanting to write might be something she would want to write about, and then she ended up writing a long piece.

But at any rate, the next thing that I wanted to mention was what happened at the very first meeting during the summer program, which was when the kids interviewed each other and they took notes and they prepared a talk about each other. In that setting, none of the kids had any problem about writing. They took at least two pages of notes on the other kids, and then we organized their notes into a list of things, but many of them wrote out a speech. And some wrote out two pages. But the point is, there wasn't any difference between Burton kids and Couzens kids. And they had no problem with writing.

So, where the focus was not on the surface of the writing, they didn't have much problem. And none of them said, "I messed up." When they took notes at the interviews, they didn't have a problem, either. We did start out thinking that these kids were not strong writers. And maybe all of us fell into not expecting as much of the neighborhood kids as some of the Burton kids, the ones who were not from the neighborhood, but we all saw it could happen.

I think we all felt, at least a little, that these kids would not be able to do as much as the Burton kids, and then we were all surprised that, given the right way of doing it, giving them the chance to write more what they wanted and working through it, they could do it. Just look at Dora, for example.

Debi acknowledges the prejudices she assumes all teachers have about the capacities of certain students to learn. She encourages us to question our assumptions and increase our expectations for all children. She also emphasizes the need to reflect on these assumptions and expectations with other teachers. The opportunity to discuss pedagogy and cultural issues that collaborative teaching provided was for her one of the central virtues of the summer program:

One of the differences between my experiences at Burton and the summer program was collaborative teaching. At Burton, you so seldom have any discussion of any kind with other teachers. You know, everything's said behind people's backs, or, you know, off the cuff; very little is handled directly. You know, I have rarely had such frank discussions in my ten years of teaching, as we did over the summer. And that was really incredible. Because we structured that in, to talk and fight the issues out.

Debi's stories, spoken from her many experiences as student, teacher, and community member in Detroit, affirm Susan Harris's and Jeanetta Cotman's calls for support and greater knowledge of black cultural conventions in teaching black children. She demonstrates that she knows this from experience; it is, for instance, important to recognize the close ties most blacks have to churches and to make use of that knowledge in working with black students and their texts. Because of those ties, as Debi points out, her students can't be seen as mere victims: "Church is really important in black families and in black culture. Church has been the political and social institution that has sustained black culture since slavery." While she does not agree with Susan and Jeanetta on the issue of black English, she nevertheless argues for building a curriculum which builds on an appreciation of difference, not deficit.

Debi points out the importance of understanding the relationship between race, class, and economics when she says, "The discrepancy between our kids and kids in the suburbs is a couple thousand dollars per kid. You have these kids with every disadvantage, more kids in every classroom, and less attention given to those disadvantages." She sees the inequities played out every day when she teaches in her overcrowded, undersupplied classroom, knowing students just a few miles away have more than enough support to help them gain a position of "social advantage." She points out the importance of institutional and community support in the effort to help her students.

Debi values the opportunity that our collaborative teaching offered, to "talk and fight things out" openly in "frank discussions." Like bell hooks, she has learned the importance of "talking back"[3] for both students and teachers when confronting oppression, but also when confronting statements that seem to run counter to one's own beliefs and commitments. She admits she values this process in part as a matter of cultural difference: in her experience, being Jewish means being open, honest, even confrontational. She also emphasizes a particular way of working with students, a way that begins with letting students "write what they want," and then working on that writing with them. Through a story, Debi illustrates how particular ways of working with students can also lead us to learn from them about how to work with them and value their ways of knowing. These ways of working with students, grounded in the work of John Dewey, provided the foundation for Toby and Debi's proposal for an alternative school.

The Dewey Center for Urban Education: Continuing to Work for Hope

Due to what some people saw as a weakened link in the community that caused a steadily declining enrollment, and the need for massive cutbacks generally in the Detroit Public Schools, the Couzens School had been scheduled for closing in fall 1989. Toby and Debi had proposed that the Couzens building be considered as a site for a kindergarten-through-eighth-grade alternative community school with an emphasis on whole language. Shirley Brice Heath says that,

> Within the United States, most teachers, administrators, and
> school boards direct far more energy to tests, textbooks, norms,
> objectives, and guidelines used to establish, measure, and record

children's incompetencies—than they commit to imaginative stories, creative problem-solving, and cooperation among educational personnel. (Bird xv)

The Couzens building was allowed to stay open as the Dewey Center for Urban Education, with a commitment to this more positive perspective on learning.

This perspective is summarized by Ken Goodman:

> Whole language learning builds around whole learners learning whole language in whole situations.
>
> Whole language learning assumes respect for language, for the learner, and for the teacher.
>
> The focus is on meaning and not on language itself, in authentic speech and literacy events.
>
> Learners are encouraged to take risks and invited to use language, in all its varieties, for their own purposes.
>
> In a whole language classroom, all the varied functions of oral and written language are appropriate and encouraged. (40)

The Dewey Center was established as a whole-language school consistent with John Dewey's progressive perspective on education—starting with what learners know, not what they need to know, learning which emphasizes doing, education as life rather than preparing for life, learning as a transaction with one's environment, and a view of teaching and learning that emphasizes whole language, not language in isolated skill sequences or in parts. "Democracy begins in conversation," Dewey (1938) said on the occasion of his ninetieth birthday. At the Dewey Center, students, parents, and community members are invited to shape together the democratic conversation of education, to have their voices included in that conversation. Dewey's goal was to "make each one of our schools an embryonic community life" (49). The school was to be an organic community not separate from the community at large; to that end, Dewey was against the kind of passivity of methods and uniformity of curriculum found in most schools, which he saw as static and inorganic. The educational center of gravity in the schools had "too long been in the teacher, the textbook, anywhere and everywhere you please except in the immediate instincts and activities of the child himself" (1899, 51).

The key educational goal for Dewey was social reform, that society might continually become more just: "The school is recalled from isolation to the center of the struggle for a better life" (1899, 119). His view of democracy was a "mode of associated living, of conjoint communicated experience," and he defined education as "that reconstruction and reorganization of experience which adds to the meaning of experience, and which increases the ability to direct the course of subsequent experience" (1916, 89, 101). Dewey wanted education not just to train productive workers but to prepare human beings who might live in such a way as to control, not just adapt to circumstances. His was progressive education, learning for praxis: reflective action for change. Dewey's own Laboratory School in Chicago was designed to "discover in administration, selection of subject matter, method of learning, teaching, and discipline, how a school could become a cooperative community while developing in individuals their own capacities and satisfying their own needs" (Mayhew and Edwards xv–xvi).

John Dewey worked to counteract "scientism" in education, which draws heavily on behavioral psychology and scientific management theories, leading at the turn of the century to standardized texts, teaching, curriculum, and evaluation. Toby and Debi, in their plan for the Dewey Center at Couzens School, took a strong stand against that still-current emphasis in elementary schools: basal-reader-driven, teacher-centered, knowledge-given, with a focus on student deficits and step-by-step rote learning. They promoted instead a program that focused positively on students and teachers as evolving makers of meaning. If we can see the "basalized" environment as one possible grand narrative shaping education, we can see that whole language is a quite different narrative about the way students and teachers learn, preserving as many voices as possible.

Why change the name of a school? Changing its name in itself is not necessarily an indication of change, but the name *Dewey,* like the name *Couzens,* is one associated with particular kinds of commitments. In an age of educational inequity, John Dewey talked of democratizing culture and bringing the school closer to life during a time of increasing formalism. Though, like James Couzens, a white male, Dewey stood for a different kind of commitment than Couzens seemed to advocate. Dewey advocated social change and certain kinds of activities to help bring about that change. These activities were inquiry, conversation, construction, and expression, seen as the natural resources of the educational process. For Dewey, knowing was inquiring, questioning. Dewey is a name of affirmation for a school that hopes to develop closer relationships with its community and to celebrate the individual and practical needs of its learners. Just as Mack Street was renamed Martin Luther King Boulevard, and Twelfth Street was renamed Rosa Parks Boulevard, renaming Couzens School the Dewey Center indicates particular changing commitments, a celebration of certain principles and a way of living that signifies the very best in a tradition of hopeful action for change.

SUSAN: TOUGH LOVE

George Cooper and I had gotten a tip about Susan Harris from Bill Ingram, the director of the Composition Studies Program at the University of Michigan, that Susan "would be perfect for the program" and would want to do it if she knew anything about it. She had a background in teaching and administration in urban schools. Working on a dissertation in the area of literacy, she was interested in teaching with us but became nervous about the location on the basis of contacts she made with certain members of urban Detroit churches. "Don't go there," she was told, "there're only drugs and guns and burned-out buildings down there. You can't do any good there anymore."

During the program, Susan usually listened and took notes in our daily teachers' meetings while those of us who were more forcefully opinionated, or who had more experience with similar programs, did most of the talking. She usually shared her feelings with George, Dana Davidson, and me later in the car on the way home to Ann Arbor. A spokesperson for what she called "Southern hospitality," she and her husband Fred cooked a feast at their house for all of our staff and families during the program, which turned out to be an important "community building" function because of all the stories we shared together that evening about our personal lives. A fine gospel and jazz musician, she sang songs and played the piano for us on occasion and was also the driving force in organizing Family Day, which involved many students' families presenting their family "artifacts" and talking about them. Students both interviewed parents and wrote about these experiences. She set this up by presenting her own artifacts, a picture of herself with her sorority sisters from Tallahassee in formal gowns, and a plate that had been handed down through several generations of her family. She was perhaps the most insistent and the most passionate among the teachers about the importance of developing close, supportive relationships with the parents and community during the program.

Born and raised in Tallahassee, she got her B.A. in secondary education from the almost entirely black Tuskeegee Institute. Of this

education, she says, "It was kind of a traditional setting in the sense
that the teachers were like the kind of teachers my mother had had.
Some of them were still there that had taught my mother. They were
very strict." Susan received an M.A. in Education from Stanford and
from there became a teacher and administrator of an urban school
in Texas.

In a phone interview several months after the conclusion of our
program, I asked Susan what her memory was of our conflict about
eating on the street and how she now interpreted it:

Susan Harris: It's very difficult for people, for white people and other
people who are not part of the black experience, to understand
some of the things that set us apart. And, for us, growing up in the
South, and that's all that I can talk about because that's all I really
know about, we have had to suffer so many stereotypes as blacks,
such as those about our supposedly smelling bad or being lazy.
Or, we're seen as walking around, not knowing how to eat without dribbling food. For many blacks that grow up in those types
of situations, our parents and teachers and everybody else work
hard to make you aware of the things that had been very detri-
mental to our race, to our people. We did not, as educated blacks,
want to be associated in any way with things that would make us
be seen as inadequate. We were seeking to set ourselves as educated people apart from what had been said about us as a race.
And the issue of hair combing—that nappy-head black boy, or
that nappy-head black girl—I think that many blacks grew up
fearing that stereotype, too. And naturally you wanted to appear
wherever you went as clean and as neat as you could. You didn't
want to be associated with those old ideas about what black people were like. Do you understand what I'm saying?

David Schaafsma: I sure do.

SH: OK. So this is what we have been striving for, and certainly this
is a major issue with blacks down South, because you were constantly faced with white people saying these things about us. And
blacks, particularly at such institutions as Tuskeegee, made it our
goal: we were to train our people, lift our people, and let not
those kinds of things be said. So when I came to Detroit there
were some things that were very disturbing that were going on
there. We noticed for example that the children were bringing
their snacks and such from their projects, and they were walking
down the street, with greasy bags and such, allowed to eat this

food directly on the street, and this was unacceptable for some of us because of our upbringing, our background. You wouldn't do anything to demean yourself in this way—eating and snapping food and just walking along the street with potato chips and sandwiches. And, are you with me?

DS: I sure am.

SH: Are you understanding why this was aggravating?

DS: I understand it clearly.

Susan also went on to point out that this difficulty with the behavior of poor black children was somewhat related to her disapproval of some aspects of Dana's—our young black colleague's—appearance, who sometimes wore her hair "all torn asunder," as Susan put it, and dressed very informally (as George and I also did, in shorts and T-shirts). She recalled why she had been so upset at the time:

SH: In the black community, you have to be neat. You have to be clean, you have to be together. Your hair has to be combed, in place. This is just part of the culture from which I come. Educated blacks are not expected to go around in a casual manner.

DS: You're very conscious of the fact that you're a model for younger black children who may still be in school, and—

SH: And are highly impressionable, and we want them to know that where it takes 75 percent for our white brother to get in, it's going to take 150 percent even now, in 1989, for our black children to get in to certain settings. You're not going to be the anchor person, you're not going to be in the bank dressed all sloppily, eating food in this sort of way; you're going to have to really be up to par. And so that was why I was so very disturbed when I saw one of our teachers there, a younger teacher, dressing in a way that I thought was not appropriate in that setting. It would have been all right maybe if we had not been in a setting where children were watching what you had on. I mean they were watching how you have your hair done. Do you understand now?

DS: I do.

SH: Because for one thing, this person was in a black setting. We had predominantly black children who were in what I would consider a deprived situation.

DS: Right.

SH: And then, why would you come in here, supposedly a role model, and a black, doing something that was almost on the level of those who were there? Because we knew that they had so much further to come. And it was certainly OK for you guys to be as casual as you like because we didn't see you in the same role as the black teachers.

DS: But that interests me, because you also said something at the time about your hopes for white teachers in predominantly black schools, that white teachers, as one teacher had done in a school where you had taught, would help to uphold black parental standards and black teacher standards for black children.

SH: Right. I was very impressed, and I remain impressed, with Toby as well as Debi, because for one thing, I felt that they were white teachers who cared. And I feel that we can have effective white teachers in black settings as long as they care enough to correct our children. We have had some white people who've come in, and they say, "Oh, that's the way black people dress," or, "Oh, that's the way they wear their hair." I mean, there had to be all kinds of lint and everything else in their hair, and they still wouldn't open their mouths. But take for example the day when Toby came back mad about all this trash that these children had thrown around on the school yard, remember?

DS: Yeah.

SH: She was openly angry and she did something about it. She said, "You are going to go out there, and you are going to clean it up right now." Now that's exactly what I would have done, and I think any other black teacher would have done, because we feel they should. She could have easily picked it up herself and said, "Oh, I'll just pick it up because these people are filthy anyway." Or she might have said, "Why, there's no need for me to even worry about it. They're not going to do any better, anyway." No! She said, "You come out here and get it cleaned up." I love that. I like that because it says "I care. I care enough to teach you what to do and what to do right. I will not put up with things that are wrong that you're doing." I really respect that and I really love that.

DS: That's somewhat related to an issue that we didn't get into yet here, the somewhat more complicated issue of the use of what some people have called black English vernacular. And I think I know your position on that, that you're doubtful that such a thing exists.

SH: I think I said I felt that black English does not exist in the sense that we have white southern English, New Orleans English, or New England English. I just don't see why we have to bear another label. I resent that as a black. I've been labeled enough. I don't want any other labels on me. Again, I feel that this is an issue that takes a lot of love and care where we're concerned. If you want to say black English exists and that there are certain patterns of speech that unfortunately have developed among black people, that's fine. We need to be aware of that, as we try to teach English, and as we try to get people to speak and write effectively. But don't keep that label there as a crutch for my people. Or say "It's OK for you to say that, because we all know that you speak black English." Because black English is never going to go in the United States, and we all know that. Nobody wants salespersons and teachers and others who speak and write ineffectively, regardless of color. We need colorless English, as far as I'm concerned. Because that's the kind of people that businesses want. They want people who can speak standard English, period. So that's my position on that: don't use black English, don't even give such a crutch to kids. Don't let folks think that you can get away with anything like that because it will not work.

DS: What about the issue of black children telling stories in school? In our program we let these kids tell stories about themselves and their communities. Are we then disempowering them by letting them tell stories and not just teaching the basics like standard English grammar and spelling?

SH: In Tallahassee Upper Middle we had black teachers who were taught in traditional ways. They were taught to speak and write in standard English. However, I remember very vividly writing a Christmas poem in black dialect that they had allowed me to write. It was something about this girl who steals Miss Loulabell's chickens. And the poem was such that they really applauded this. I was asked to read it in assembly, other teachers heard it, and they thought this was just splendid. I also did a story that I put in first person. Actually it was my grandmother's story about coming home from school and the perils of trying to cross a log over a creek to the other side. It was about the fear of trying to cross that log every day, because they didn't have any other passageway to get home. And how frightening it was because she didn't swim. These things that were related to my background and my way of life were accepted. But when we come to writing in a normal setting, we're going to do standard English. So I liked what you did this summer, because it was very similar to what I had experienced, too. You allowed the community stories of Ms. Bell to come in, which was good. And you let these children talk and write about the things that were important to them, and applauded them, and said, "Oh, this is good. This, I like." I think the children need to hear that, and black children in particular. I love that. That was one highlight of the program for me, something that I felt really really good about. And we did talk about grammar with the children, but in terms of their writing, which I think was good. And I think that the children felt real positive about you and George, and in terms of how open you were to what they were doing. And in Camille's story, for instance, she does both standard English and the—what shall I call it?—maybe community dialect.[4] And I think that in order for you to be successful as a black person you have to be able to do both. Everybody is supposedly equal, but it's still not quite that way.

A key to Susan's view of teaching was her faith:

SH: Certainly I have great faith in the Lord, and I credit him with all of the accomplishments and the great things that have happened to me. All of this I attribute to God Almighty. You know, there's a lot of talk about positive thinking, and there are optimist groups all over the United States, and that's good, but to me the greatest source of optimism is one's faith in the Lord because you get so much beauty out of that, there's hope in that, there's a way out in faith, something that I think can and will deliver our people from some of the situations that they have found themselves in. We certainly have seen the work of the church and the work of the Lord with Dr. Martin Luther King, with the civil rights movement—that is certainly a great testimony to what I am saying. Regardless of what people want to say, the black church is still the strongest institution available to black people on a regular basis, since they go there every week, you see. So that's why I'm saying that I see hope there, and I'm seeing a lot of possibility through the church.

DS: I think that not only shapes your way of looking at the students and the way you care about them, but it also shapes these kids' view of their future.

SH: Right. You know, David, I believe in tough love. And I also credit my grandmother, who was a very influential person in my life, and a tough woman. She didn't put up with things that were not right, and if she felt that we were doing something wrong, she told you that you're doing this wrong, I don't like this. And to me, that was the most loving thing a person could do, to try to make sure you get on the right track. And if you stay on the right track after finding out what it takes to be successful, then you are well on your way. And we know what it's going to take to be successful: You have to have some faith. You have to have self-confidence. And that's what a lot of black children don't have. They do not believe in themselves. But you can believe in yourself through Christ. If you believe in God, and know you're one of his creations, you can believe that you are beautiful. See, that's the thing that we've got to use to help our people come up and become the beautiful persons and positive contributors that they can be. Regardless of the circumstance, regardless of where they are, like they used to say: if you can't be the sun, be a star. Be the best at whatever you are. Be a positive contributor to your community and to this country. And see, that's what we need for black people. We don't need black people running around killing folks and stealing and being a problem. We need to take our problems and work out some solutions ourselves and not depend on people to do it for us. We've got to pull ourselves up by our bootstraps, if you will, which is an old Booker T. Washington notion, but I believe in that.

DS: Faith is your first and the most fundamental part of your answer to how to deal with the problems of urban poverty?

SH: It is. And you know, I don't presume to have all the answers to these problems because these are big problems, and I don't know if anyone has all the answers, but for me, I think it begins with the family becoming positive, with each person becoming a positive family member and building up confidence in yourself and building up confidence in your group, your own group, by commenting on and complimenting each other and encouraging each other. I love that about you and George, because you did that for each other all the time, and I think the children picked up on that, too. That was a marvelous example and role model, how you encouraged each other, and how you seemed to be almost brotherly in the way you conducted yourselves in front of the children. I liked that.

Building up self-confidence in blacks. If you can get a boy, a girl, believing in themselves, believing that they can accomplish things, there's power in that, there's a lot of power in that. I don't care if he's in prison, I don't care if he's living in the sewer. If he believes he can come out of the sewer, honey, you've done something for him. If I really believe that, I don't care, I might be living in the sewer now, but if I have within me the capability and the possibility of getting out of here, then I'm going to get out of here. That to me is the key, that's the thing that will unlock the door for them, from the projects, from prison, wherever they are, if they can start believing in themselves. And we did a lot, we did more than we realized. We did a lot with that this summer, not only providing a program for them like that, helping them get through the program, but saying, "Oh, I like that. Oh, you're doing so well." You know, when you say to a child, "You've done a good job; I'm proud of you," that means a lot.

Susan articulates a perspective of "eating on the street," and a perspective on literacy learning, through her stories, which those of us who taught with her learned much from. Hers is the view of a traditional black teacher and administrator who, like Jeanetta, is a strong disciplinarian. Her discipline is one informed by a strong religious faith and a belief—inspired by, among others, Booker T. Washington, the founder of the Tuskegee Institute—that observing the social conventions of the middle class, even acknowledging that they have been largely formed by the white population, remains the best means to social success in today's society. Her view depends heavily on models for these "high standards of correctness," both demonstrating these models with stories of the past and present, but also by being one of these models in every interaction with black youth. It is a view which Janice Hale-Benson explains: "Black parents have always stressed to their children the importance of their exceeding white children's behavior and performance because falling short would reflect unfavorably upon the group" (48).

Susan liked what she perceived to be the "motivational" aspects of the writing program. She, like Debi, appreciated the positive emphasis on the abilities—and not the deficiencies—of our students and noted the apparent improvement in students' self-worth. She came to the program with a firm perspective on life and learning that she says was changed to some extent by working in the program. She told me she learned "to some extent how to be less rigid" in her perspective on teaching, which she described as an essentially skills-oriented approach to teaching. She also said: "The collaborative teaching was wonderful because everybody brought something unique to the setting." But she never fully accepted George's and my insistence on everyone having a voice in planning, in every aspect of decision making:

> I was not too happy with the fact of so much ownership. You know, I think it's a good thing, in the sense that everybody needs to be a contributor, and people did emerge taking on roles, but to me, that made it kind of floundering. I mean, I thought it was interesting, but I also thought we messed around too much. If we had spent more time working on being focused before we got in there, spent more time deciding what direction we wanted to go, what contribution we would each be making, then I think we would have had a better program. I think if you do it again, you're going to be in a better position to be more focused.

Susan articulates a perspective that questions the usefulness of the collaboration I have advocated here. It is a perspective on negotiated curriculum planning consistent with her view of students' eating on the street; in her view, certain issues should not be negotiated. These ethical issues for students and teachers involve serious commitments, about which one should not be "floundering," since they have implications for students' lives.

Susan also recognizes that there is a double responsibility required of black children. As Hale-Benson explains: "A duality of socialization is required of Black people. Black children have to be prepared to imitate the 'hip,' cool behavior of the culture in which they live and at the same time take on those behaviors that are necessary to be upwardly mobile" (62). The place of schooling for Susan in this double task is to provide the skills needed to survive in a world where black culture is largely ignored and hardly respected.

Helping black children get "up to par" in order to get jobs means for Susan helping them adopt a "colorless English," primarily because she knows that a history of labeling blacks, even when the labelers are well intentioned, has meant a history of exclusion and inequality. She suggests that the term *community dialect* might be more appropriate than labels such as *black English* or *black dialect* for discussing issues of student language differences, a notion similar to Toby's "color-blind" approach to working with students. Though her view of black language and abilities was one with which some of the other teachers sometimes disagreed, Susan was nevertheless passionate about developing closer relations between schools and communities, about the importance of the family and the church in their relation to urban literacy, and the necessity of a positive attitude in the face of the complexity of these difficult issues. Angela Davis, speaking from a very different political perspective, sees the virtue of Susan's way: "The concept of empowerment is hardly new to Afro-American women. For almost a century, we have been organized in bodies that have sought collectively to develop strategies that illuminate the way to economic and political power for ourselves and our communities" (348).

While she admits that oppression and injustice exist for many African Americans, Susan refuses to admit that degradation and humiliation have been the defining motifs of African American history, and her "version" or story is one with a more hopeful emphasis, infused with faith. Survival is the central theme of Susan's history, perhaps even more than Jeanetta Cotman's, because of its consistently positive stories. However, Susan's way to survival differs sharply from Angela Davis's notion of how collective strategies might lead to economic and political power. Whereas Davis sought revolutionary social change in part through resistance and action against mainstream American values, Susan believes that the means to power is in part adapting differences to broader societal expectations.

While Debi Goodman and Susan seem to agree that black students need to learn middle-class norms for language and behavior, and both emphasize students' abilities as learners, they also speak in different ways about language and language learning. But how do we negotiate the apparently contradictory perspectives that Susan and Debi seem to assert through their stories? How do we build a curriculum out of diverse perspectives? My own view of black language use and culture, informed by my limited experience working with African American students, and by reading into various theorists, follows Debi's perspective more closely than Susan's.

My reading has led to me to recognize and appreciate language diversity. As Debi's father, Ken Goodman, puts it, "In a whole language classroom, all the varied functions of oral and written language are appropriate and encouraged" (40). Geneva Smitherman similarly encouraged me to have "an attitude that sincerely accepts the inherent legitimacy of the many varieties of English" (219). As a longtime Detroit resident, linguist, and historian of black literacy, she tells about one of the first government-financed programs for the black "disadvantaged" student established in Detroit in 1959, which espoused the following principles: "Negro students of a low socioeconomic level in Detroit must change their patterns of speech"

(204). She tells her own story of being forced to take a "speech correction" class in order to be certified in the classroom in the state of Michigan. As she says, "Certainly, it is easier to work on fitting people into the mainstream than to try to change the course of the stream" (241). She has worked nearly two decades for a national public policy on language which would reassert the legitimacy of languages other than English, which for her includes black English. Rather than attempt to "eliminate black communication, she encourages whites to learn the fundamentals of black communication" (231). I have been persuaded by Smitherman's work to celebrate linguistic and cultural diversity.

I have also been persuaded by Henry Louis Gates, who reminds us: "Eager to 'domesticate' the African slave by denying him and her their language, their religion, their values and belief systems, and indeed their entire sense of order, the slave owners, first, forbade the usage of African languages on their plantations" (15). I am led by writers such as James Sledd and Harvey Daniels to be "tolerant, open-minded, curious, even enthusiastic about linguistic and cultural variety" (Daniels 127). I am eager as a white middle-class teacher to participate in a celebration, and not a further renunciation, of African American language and culture.

While I in some ways disagreed with Susan, I was persuaded by her stories to explore her perspective further. As an outsider to the world of black culture, I knew it to be a necessary voice in building a perspective on literacy work in multicultural settings. I turned to other voices, storytellers, and theorists, to help me better understand. Lisa Delpit's perspective is one shared by many black educators facing the overwhelming embrace of "process" pedagogy. While recognizing that students should learn to write in meaningful contexts, she also sees that many of her fellow black educators teach with a focus on skills, with a largely unquestioning endorsement of mainstream, white, middle-class oral and written grammar "correctness." These are teachers who insist on enforcing quiet and do not encourage interaction, teachers who teach the way they learned to succeed, and, while not wholly endorsing it, Delpit understands and defends this perspective, seeing the teaching of skills as essential to black students' survival and not just further oppression:

> Many liberal educators hold that the primary goal for education is for children to become autonomous, to develop fully who they are in the classroom setting without having arbitrary, outside standards forced upon them. This is a very reasonable goal

for people whose children are already participants in the culture of power and who have already internalized its codes.

But parents who don't function within that culture often want something else. It's not that they disagree with the former aim, it's just that they want something more. They want to ensure that the school provides their children with discourse patterns, interactional styles, and spoken and written language codes that will allow them success in the larger society. (1988, 89)

As Delpit says, it is not an issue of either/or: "Students must be encouraged to understand the value of the code they already possess as well as to understand the power realities in this country. Otherwise they will be unable to work to change these realities." (1988, 97). As she puts it, "There is a political power game that is being played, and if they want to be in on the game there are certain games that they too must play" (97).

Janice Hale-Benson echoes this view: "Black children must achieve competency in mastering the tools of this culture if they are to survive. It is not enough to wear dashikis, speak Swahili and eat 'soul food' in educational settings, as desirable as those activities are" (3). Hale-Benson advocates real sensitivity to cultural ways of knowing, while at the same time recognizing the very real demands for high performance on ACT and SAT tests for getting accepted in colleges.

Hale-Benson, much like Susan and Jeanetta, speaks in a way which denounces predominantly white liberal presumptions (such as those that informed the open classroom concept in the late sixties and early seventies) about "what poor black kids need" and what primarily white educators can do to begin to address racial and social inequalities. She reminds us that talk about language and language learning inevitably involves multiple perspectives somewhat like Bakhtin's heteroglossia: talk about language will inevitably reveal a complex of ideologies.

Susan, an encouraging and supportive teacher, demonstrates the truth of the power of learning through the stories she embeds in her response to my questions, in her stories of hope and faith and triumph, from her "upbringing" and her own schooling and teaching, from her perspective on African American history and the "tough love" gospel tradition which has sustained her. She encourages me to speak my particular—and different—commitments about African American language use, but hearing her words changes mine, to some extent. Her story of eating on the street informs and reshapes my story about the realities of work in a multicultural classroom for both white and black educators and my understanding about how I as a white teacher can work with black educators in developing an empowering perspective for teaching literacy in multicultural settings.

I turn to more storytellers and cultural historians of eating on the street to further problematize, further complicate, our evolving story. As in Richard Price's study of the Saramakans, our messy, incremental tale of curriculum building and theory making is told again from still other conflicting and enriching perspectives. Dana Davidson and George Cooper both tell stories which for me lead to a consideration of student stories, student perspectives. Dana, a black Detroit resident who was quiet during the discussion of eating on the street, tells a story that reinforces aspects of Jeanetta's and Susan's stories with their emphases on tradition, but she complicates the issue by asserting notions of Black Power and individual identity. Dana's concern for individual and not just cultural differences is consistent in some important ways with George's view. George, who with Jeanetta Cotman walked to the Cultural Center with a group of students and was first confronted by her, tells an outsider's story of trying to make friends with children while being unfamiliar with cultural expectations.

Both Dana and George tell very different histories; nevertheless, their stories of eating on the street seem to me to place a similar emphasis on valuing individual student perspectives while at the same time raising concerns about the nature of teacher and student authority. Their stories led me to students' stories, students' perspectives on Children's Day at the Cultural Center, stories which also deal with issues of authority, helping us to see all the teachers' stories in a slightly different light.

4

DANA AND GEORGE: Valuing Each Student's Way of Knowing

WHY I WANTED TO BE IN THE DEWEY CENTER
Ifeoma Okafor

I wanted to be in the Dewey Center because I really enjoy writing and doing other things. I like taking and giving ideas, working with other people, and doing projects. I also wanted to be in the Dewey Center for reasons such as we go on field trips and get to see fascinating things. We get to share the things we've written and listen to other people share their writing. I am learning so far that learning itself is fun. Education is fun. (*Corridors* 70)

"In trying to find new ways to teach students who find themselves at risk both in the classroom and in the worlds that surround it, we are trying to find ways to encourage agency, to find sources for its exercise, to give latitude for its development. We are encouraging students to tell stories and to write them about the worlds they live in and to be critical about their presences in those worlds; we are encouraging students to read stories in which others have found critical presence in other worlds. We are, quite deliberately, trying to fashion in the classroom an inhabitable world for students, one in which they might safely raise such voices as they have to make meanings for themselves and others, voices that will be valued for such agency as they can manage." (J. Robinson 312)

"The challenge in teaching is to find a way of communicating to each child the idea that his or her special quality is understood, is valued, and can be talked about." (Paley 1989, xvi)

115

DANA: BLACK BY POPULAR DEMAND

A graduate of Cass Tech High School in Detroit and the University of Michigan, Dana was committed to teaching in the city and politically committed to issues of urban literacy. I got to know her as my student at the University of Michigan, and through supervising her student teaching at Detroit Henry Ford High School and on the basis of observing her teaching and learning, knew her as strong, opinionated, passionately committed to teaching, and loved by kids.[1] Because she was a good teacher, because she was African American, and because she was committed to teaching in inner-city Detroit, I felt she would be an ideal addition to our program, and asked I her to join the staff.

In the planning and in the teaching of the program, Dana was assertive and more than capable as a teacher, even though she had only just completed her student teaching semester. In part because she was more than ten years younger than the other teachers, she was the students' most "popular" teacher in the program and received many gifts from them when it was over. She got along well with the teachers, although there were differences of opinion with regard to her choice of hairstyle and clothing. I recall a T-shirt she wore two or three times during the program which read: "Too Black, Too Proud" from her membership in the University of Michigan Black Student Union, a politically active campus group known for its extreme stances. I knew from observing her student teaching that she had struggled with issues of authority in her own teaching, having graduated from a school where "respect" for the authority of the teacher had been unquestioned, but having thought hard, too, about Black Power issues. I first asked her to reflect on her experience in the Dewey program on November 7, 1989, during her first semester of full-time teaching in the Detroit Public Schools. I began by asking her to tell me something about her life.

Dana Davidson: I went to school here in Detroit, on the East side, Miller Middle School, and then Cass Technical High School, which is kind of a magnet school. You have to apply and be tested to be accepted. You have to be one of the top students in the city to get in. I graduated from there and went to Michigan. Cass was a good school to graduate from if you're a black person going to a large university because the school was big. There were almost seven hundred kids that graduated from Cass. And then it's just assumed that everybody's going to college. Like 98 percent of us go to college. So you were already taught to be competitive, and that you could do well, and that a lot was expected from you. The school was like the opposite of Michigan, like maybe 95 percent black, 2 percent white.

I ran track for Michigan, and that went pretty well. I qualified for nationals my senior year, made All Big Ten every year, traveled to every away meet. So I've had actually a very fortunate life. And I'm saved. I've been saved for a long time but I haven't been committed to Christ like I am now—for two years actually—as long as I've been married. Marriage made me more seriously committed to Christ.

Dana establishes herself as a woman who has had academic and athletic success in both predominantly black and white school settings. She is clear about the two relationships that guide her life—the one with her husband Omar and another with Jesus Christ. But knowing something about her political stance as a black woman in the university, I knew that another guiding force in her life was also her commitment to equal rights for black people. I was curious, since our discussion focused on a relevant issue, why Dana had been uncharacteristically quiet during our teacher meeting about the issue of eating on the street. I discovered that it was not because she disagreed with Susan and Jeanetta and wanted to avoid being disrespectful to the older black women, as I had suspected; rather, Dana revealed that she basically shared Susan and Jeanetta's perspective about eating on the street, though not in all respects, but they disagreed on other issues. At first, though, it seemed to me she and the other two black women were in complete agreement:

DD: We went down to the Cultural Center in Detroit. And some of the girls, I've even forgotten which ones they were, but they were eating potato chips and sandwiches and stuff and they walked down the street, looking around from each exhibit. Jeanetta and George were with them, and Jeanetta saw the girls doing this and it immediately grated against her nerves, but George couldn't even see what the problem was. I guess he had never even considered such an issue, at least that's what it seemed from the sound of it. It's like, so what, they're eating on the street. To George it seemed like: So, they're using their left foot when they walk—it's a normal, natural thing to occur. But as it turned out, when we had our little meeting, I didn't know it had happened until Jeanetta first brought it up. And as blacks, you don't eat on the street. It's just that simple. Oh, well, potato chips, you drink a soda, something like that, those are mobile, at least in my mind, a snack. But you don't eat a hot dog as you go along or a piece of chicken or a sandwich.

DS: But that's what they were eating, chips and pop.

DD: Well, I didn't know what the actual food was, and I might disagree with Susan and Jeanetta about what kind of food would be OK or not OK to eat, but on the basic issue we are agreed. Because that's just how we view ourselves—you know what I mean? That's just like, you know, white people have conceptions about how people should dress—most of your body should be covered—and just different ideas about family. They assume that that's how all people should behave if they're going to be decent like white people. So black people don't think that you or anyone should be eating on the street.

DS: Right. But the issue on that day wasn't how all people eat—

DD: But it was particularly bad for black kids to do it because they represent us, and we know better, right?

DS: Yeah—

DD: And then there are certain stereotypes that can follow behind. We always assume—I'm gonna say it flat out—as a black person you always assume, if you're going to play it safe, that white people are not on your side until you get to know them. There's just no sense in doing it any other way, because culturally and emotionally you have to defend yourself. And then if the person seems cool, then you can relax. So you just don't walk down the street doing that because you assume that white people in general want to think badly of you as a black person. They want an excuse to validate how they feel. So you don't walk around eating a piece of chicken on the street because it looks kind of barbaric, and you don't walk around eating a sandwich because it looks like you don't have any home training, you're not decent, you don't know how to behave, you're not proper.

DS: Manners, proper training, right.

DD: Yeah, and so you don't eat on the street. You just don't. I can't even think of—there's no further rationale. When I really think about it, that's just it, you just don't do it.

DS: Saying it out loud may seem a little silly in one way because it's arbitrary, or specific to a particular culture—

DD: That's true, it's a cultural thing. And if you let yourself live in a black neighborhood for a while, you won't often see people hanging outside with a piece of pizza or taking their hamburger out of their McDonald's bag and starting to eat, no. If they're waiting to take the bus to Caston Park, then they wouldn't do it. They wouldn't even do it standing up on the bus. There's something about standing up and eating where you don't have a home with a table and a chair. You can sit down and eat. You can always find the time to do that, you know, and preserve your dignity. So that's what it was about to Jeanetta, Susan, and me—

DS: You were actually quiet during our teacher discussion about it. My memory of this differs from Toby's and Debi's. They said you were in complete agreement with Susan and Jeanetta.

DD: Well, I definitely agreed with them totally, so it wasn't necessary for me to say anything because they were saying everything I was thinking.

DS: Oh, I see—

DD: At the same time, there are certain things that we don't quite agree on; maybe it's because of how I am and when I grew up. You know, Jeanetta and Susan are from a different time, where *they* knew they were together black women, but *society* blatantly told them that they were not.

DS: Right—

DD: Then you know how I am, I am who I am. I'm strong, I'm intelligent, I'm a woman, I know what I'm about, *I'm black.* I'm black, and I don't care what you think, you know? So, my idea was basically this: The kids eat on the street, but I know the kids are good, they're intelligent, and it's still bad, they still shouldn't do it, but I'm not going to be preoccupied with what other people think so much.

At this point, Dana shows ways in which she might differ from Susan and Jeanetta due to her age, and due to her political position. She makes it clear that her position is one that focuses on cultural difference and not primarily class, as she interprets Susan's and Jeanetta's to be. She also begins to assert her individuality and her concern for recognizing individual differences in her students. She suggests how she and other blacks take different perspectives on issues if they are from another generation, or have different personalities.

DS: That has maybe something to do with you personally, as a younger, more militant person, living in a different age and time than Susan and Jeanetta.

DD: Different time, yeah, different time. Now I'm sure twenty years ago, fifteen years ago, I wouldn't have had taken that stance. No.

"Immediately, put that sandwich back in the bag, wipe your mouth, and explain yourself to me. You know better. You know what you're supposed to represent, and you know what things are like now." But today it's different kids, and I know that those kids don't feel the same pressures that Jeanetta and Susan would have felt at their age.

DS: Susan had said she was concerned about poor blacks eating on the street because you are showing your poverty, your low place in society. You're showing them that you don't have what it takes to rise up if you are eating on the street.

DD: I don't remember Susan saying this, but I don't agree with it at all. You are who you are, essentially. There are certain things you should know how to do because you do represent a whole people; you're not just a black individual. But at the same time, you can essentially decide what type of person you're going to be, you know, and eating a sandwich on the street at the age of twelve is not going to negate what they're going to grow up to be. She's still going to be a doctor, if she wants to be doctor. I'm sure I did plenty of things where adults were thinking, "Gosh, she shouldn't have done that without her parents around," but I am who I am today, and I am still going to be that whether I spit on the street with an old woman coming towards me or not.

DS: I want to talk about a conflict that you were only dimly aware of at the time of the summer program. And I think it's slightly related to this business of manners and cultures. You said that white people have a certain conception of dress, but it's certainly true that black people have a certain conception of dress, too, in certain places. You know, in church, for instance. Well, one of those places for Jeanetta and Susan certainly was where she teaches. The classroom is a place where you wear a dress, if you're a woman. The first time she ever wore shorts in front of students was this summer. And Susan never did. And still never has. Now, there may be lots of other reasons for it, but they were concerned about that, and Susan in particular was concerned about the way you dressed, early on in the program, and about the way you wore your hair.

DD: So what bothered her about it?

DS: The same issue of how black adults should be models for black children.

DD: Well, I wasn't worried about that because my hair was clean, well kept, and styled. It wasn't just like I woke up out of bed and *poof* here am I. It was a conscious choice I made to wear my hair in that way.

DS: This was also an issue that I disagreed with her about, though I wanted to respect her feelings. But I wondered what the deal was, since you say there are black and white conventions.

DD: Well, let me tell you something about it. Black people of Jeanetta's and Susan's generation have an idea of what a black woman's hair ought to look like. My mother has this same idea. They don't mean it in a mean way—some of them don't even mean it consciously to reflect a Eurocentric view of hair, but that's what it is. The hair should be straight. It's not neat and taken care of unless you pressed it, unless you conged it, unless you're keeping both those things up. You know what I'm saying—you don't let the kink come back into it. My hair was wildly kinky when Jeanetta and Susan first saw me, I'm sure, and she probably couldn't deal with it. I'm not down on her about that, it's not an uncommon thing at all—in fact, most black people think like that. If you drive around Detroit, the black young girls my age and younger have straightened hair. It's just something we do. So she's definitely not alone in that idea that in order to show that you are keeping up your appearances, your hair is in some way straightened, and I just disagree.

DS: Also, you wore T-shirts and shorts and tennis shoes.

DD: Right, but the thing is, when I teach in a classroom setting and that's what I'm supposed to be—*The Teacher*—I dress differently. I dress differently going to work every day than I did this summer. But the idea that was gotten across to me about the Dewey program is that it would be a community project, not just in the sense that we were writing about the community, but also in that the students would have just as much authority as me. You know, so far as what they want to write, when they want to write, how they want to write. So what is the point of my always looking set apart from them, more businesslike than them, if you are trying to make that point in a summer program? You know, what's the point? Since I didn't see any point, I didn't take out my nice linen skirt or my tweed pants.

And you know, I don't know necessarily that blacks as a whole would be upset about my particular instance, concerning hair or clothes. Then again they might be. But here we're dealing with an issue where a black adult just sees the issue differently. I see the issue of what a black woman's hair has to look like dif-

ferently. I think that it's our natural form of hair and if that's what
we want to have, there's nothing wrong it—there's no basis to say
that it's not right. You know what I'm saying? I just see it differently, and lots more black women are seeing it that way, and that's
why you saw so many Afros, so many natural styles during the late
sixties, early seventies. That's when you saw so many natural hair
styles because at that time they felt that it identified them more
strongly as black: "This is our natural hair, this is our natural state;
we won't deny it as a way to fit in to this culture." Now, I agree
with that idea. You don't tell a white person,"You really need to
kink up your hair." No. They wear their hair with its natural tex-
ture. And if they want to wear it pressed, that's their business, too.
But a lot of black people don't feel that way. They feel that if it
isn't straightened somehow, it isn't done.

DS: I'm thinking of your T-shirts that say "Black by Popular Demand,"
and "Black History: The Universal Truth."

DD: Oh yeah, right, right. Black inner-city kids made those leather
pendants with the continent of Africa on them. They made those
popular. Inner-city kids. Not the kids at the university. A lot of our
styles come from home, and then we take them to the university.
We're not going to get them from the university. Sometimes the
children from the city set the standards; they don't always come
from the adults.

I asked Dana, as I had asked others, about what I had felt was a
closely related issue to that of eating on the street, and the issue of
cultural conventions for dress and appearance—the issue of black
English.

DD: This whole black English thing isn't as big an issue to me as they
put it out in those books, as it was in all the papers, and in aca-
demia. It wasn't as big a deal to me. It still isn't. Because it isn't
that different. It really isn't. I mean, I work with these kids every
day, I grew up in their neighborhoods. A little verb change is
mostly what occurs, and it's only with the *to be's,* mostly. You
know what I mean? It's not like the whole language is different or
anything like that, and for black people who are not all that politically and socially interested, or who don't know that there's all
this literature being written about them and their language—and
most of us don't know all the junk they're throwing out about
us—it's no big deal. It really isn't.

DS: Right. I understand. Though you went a different route than
many of these kids may be heading.

DD: No, but I still grew up in neighborhoods where people talk what I'm sure they consider black English. I teach at a school where the kids are not from middle-class, black families, and I hear some of the verb changes, they do some of the things that would not be grammatically correct if you wrote them down and presented them, and you want to be a news editor or something. But it's not a big thing.

DS: But it is a big thing if you're denied entrance to a university on the basis of the writing that you do, and—

DD: Yeah, but they don't write like that, in general, except for occasional mistakes that you would correct on anyone else's paper who's twelve or thirteen. They write like what they read. I remember my papers from when I was young. I'm sure I talked and my friends talked in what was considered black English, like, "You ain't gonna be tellin me what to do." There is nothing wrong with that sentence in my community. I mean, it may grate on my nerves, because my mother doesn't talk like that, and I didn't grow up like that, but it's just a natural phrasing. That language thing isn't that big of a thing because even when they talk, I don't have to correct kids frequently. I mean, if I keep hearing it from a student, then I will say something, but I don't hear it enough to do that.

DS: Susan has said that she doesn't believe that there's anything like black English vernacular.

DD: I don't think so, either. That's what I mean when I say it was made into a much bigger deal. Otherwise I would have noticed. Because I always talk the way that I talk. And most of my peers didn't, because they would be teased about it. You know, at certain times you talk proper, is what black folks call it.

DS: Well, the reason why people started to focus on this thing that they call black English vernacular is because they saw that some people were being denied freedoms, denied rights, on the basis of the way they spoke. They saw that society was making judgments about what was proper and improper and saying that the way that black people spoke was not proper. Not just different, but not as good. And they were denied rights because of the different way they spoke.

DD: Right. Oh, I definitely know the political agenda behind the whole thing. I'm not confused about that. I mean that's why I don't teach my kids that they are wrong to speak as they do with their friends and at home; I don't try to constrict the way that they talk. That's the way that they talk, and they speak clearly and articulately to me as far as I'm concerned, but I teach them how to write in standard English so that they can compete.

But see, I used to think that only black people talked like that because that's what academics kept talking about. And then I took a ride on the east side of Detroit, way east, like near the river, probably east Detroit. And I went to a gas station there, and a woman was talking, and if I wasn't looking in that woman's face, she could have been black. You know what I mean?

I guess what I'm saying is I think they wouldn't hire anyone who spoke nonstandard. But they wouldn't hire us because we're black. Language is just a small part of it. You know what I mean? But black people in general just do not talk the same way in the white community that they do outside of the white community. On the whole, I agree with Susan that black people have been hurt more than helped by people calling attention to it as black English.

DS: So what do black, and other minority, kids need to survive, in terms of language? They have to realize that—

DD: They need both.

DS: They need both.

DD: I absolutely and thoroughly believe that.

DS: I do, too. And on that general point I think all of us basically agree.

Dana's interpretation is crucial to our understanding of several issues regarding cultural, racial, and individual differences. She initially seemed to be in full agreement with Susan's and Jeanetta's perspective on the issue of eating on the street, but she makes it clear that her reason for opposing the practice is based in tradition and not in altering the deficiencies of poor black children. In her experience, it is just "not something black people do"; black cultural standards do not or should not exist in terms of mainstream white traditions. While she reinforces black cultural tradition by showing how eating on the street has been viewed in her own family and community history, she also demonstrates that *what* is acceptable to eat on the street might vary in particular communities.

With regard to accepting certain hairstyles, Dana points out that generational and political factors often play an important role; she acknowledges that her view may not be in keeping with the majority black position. With regard to the issue of cultural conventions generally, she makes room for individual student difference by pointing to her own experience as a person to some extent on the margins of mainstream African American life.

Dana is a teacher whose stories about eating on the street and black culture help remind me that broad concepts like culture and race are continually shifting and complex. Eating on the street may be appropriate or inappropriate within a given culture, depending on various specifically local considerations. The conventions within particular communities also change, and thus our approaches to cultural and racial issues must be sensitive to the ways these conventions intersect with different community and individual histories—and are continually changed to some extent by them. Dana tells us that there is no single "black perspective" on any issue: "I am who I am," she says, asserting her own individuality, while at the same time asserting pride in her black identity. Her voice reminds us that multiple and conflicting voices within any given culture inform a collaborative teaching and learning environment.

Several months after the interview excerpted above, I talked with Dana about her first year of teaching and how it differed from teaching in the summer program. She said she liked having the opportunity to talk with other teachers and work with students on a more one-to-one basis, as she had been able to do in the summer program, but also liked teaching in the regular classroom, trying things out on her own. In September 1989, Dana was hired as a substitute teacher in the Detroit Public Schools, and by October she was given a full-time position as an eighth-grade teacher. I asked her whether she had solved the initial "discipline problem" she had been having and some of the other difficulties she had encountered when beginning teaching:

DD: At first, the school was having administrative problems, and, as a result, certain academic things didn't occur, and then, in terms of discipline, the kids were in control of some situations. And with my being new at the time that I substituted . . . they also had had two teachers before me, one who just really did not want to be in a middle school, and he told the kids that. You know, he was telling every staff person that would listen, when he got a transfer, "Thank God I'm getting out of here. I can't stand this blank blank place." So you know, I'm coming in after him and his attitude, and it's hard to get the kids at first to realize that I'm serious, I intend to stay. But at that time I came home exhausted every day. I was losing weight, I was tired, you know what I mean?

DS: So emotionally it was really bad.

DD: Actually it wasn't so much emotional it was like physically draining to get those kids to keep still. And that would make me mentally tired. You know, because I made all these lesson plans up, had all these ideas for teaching, and nothing came of it. For the first four or five days, nothing. And then, finally, when I started calling folks' homes, kicking kids out of my classrooms, talking to them like they had some sense, you know, getting on them to be quiet. I said, "Sit down, act right, or get out, because I'll call your parents *to*night, have them come in *from* work, and you know they're going to be mad if they have to miss work because you're acting crazy up here." So they started to think that I was serious and that I was willing to discipline them. Things are a lot better now. So I like teaching the kids, and I like the school. I like the school a lot.

I had visited the class in which Dana student taught several times. I liked her energy, I admired her commitment to individual students and to teaching in the city, and I found her struggling to create her own teaching philosophy, drawing on both traditional and progressive perspectives. Early in her public school teaching she had experienced difficulties with student discipline, but she found a way to gain some control of the situation. In the summer program, she had defended her way of dressing and acting as consistent with her understanding of the intentions of the summer program. She questioned the presumed authority of the "Teacher" that other staff members seemed to assert, seeing the summer program as an opportunity to explore the boundaries of received notions about teacher-student relationships. Partly as a result of that exploration, she seemed willing to allow black students to eat on the street, even though she had agreed with Susan and Jeanetta that it was something blacks traditionally "just didn't do."

One of the virtues of collaborative teaching for Dana, as a young teacher, was having the opportunity to test out her own ideas about teaching. She seemed to be exploring how to value individual student differences while at the same time asserting the importance of racial and cultural identity. George Cooper, having grown up in very different circumstances, reinforces a similar view; he, like Dana, sees the necessity of valuing individual students' ways of living and learning.

GEORGE: MAKING FRIENDS

"From the other negative function of judge and jury, the teacher can rise to the far more useful and satisfying position of friend." (Paley 1989, xv)

George Cooper: I grew up in Wanakah, a little village which is a sub-
urb of the city of Buffalo, in Erie County, New York, on the shores
of Lake Erie. I grew up in an upper-middle-class family, went to an
all-white high school, was a jock there, lettered in football four
years, and was an All-Star my senior year. I remember going to get
my picture taken, and I remember whenever I had my picture
taken I had the most serious look on my face that I could muster.
So I have this picture, like most sports pictures, where you are
trying to assume a pose, and it's really funny to look at when you
think of it that way. I wasn't much of a student, really, although I
was in the upper track. They started us in the seventh grade, and
I was in the "A" track, which allowed me to take languages and
advanced math, and I took some advanced courses, but I also
screwed around a lot. I went to Bowling Green University in Ohio
with no real goal in mind but to get away from home. I knew I
was supposed to go to college. I enjoyed the writing and philosophy courses, I remember, and I recall that this was a time when
we were protesting various things, such as the war and our right
to smoke marijuana in the dorms. This was in the early seventies.

George left Bowling Green and for a few years worked in various
jobs across the country before returning to Ohio State University in
1979 to finish his degree. There he married, he and his wife JoAnn
had a son, and soon after they moved to Ann Arbor. He worked
through an M.A. to candidacy in the Ph.D. program in English Language and Literature at the University of Michigan but left the program to become a full-time lecturer with the English Composition
Board (ECB). In the year following the first summer program, he continued to work at the Dewey Center in Debi Goodman's fifth grade
class as a volunteer and team teacher. Relaxed, jovial, even-tempered,
yet also deeply serious about teaching issues and eager to learn more,
in many ways George was the "spiritual hub" of our teaching team,
a trusted friend and respected by all of us for his love of kids and
his advocacy of their ways of learning. In November 1989, I talked
with him about his involvement in the Dewey Center Community
Writing Project.

David Schaafsma: What attracted you to working in Detroit?

George Cooper: Well, we had been working in Rogers City, enjoying
the work that we did there and seeing that it was profitable, it
was productive for kids. We saw them writing more, we saw
them having fun writing, we saw them taking care more, a different kind of care with the writing they were doing than I saw in

my college students. They were not only trying to make their writing look good in a way that would please the teacher, but they were actually digging deeper into the subject matter in a way that was motivated from inside, not from outside. We thought that, well, if this was working for kids in rural Michigan, it should work for kids in inner-city Michigan, and since we're close to Detroit, why not try to do a similar project there? And see if in fact it would work with kids who have not had many advantages in terms of their lives and education. We were excited about working with these great kids, and learning with talented teachers about teaching there, and offering what we knew, or thought we knew, about teaching.

DS: What was it like to go to Detroit, and starting a writing project?

GC: Exciting. Challenging and scary. It was exciting in that the idea of actually being able to do it seemed beyond anything I would have imagined myself doing—although I knew those were things that educators should be doing. I think education should meet the needs of people, to look at education as serving people rather than serving industry—turning out people who have nice bright diplomas, who can go to work and serve the society that way. But I also think that education needs to meet the needs of those people who are coming into education, and I think that it should adapt itself to every situation that's conceivable. But I think that it should meet the kids' needs, and not the school's needs or society, primarily. We all felt this.

I thought that was exciting, challenging, because you have a white person going in to the middle of a black inner city, and this was scary because I didn't know, I don't know black culture that well. And I can be a person who would say, "Oh well, you know, black folks and white folks are about the same." And certainly a liberal ought to say that, "We're all the same, we're all people," but indeed, there are a lot of different perspectives embedded in each culture, and I think it's dangerous for that to be overlooked and for someone to say, "Oh well, everyone's the same." It can lead to major oversights of important things.

So I was worried. I felt like a minority for the first time in a way, which I guess I was, and yes, I was excited. I was excited to be working with these wonderful kids and with equally wonderful and experienced teachers like those we had met in Toby and Debi and Jeanetta. Our desire to start a project in in Detroit led us to meet with them, and we wanted to ask them the best way to get into Detroit, and they immediately responded, "Through us! We want to work with you. We want to do this. Yeah, we're interested!" And that wasn't the way we approached them. It was to ask them for advice. And they immediately got excited about the relationship between the program and the development of the alternative school, the Dewey School. These Detroit teachers, like us, were interested in teaching together.

As I had done with the other teachers and some of the students, I asked George about the conflict with which he had been intimately involved, the conflict about eating on the street, but I also asked him about Dora and her writing. Because Dora had been one of the students involved in his group on that day, and because George had come to know Dora through his spending time with her on this day, he often intertwined comments about the two "issues of interpretation":

DS: What do you remember about Dora?

GC: Well, she's kind of an awkward, preadolescent, lively kid. I think of her that way. She's gangly, has long arms, long legs, glasses. My first recollection of her was the third day, the Cultural Center day. I went with Jeanetta, and I was really happy to go with Jeanetta because I figured I could stall a little about being the authority figure. Jeanetta thinks of herself as such a leader, she also knows the community and these kids, and I didn't feel comfortable being the authority figure with them at this point. I felt it was easier to follow Jeanetta's lead.

We had all girls in our group—Dora, Tameka, Aquileth, Farrah, LaShunda. So we went on this walking trip to the Cultural Center, and you know, in walking with a group some place there is a kind of community that is established because there're conventions to watch: where are you going to cross the street, what route are you going to go, who are you going to talk with? As teachers, are you going to talk with students, or among one another as teachers? And so, I'm trying to talk to the group and be a part of the group, the only white person in this group in a black neighborhood, and feeling a bit of an outsider, so I was uncomfortable. But I was taking pictures along the way. And they liked me because I was taking pictures, and as we got further and further along in this journey, they would more and more mug up to the camera.

But right from the beginning there was a tension because

they were determined to go under their own power. The kids were indicating to us that they were going to travel on their own time and on their own terms. They weren't necessarily going to listen to us. We had partly set that up in the program—to be independent—yet this was also in a sense a class trip of sorts. And Jeanetta by the third day is a changed person. Ordinarily she would have marched these kids right up in line, and she was kind of referring to that under her breath to me, and she started talking to me: "You know—if it weren't for you guys, I would have these kids in line, and we wouldn't be giving them any space at all. But I'm trying to be good, you know, I'm trying to do it your way. And I think it's important. I'm interested in seeing what will happen." So we're giving them room, and things are going OK.

We went along for about five blocks, stopped at a grocery store to get paper bags because at the Cultural Center there was a mask-making exhibit, and we needed paper bags for that, but at the store the kids were almost uncontrollable. They all wanted to run into the store, and Jeanetta wouldn't have it; she said absolutely no. And I was glad of that, because I thought, they don't listen to me, they're on their own, and to get their attention I would have to yell. And I didn't want to yell. So I was kind of glad that Jeanetta was doing the yelling, and she said, "OK, I'm going to go into the store, and I'll get the bags." So she's gone for a while and I got my camera out, and these five girls started climbing on this metal structure that was in front of this store. They loved it, that I was taking pictures. And I felt great about that, because they were really loosening up as a group, in their acting out; there were a couple of guys, too, hanging out in front of the store, and I took their pictures too. And I was starting to feel more comfortable.

Jeanetta returned from the store, and I was wondering what was going on because Jeanetta was talking under her breath about something, and I didn't know what. I mean, part of it was how she's a changed person, she's not disciplining kids as much, and she's doing it because she's trying hard to live by the kind of philosophy that we've advocated, that we've invited her to live by. These kids really wanted to go into the store to buy some stuff. They said, "We've got money, we've got money." And Jeanetta was saying, "No, no, you're not going to buy anything."

So after she came out of the store, we're walking down Second Street toward Wayne State, and the kids start pulling bags of

food and juice out of their shoulder bags. Jeanetta's talking to herself, louder now, and she starts talking about these kids eating this
stuff. I really didn't understand what she was getting at, so I asked
her, "What are you talking about? The kids eating?" And she said,
"Oh, you don't even know. These kids: look at them all now,
they're all eating." And suddenly—it was like it was happening in
a movie or something—suddenly everyone had something in
their hands. They had either a bottle of juice, or a bag of chips as
they were walking down the street, as though they had been produced out of nowhere. It could have been that they had them all
along, and I just wasn't paying attention to it. For some reason,
eating on the street didn't seem such a strange thing to me.

DS: Why not?

GC: Well, I don't know. I eat in a whole variety of places. I get an ice
cream cone on a hot summer day and I walk down the street eating the ice-cream cone. I'll go into the store, get a bottle of pop.
I'm walking down the street, and I drink a bottle of pop.

DS: So in terms of your comment earlier about conventions, this
doesn't disturb your personal notion of the conventions of eating.

GC: In fact, I didn't even notice it until Jeanetta drew my attention to
it. So Jeanetta and I talked about it as we progressed toward
Wayne State. She, more and more tempted to say something to
the kids, and me, just happy that we were walking along, and the
kids were more or less hanging together with us. As we got closer
to Wayne State, with Jeanetta's more and more constant banter
about it to me, the eating became a bit more noticeable to me
and actually in a way irritating. The kids were carrying these purple plastic things, plastic containers of grape juice, and as they
drank it and spilled it on themselves, you know, they did take on
the appearance of being a bit sloppy and all. Again, this sloppiness
never really occurred to me, but you know, I felt for them, "Hey,
we're 'going out,' you don't want to get that stuff all over you." I
would have told my own kids the same thing.

The other thing that was involved in it was that we had this
big snack prepared for them, not more than an hour away. So this
wasn't a matter of being hungry, I didn't think; it was a matter of
kind of enjoying that they're being out and about, and eating is
one part of it. But it wasn't a matter of necessity. It wasn't such a
hot morning that they had to have something to drink. Well, they
didn't generally like our snacks all that much, so their argument
might be, "Well, I won't like their snack. Let me bring my own."

DS: Right. And Toby might have stopped them from eating on the street because she hated the junk food they were eating.

GC: But I would have taken a practical view: "You're going to spill that stuff all over you, and we have a good snack coming up, why don't you at least wait until we all get together to eat?" The complaint of Jeanetta's finally was that maybe there's a certain practicality to it, but she was saying it was a matter of the attention that it brings on a person, and that these are young, underprivileged kids from the inner city who will draw negative attention to themselves because they're eating in the street. She tried to illustrate this to me as we got closer to the Cultural Center, when she insisted that the kids put this food away, and she said, "You see, George? No one else is eating on the street here." And I looked around, and sure enough, no one else was eating on the street. But I said, "Jeanetta, white folks do that all the time." "You can do that," she said, "But black folks can't. White folks can get away with that because no one really pays attention to them."

She said, "This is a double standard, but there's a double standard being held by this country and you have to be aware of it." So she spoke about it as a matter of culture, that it's not acceptable among black folks who want the best for their kids. Because black folks have more to face, the road is harder for them. So that to act out in the same way even a white person would do is less acceptable for a black person; they have more to prove. And all of this of course says a lot about Jeanetta. It's the way in which she's raised her own kids, and it's the way in which she herself had been brought up to be.

DS: What happened when we got back to the school?

GC: Oh God, that is a tough one, because I haven't thought about that for a long time. And what you have coming from me is probably not an exact rendition of what I thought that day, but my recollection of what I thought that day. One thing that I anticipated already in our discussion now is how I felt about Jeanetta saying that there is a double standard in existence. That white people can do certain things that black people can't, because of this double standard. Black people are held to a tougher standard than white people. They're held to a tougher standard by their own people than white people are. I was interested in Jeanetta saying that, and I think it reflects my own uncertainty about entering that environment, you know, not knowing what the standards are that people, especially outsiders, are called to follow.

You know, me coming from another community.

I understood what Jeanetta was talking about, and I guess Susan shared that same view. When they say they want the best for "our people," they are expressing a concern about black culture in particular. White folks can say we are color blind, we see no difference. And yet it's not our people, our race who is going to suffer because of the prejudices of others. It is Jeanetta's and Susan's people, their race who will suffer because of the prejudices of others. And if we don't share those prejudices, I suppose that that's nice for us, and maybe it's nice for them, but there's something else involved in this too, I think. It's not just about the way in which black folks are perceived by others, it's a concern about discipline that Jeanetta has, and I think Susan shared, for her own people. A worry that these kids weren't being coached thoroughly enough at home.

DS: According to what society thought was proper.

GC: And I hear Jeanetta, when I see her even now, you know, day after day, talking about discipline within her classroom, and she'll say, "These kids"—and I think when she says "these kids" she's speaking about the kids from the area of the Dewey Center— "These kids lack self-discipline. It's not expected from them at home. They come home, they watch TV with their parents, and then they don't talk to their parents about anything. They're allowed to do just about anything they want to do, so that they have a harder time living up to social expectations than other people. They are doing what will keep them oppressed. They contribute to their own oppression, in a sense," I think she and Susan are saying.

DS: Sounds a little like blaming the victim. They certainly have a view that you have to very vigilantly guard against behavior near that "socially unacceptable" line, and those people who are creeping near that line are those who speak in "nonstandard" ways, for example, black English vernacular, and those who also act in certain ways. Susan and Jeanetta obviously, without question, care very much about "their" people, their (and our) students, fellow African Americans, and how we all will interact with students. And they should be wary. There's a history of abuse that should tell them to run the other way when they hear white folks from the university offering to "help."

GC: Jeanetta had been talked to about the white world and black world as she grew up, I think. And Jeanetta was told, "You need to deal with these white people, so you better know their ways. Because until you learn them, you're not going to be able to teach in the schools," you know? So I kind of figured that it came from their own background. I guess the prominent point in this is that they were saying that white teachers will sometimes let their black students get away with things that they shouldn't get away with, like eating in the street, or like black English, in the name of liberal ideas like freedom and democracy.

DS: Which is, or can be perceived as, just another form of racism. At the very least this made us more sensitive to cultural difference. In some sense, though, I felt at the time that we were being told that we as white teachers, all of us, couldn't really understand what it was like to work with black kids in the same way that black teachers could, and our only option was to look at black teachers for how to work with black kids. But then what do you do?

GC: But we do need to look to black teachers, and they need to look to us. And we all learned some things from working together. We went in saying that we would accept them and their ways of language and wanted to work with their ways of learning. And we do, but now because we have talked we know a little better, that it's more complicated, it's not just a matter of accepting. But you can get in trouble either way, being authoritarian or liberal in terms of encountering another culture. I just didn't want to get into any kind of authority struggles, and neither did you.

DS: You have a different perspective on discipline than Jeanetta and Susan, too.

GC: I do, and I think so do you. We are not disciplinarians, generally. And don't often have to be. Although I discipline my own child, and my students, in a way, questions about good or bad behavior hardly ever enter into it, or not in the same way. In my classes at the university, it enters in if in a peer review, for instance, they're not putting any energy into it. You know, you can talk about giving productive responses because their peers depend upon it. We did that in the summer program, too. Or if someone is going to sleep in class or something.

DS: That doesn't happen in your class, does it?

GC: No, because my class is so exciting.

George said the issue of discipline was in part related to his discomfort in this situation; if he knew kids better and the situation better he would feel more comfortable with confronting students according to his understanding of the expectations of that situation. If he were aware of the conventions within a particular community, he would respect them and learn how to support them, up to a point. That point would mean disagreement, conflict, and require negotiation. We discussed corporal punishment as one example of a cultural convention we could not act on, for instance. Though he would certainly support parents' standards for dress and behavior, he said that he wouldn't hit kids just because they were hit at home. I recalled a related occasion we both had experienced and considered startling:

David Schaafsma: We ran into a conflict when we were interviewing Hattie Montague at a whole language seminar in March of '89, where Hattie Montague was asked, if she could take control of the school, what she would do to restore it to its former glory. She said she'd restore corporal punishment. And we thought, "Well that's quaint." We kind of smiled a little bit, we thought that was interesting; she amused us almost with what we felt to be her "barbarism" in saying, "I would put a stick on the table and if anybody'd move, I'd kill that child. You do that, then you'll get results."

Many (though not all) African American teachers at the whole language seminar that day nodded in agreement. One teacher admitted it was a "touchy" cultural issue for whites to deal with, but he said it was a reality that was necessary for white teachers to confront that a central means of discipline in most black homes is the use of physical force. This issue helps to extend our sense of the range of cultural conflicts we felt we had to negotiate as a staff in the summer program—cultural conflicts teachers in inner city schools face and deal with in a variety of ways every day.

George Cooper is a white university teacher who, like me, sought to bring his skills as a teacher to bear in an inner-city teaching and learning program in Detroit. He and I also sought to create a collaboratively planned, community-based writing program that would provide opportunities for thirty inner-city students to write about their worlds and opportunities for teachers to talk about teaching in the city. We saw our goal met with success by the publication of *Corridors,* through a book-signing party, through the considerable media attention for the students which followed, and, most importantly, through an increased investment in writing and learning that we observed and students attested to. In addition, those of us from the university were enthusiastically welcomed by Jeanetta, Toby, and Debi as team teachers in the coming year to extend the kind of collaborative learning that had begun in the summer program.

George's story of the conflict of eating on the street, while it shared certain affinities with other teachers' stories, was a slightly different interpretation of the event, a different version of what happened, reflecting somewhat different beliefs about language and language learning. Still, he demonstrates that he was sensitive to Jeanetta's perspective, as she was to his. He acknowledged that he had been led to rethink "what we knew, or thought we knew." He admitted rethinking his "liberal agenda": "we're all the same, we're all people" in the process of learning to accommodate cultural and individual differences in his approach to teaching. He, confident about what a "nondirective" approach might accomplish in empowering students, learned to listen to other perspectives to some extent: "We know a little better, that it's more complicated." He learned through discussion with Jeanetta the difficulty she had with "public eating," and she learned to appreciate the various reasons why he seemed to have no problem with it and why he was reluctant to discipline students for doing it. As an outsider, he was unaware of the cultural conventions attendant on poor black children eating on the street, at least the conventions as perceived by these particular black teachers. At this early point on the third day in the program, he was also struggling to develop relationships with students. He was trying to make friends and succeeding—but unfortunately at Jeanetta's expense. He, like she, was caught in conflict, and by sharing in it we all came to the kind of resolution we all must come to in such a situation, a decision that comes from the best of our collective understandings at that point.

Though he came like them from a middle-class family, and though as a white male he did not suffer from racism, his stories reflect a clear sensitivity and commitment to confronting racial issues—and issues of difference, generally—which all the teachers recognized and appreciated. While the stories show his willingness to learn from other teachers, they also demonstrate his respect and advocacy for student interests, their language, their ways of knowing. George seemed to place a priority on developing what Jay Robinson and Patricia Stock call "an inhabitable world for students," a place where student agency, student choices, are of foremost importance, a place where student voices are given room "to make meanings for themselves and others, voices that will be valued for such agency as they can manage" (Robinson 312). As he says, he is more interested in students' needs than institutional demands.

George was enthusiastic about working with students and initially joined me in opposing, for instance, teachers' efforts to change students' language to make it consistent with standard English grammar. His view of literacy seems to me consistent with Michael Clark's: "Real literacy is always a specific response to a concrete situation and never a generalized touchstone for personal development, social responsibility or pedagogical success" (60). Like Geneva Smitherman, he was more interested in trying "to change the *course* of the stream" than "fitting people into the mainstream" (241). He was, with Jay Robinson and Patricia Stock, "encouraging students to tell stories and to write them about the worlds they live in and to be critical about their presences in those worlds; we are encouraging students to read stories in which others have found critical presence in other worlds" (Robinson 312). George's positive approach to teaching and learning as a way of validating students' ways of knowing leads me to consider student stories about eating on the street.

STUDENT VERSIONS: THE GENERATION GAP AND ISSUES OF AUTHORITY

Three students, none of whom was in George and Jeanetta's group, wrote about their experiences on Children's Day at the Cultural Center, June 28, 1989. Their daily diaries of the Dewey Center Community Writing Project were part of what they chose to publish in *Corridors:*

ONE WRITER'S SUMMER DIARY: OUR COMMUNITY WRITING PROJECT
Billie Jo Roark

Dear Diary,

Today we went to the Cultural Center Children's Day. It was a lot of fun to see all of the children play and watch the parade. And the best part about the parade that I saw was the guy on stilts. He was good. He even danced with them.
That's all I have to say today,
Billie Jo Roark (*Corridors* 5)

THE SUMMER STORY
Thadd McGaffey

Wednesday when he got to the Dewey Center he was late as usual. The group talked awhile then headed over to the Cultural Center for Children's Day. The group Thadd was in headed for

the instrument-making place, but it was closed so they started
for face painting. They passed the place where the African dancers would be, so Dana made his group stop to watch. Thadd and
a few of his friends decided to go where not too many people
were and played team keep away. They did that until Dave told
them to sit down. Pedro, Jason and Thadd walked over to the
science center. They watched the dance from there. On the way
home Thadd and Jason carried Jon and Dale on their shoulders.
(*Corridors* 131–32)

DEWEY CENTER WRITING PROJECT
Walter Fahoome

Then on Children's Day we all went to different places. My
group was supposed to go to the instrument factory but it was
closed for reasons we don't know. Then after wasting 30 minutes of our time we went to the African Dances. That was kind
of interesting for the minute I watched it. For about the other 30
minutes Jon, Santiaro, Dale and I were on teams "vs" Pedro,
Thadd, Jason, and James in keep away. It was better than the African Dances. Me, Santiaro, Dale, and I went to get pizza. We
were getting the pizza when George and Dave came. "We're having snack," George said. (*Corridors* 127)

These versions of the day clearly reflect differences in tone and
tell of different experiences, but both Thadd's and Walter's stories address an interesting issue. Both note conflicts with teachers and their
disagreement with them on issues of discipline or of having the freedom to choose what to do on that day. Part of the reason for their
remarking on "conflicts in authority," as they seemed to see them,
may have been the teachers' emphasis on student ownership of the
program. Teachers had repeatedly involved students in the planning
of the program. We had asked them to imagine how learning could
take place in a "nonschool" environment. We had asked students to
think of how they could best learn and had pledged to them that,
since this was "their" program, we would give them opportunities to
shape their own experiences for themselves.

We had not originally planned to go to the Cultural Center, but
when we heard that Children's Day was taking place, we seized the
opportunity to go, pleased to have the flexibility to meet students'
various needs. After all, this was a student-centered program, and we
reasoned we had to take every opportunity to think of student inter-

ests and change our program plans to meet that goal. We gave students the opportunity to sign up for a variety of experiences on that day; thus, taking advantage of our excellent student-teacher ratio, we arranged for students to walk with peers who had similar interests. Debi handled the difficult job of organizing the day, and, given the fact that we had little time to plan it, we were generally pleased with how the day went, at least in terms of the way we had structured it. However, because it was an outing in which the students were, in a sense, representing the Dewey Center (we all wore our Dewey Center T-shirts on that day), we also asked them to "be responsible," to stay with their groups, and designated a teacher in charge of each group. We explained to students it was because of insurance purposes and more importantly because their parents had entrusted us as teachers with their safekeeping. Some students like Thadd and Walter recognized this move and characterized the day at least partly in terms of school authority considerations. This was still school, they were telling us.

Several months after the summer program, I asked some of the students who had been there to tell me what they recalled about their experiences that day. LaShunda, who was in George and Jeanetta's group, and Allen, who was not, both black students, responded in this way:

David Schaafsma: What do you remember about Children's Day, Allen?

Allen: It was boring, Dave. And hot. Too hot.

DS: What else do you recall about the day? Anything you want to say.

A [he is teasing]: Nothing. It was terrible. The teachers all made us go and some of us didn't want to, but we had to anyway, and we had to walk about twenty miles and it took about three-and-a-half hours. It was terrible, Dave.

DS: I know, Allen. You really have suffered. But it was only a mile and we were there in about a half an hour.

A [smiles; he is still teasing]: No, it was hours. It was awful. Lots of things were canceled, we had to sit outside to watch the dancers in a hot parking lot, the lines were long, there was nothing good to eat. And everywhere you looked there were mobs and mobs of screaming kids.

DS [smiles]: You mean people like you? Sounds horrible, Allen. LaShunda, what do you remember about Children's Day from last summer?

LaShunda: Well, we all got into groups, and some of us went with different teachers.

DS: Who did you go with?

L: George, and Ms. Cotman, and let's see, Farrah, and KeeKee, and there was Dora and Tameka, too. I don't remember anyone else.

DS: Tell me what you remember about that day.

L: We walked to the cultural area, and it was hot, and we couldn't buy snacks, Ms. Cotman wouldn't let us, but I had already had some along from home. We watched some dancing with drums. There was a parade with a man on stilts. We walked home, and I don't remember what else happened.

DS: Was it fun?

L: Yeah. It was OK, except it was too hot. I liked the train trip to Ann Arbor a lot better.

Without my having prompted either of them, and not knowing about the teacher discussion about the cultural issues involved in discipline, both Allen and LaShunda recalled disagreements with teachers about power issues on that day. LaShunda specifically recalled being denied the opportunity by Jeanetta to buy snacks. But I didn't ask either of these students to expand upon or explain their answers. In talking about the issue with Dora, however, in February 1990, I did ask her to elaborate more on her experience of the day. I began by asking her to tell me what she recalled about Children's Day. She was, like many of the other students, characteristically candid and direct.

Dora: OK, the adults with us was George Cooper and Mrs. Cotman. The kids was me, Tameka, Lashunda, Farrah, and KeeKee. We walked there, and we had lots of money, and we wanted to go to the store. Mrs. Cotman said "No, we've got to keep walking so we can get to the pop machine before the stuff start." We said, "It's boring, it's boring," and then we said, "We're hot, we're tired." We walked around a couple times, Mrs. Cotman wouldn't let us do what we wanted to do. We say, "Let's go over to the museum," we couldn't do that, we wanted to buy different things, she wouldn't let us do that. We were lucky to buy some lemonade. It was fun, but it was too hot. If you wanted to, you could probably fry something on the sidewalk.

DS: Remember anything else?

D: Not really. It was just a boring, hot day.

DS: Did you bring some food along, too?

D: Yes, I had some chips, and some stuff like that.

DS: In case you got hungry.

D: We took pictures at Wayne State and in front of the store Mrs. Cotman wouldn't let us go into.

DS: So that's what happened at Children's Day. Did you see the dancing or not?

D: Yeah.

Dora, like LaShunda, recalled specifically being denied what they felt was their "right" to buy snacks on this particular school trip. Like the other students, she saw the day partly in terms of her concerns about authority and autonomy. I asked Dora about the specific issue of eating on the street and told her that it was an issue which had been a source of conflict for teachers.

DS: I wanted to ask you about this eating on the street. Some of the teachers didn't like it. Can you figure out why?

D: Yeah, they say little kids who eat stuff on the street, when they buy chips and stuff, they pass it around, and their friends be eating it, and you don't know what your friend had, and then teachers tell you you have to go back and get your chips and just sit. If you sit then you miss out on school, and if it's in the summertime you miss out on fun things to do. And you could get sick if you eat on the street, so like they don't want you to get sick, and they don't want you to die, either.

DS: So that would be the problem with eating on the street. So you think that's what they might have been upset about. Let me say this: they said they thought it was sloppy, that it made a bad impression if people see kids eating on the street.

D: It's not sloppy to eat on the street, because little kids get hungry more often than what grown ups did when they was little. Adults don't understand the way that kids be like.

DS: So you think that's all right, that's what kids do. And you think that adults just tell kids that they don't like to see kids doing that?

D: Because they didn't do it when they was little.

DS: It's just an example of adults not understanding the way kids are today, maybe?

D: Yeah.

For Dora, like many of the sixth-through-eighth-grade students, the day involved several sticky issues of freedom and self-determination. Dora didn't seem to characterize the conflicts of the day in terms of issues of race or class, particularly, but as an issue of age (younger people should have the right to "be themselves" and are misunderstood by adults), as a matter of a difference of opinion about what constitutes "sloppiness," and as a function of the usual student-teacher power relations (teachers, like most adults, tell you what to do, how to live). Besides, she says, teachers do not realize how hungry students get, implying that not letting kids buy food on this day is being insensitive to their different physical needs. Her version of eating on the street, like the other students' versions, conflicts with the teachers' versions in some important ways and enriches our storied understanding of Children's Day at the Cultural Center. The students' accounts remind us that in imagining new notions about literacy learning, student stories, student voices, must be part of the evolving story.

The teachers were caught in conflict on Children's Day about the issue of eating on the street. By sharing stories with each other about it, stories embedded in our daily conversations, we came to a decision which resulted from the best of our collective understandings of each others' points of view. Ultimately, we never came to a formal decision about whether we would *all* try to discourage students at *all* times from eating on the street, although there seemed to be a general agreement that we would do so. Eight days after the trip to the Cultural Center, we did have to confront the issue. We were to travel to Ann Arbor by train, and Toby specifically asked that students bring no food on the trip since we would be eating lunch at one of the university cafeterias, and we would also bring additional food. On the morning of the trip, while we were waiting in front of the Dewey Center for the school bus to take us to the Amtrak station, some parents who had been invited to accompany us brought with them a grocery bag of snacks, from which they were eating on the street. Toby explained to them what we had told the children and asked the parents to put the food away.

The issue of eating on the street was just one of many issues we had to confront in our collaborative teaching. Other cultural issues, other conflicts, needed to be negotiated daily. For instance, trash disposal was a problem on Family Day, leading Debi and Toby to confront students. The use of black English (or what Susan might call the community dialect), became a matter of controversy, especially when we anticipated publication of *Corridors.* The nature of what constituted "community writing" was also debated, particularly as we read fantasy stories such as Joe Hammer's "The Unstoppable Knight," about a black knight who destroys the universe armed with a razor-sharp blade and an impenetrable shield. Each issue, while confronted in slightly different ways, was nevertheless confronted in teachers' meetings and inevitably involved teachers' storytelling to shape our developing policies and curriculum. But, as the conflict about eating on the street is represented in the stories teachers told in conversations months after the program ended, it is clear that the issue is not and can never be finally resolved into easy consensus.

In addition, the students' voices, missing from our discussions during the teachers' meetings, would have also been a useful contribution to our discussion on that and following days. Patricia Stock speaks of "the dialogic curriculum, a curriculum realized when students translate teachers' plans into intellectual projects that make sense to them, a course of study in which learning and teaching are best understood as reciprocally realized" ("Dialogic" 4). We would do well to consider, in our curriculum planning, the ways in which students can and inevitably do shape that curriculum by asserting their needs.[2]

From a story of eating on the street, a story of a cultural issue that is important to negotiate, we come to another story, the story of one young African American girl, Dora, and her texts, "961-BABY" and "I Am a Cat," told by those of us who were her teachers in the Dewey Center Community Writing Project through our separate and mutually informing stories. One's own language, as I said above, is never a single language. The voices present in Dora's story, "961-BABY," for instance, are the voices of the people she interviewed, including primarily Rose Bell; the voices of her peer, teacher, and family readers and writers; the voices of characters in other texts she has read, interacting with her own emerging voices. In many respects, her story can be seen as an artistically organized means for bringing different languages in contact with one another, testing them against each other. The languages of the others whom we learn from and with are present in each instance of our language use, in all of our talk and writing with each other; but they are voices, often consciously suppressed in other forms, which are emphasized in the social exploration which is narrative. The notion of the isolated, individual self, separable from other selves, learning on one's own, is a limited and limiting fiction. Self is social; thus, Dora is a collective of many selves, many languages and voices of others, not merely words, but whole systems of meaning, each language or voice itself constituting an interrelated set of beliefs and norms.

In a similar way, the teachers' voices, with Dora's voice, construct Dora and the meaning of her texts in a story. The stories these teachers tell are provisional, for the moment, but through these stories the curriculum was designed and theories about teaching and learning developed. The story I tell in chapter 5 was not written during the three weeks of the program, but it was, in part, shaped there through the daily stories we told each day about Dora and her peers. Those daily stories informed our planning, our curriculum, and revealed our differences.

What do teachers' differences have to do with teaching and learning? As Margaret Himley says about a group of teachers with whom she had worked, "Group participants bring all that makes them human to the project of understanding how children, and their works, come to 'mean'—experiences, knowledge, intuitions, memories, related stories" (10). The multiple perspectives on Dora and her texts yield an increasingly complex story of the nature of interpretation and give some indication of the possible virtues of collaborative teaching and learning. The teachers' values about teaching and learning—practical wisdom about practices—are there in our stories about eating on the street and in our researching Dora's self-construction. Stories about the classroom are always tentative, including occasional wrong turns and false starts, a provisional exploration that never quite achieves understanding, always out of grasp. But these are necessary conditions for leading into other ways of knowing, possible worlds for learning and teaching.

This is my story, and, like Dora's story, it is an artistically organized means for bringing different voices in contact with each other. I tell my story for several reasons, not the least of which is that I care about Dora—and students like her—and hope that, by sharing the various perspectives some of us have about her and her work, we will begin to appreciate the complexity and importance of her life and work. I also hope through this process to examine competing claims for understanding—different versions of—Dora and her story, to explore ethical and political implications of certain kinds of instruction, to seek out ways to incorporate social, cultural, and historical issues into our working with students and their texts. I also hope, through the telling of my story, to explore the uses of storytelling itself in the process of learning about the nature of teaching and learning. This story represents my—one learner's—attempt to incorporate different voices in an inquiry into useful ways to begin to talk about teaching literacy in a multicultural society.

5

DORA:
Collaborative Myth Making, Teaching, and Learning

961-BABY[1]
Dora Simpson

Lynn was having a baby. As she get out of the car at the hospital, she looked like she had a pillow under her coat. She said to Don, "I can't take it any more, O.K."

Don didn't answer.

"I knew it was about to come," said Lynn.

"How are you doing," Don asked.

"Just fine . . . Ohhhhh."

Lynn was 23 and had four kids and one on the way. She dropped out of high school at the age of 15. When she was 16, she got pregnant. Her mom put her out when she found out that she dropped out of school. Her mom was very sad that she had put out her only child.

"Right on time, honey."

"You know I can't take care of all these children."

"You only have four, and one on the way," Don said.

Lynn walked into emergency and Don left. On the way home, Don didn't think about what Lynn said.

*

Three days later Lynn came home with a new baby. Lynn walked in the bedroom, and found Don's clothes were gone.

Now she had five children. It was very hard to get things done around the house. The seven year old wouldn't obey her and wouldn't help her. The two year old threw paper and milk. The baby would holler. The four and five year olds were always fighting.

145

Lynn felt exhausted. She would go outside and get a stick and hit the kids. Then she felt bad. She didn't want to hit her children.

She looked in the newspaper and saw an ad that said, "If you can't take care of your kids, call us, and we will help you; 961-BABY. So she called. Mrs. Bell answered the phone, "Hello, how may we help you?"

"I need help with my children."

"I can help you but you have to promise to get your G.E.D., OK?"

"I'll try."

Mrs. Bell then asked, "You have to help us, too. What do you know how to do?"

Lynn said, "Nothing."

"Can you wash clothes? Can you cook? Can you clean?"

"Yes," said Lynn.

Mrs. Bell found day care for Lynn's kids, so Lynn could go to school in the morning. The teacher at the day care helped Lynn and the children learned to cooperate. The kids started to obey and help. Lynn got the rest that she needed.

Lynn called her mother and told her mother what she was doing. Lynn's mother helped her with the kids, too.

Then two years later, Lynn came to Mrs. Bell and said, "I made it." (*Corridors* 32–33)

I Am a Cat
Dora Simpson

I am a cat so soft and cute.
I'm a rose with sharp thorns.
I'm a Limo, so long and black.
I'm Dora, so cute and so nice.
but don't mess with me
or I'll dice you to pieces. (*Corridors* 34)

"It is helpful for me to change from theory-maker to storyteller if I am to follow the classroom lives of children who do not assume expected roles. A storyteller, above all, likes suspense. It is the not knowing about characters that makes them interesting." (Paley 1990, 31)

"You must invent your own literature if you are to connect your ideas to the ideas of others." (Paley 1990, 18)

The story that follows reveals multiple perspectives on one student's texts—Dora's "961-BABY" and her poem, "I Am a Cat"—which emerged from the collaborative teaching and learning in the Dewey program. Following the program, when I suggested to teachers the possibility of my writing about one student, we came upwith many possibilities, of course, but chose Dora because "She was interesting," as Debi Goodman said, "someone weall disagreed about from time to time and because we have done a good job of keeping track of her progress." Beginning with Dora's own story of "961-BABY," and some background from her own perspective on her life, my story of Dora's story follows. In another study, I plan to examine some of her fellow students' perspectives, but the focus of this chapter will be on the seven teachers' perspectives, their interpretations or stories about Dora and her writing, seven different and somewhat conflicting voices that tell us something about the nature of stories as they represent Dora and her writing.

All teachers told stories about different aspects of Dora's texts. Those who knew her well said much; those who knew her less said less. Some of the teachers talked little about Dora's story "961-BABY" itself, but chose to discuss relevant cultural issues. Debi talks more than others in her story of Dora since she has known Dora longest and worked the closest with her as she composed "961-BABY," more closely than any other teacher. But each of our stories problematizes and enriches the others. All teachers' voices in my story demonstrate not only the importance of multiple perspectives in learning and representing and teaching in the classroom but also the impossibility of silencing those multiple perspectives once they have been entertained.

I begin with my own story, and the section about student stories and the politics of schooling, in part to illustrate how I saw Dora and her writing before I began to discuss it with my colleagues. Except for a few small changes, it is the story I constructed in September 1989, a primarily "biographical" interpretation of her writing: where Dora lives, who she knows and lives with, the social, cultural, and economic circumstances of her life in part shape what she writes.

Mrs. Bell was born in Oil City Pennsyltargl. She thinks that when you talk about somebody who have die. Her son jump off a bridg. She help young girls who have babes.

Dora's journal entry for June 27, 1989. Notes from Ms. Rose Bell interview.

DAVID TELLING DORA

Dora lives with several other family members in a three-bedroom apartment in the Jeffries homes. Besides the small bedrooms, there is a bathroom upstairs and a small kitchen and living room downstairs. Her mother, her two brothers, and her sister live there all the time, but her three cousins, who usually live with Dora's grandmother nearby, often stay at her house too. Lanette (Dora's mother) and Dora's grandmother share in taking care of Dora's cousins since Lanette's sister was killed twelve years ago. One of these cousins, Tameka, is Dora's best friend. The two girls spend much of their time together; both were in the Dewey Center Community Writing Project, though Tameka left for camp after two weeks. The first time I visited their apartment to talk with Dora about her writing was July 25, 1989, soon after the project ended. Though I had initially (and naively) hoped to have a "private" interview with Dora at her home, I soon found that this would be impossible. Thus, for our interview, Tameka was also present in the living room, as was Sherman, eight months old, Justin, three years, Kimberly, five, and John, seventeen. Dora and Tameka are the same age—eleven, at the time of the first interview. Farrah and Aquileth, who live in the neighborhood, came for part of the time. Phone calls from three neighbors also took place during my visit, during which Lanette explained to the callers why I was there. For much of this first visit the room was quiet and the attention was focused on me. Later, and often, I talked with Dora alone at Burton International School where she and Tameka were seventh graders.

Because she consistently performs poorly by various school measures, and partly because she is feisty and tough and gets in occasional fights, Dora had for years generally been assigned to the reading lab at Burton. When Dora was in the second and third grades,

Debi Goodman worked with her and helped her learn to write. She was also a student in Debi's fifth-grade class, and through it Debi recruited her for the summer program.

My first impression of Dora in the program was a rather negative one. My notes for the first day of the program are sketchy but useful in indicating my own observations, independent of others' talk about her, and what I learned through others' stories about her. I wrote, after the first morning, "Dora—Hyper kid, bossy, didn't do much today, hung out with other Couzens kids Farrah, Aquileth, Tameka," then added, during our teacher meeting, "Dora: Tameka's cousin, grandmother matriarch from opening banquet, average writer, *is* bossy," information I secured from Debi. And I added one more note, information which I obtained from Toby after Jeanetta and I reported similar stories about Dora and her group of friends "doing nothing": "Wrote much in journal by herself—missed it! Toby." We all took notes on each student and learned similarly to build an image of each of them, a story of her or his day.

Toby's information helped me watch Dora more carefully, and when Dana the next day mentioned she saw Dora outside on the swings with Tameka during open-writing time, I joined others to say I saw Dora's notes on the Rose Bell interview and saw her listening to what Julia Pointer, a fellow student, had written. Each day, with each anecdote, with each item of shared information, we were all contributing to the narrative of Dora, the construction and interpretation of which differed for each individual. In the last week of the program, Dora became a very active member of the book publication committee in a way that others could not have known about. Since I was the committee's advisor, I saw her take responsibility for deciding how we would resolve certain important publication issues—for instance helping bring title and organization questions to the group as a whole for a discussion and vote.

The notes I took after my first visit with Dora at her house reflect my inexperience with life in the projects:

> Initially I had to wait outside, where I noticed the broken windows, the broken screen door, the angry scars on the walls of the building outside. No one seemed to be around, but then Farrah and Aquileth came by. When I went in, every corner of the limited main floor living space seemed to be filled with boxes and bags, and in the kitchen there were dishes and groceries everywhere. Lanette, Justin, John, and Kimberly sat on the couch, and Dora sat in a chair across from them, and though Lanette and

Dora offered me their seats, I sat on the floor. No one seemed to notice that bugs were crawling everywhere.

Later in the journal I noted:

> Contrary to my initial negative response to the mess, I came away with an impression about how well-behaved and fun the kids were, and my dominant impression is admiration for Dora for her mature response to all my questions and her dedication to "doing well" in life, but especially admiration and respect for Lanette for doing the best possible job for her kids under amazing circumstances—man gone, many kids, caring for sister's kids, getting kids into best school she can.

As I see it, "961-BABY" usefully builds from multiple voices and perspectives. The impetus for the story came from a group interview with Rose Bell. In order to further understand this story, we need to know that Rose Bell's words are here in Dora's text. For instance, when in "961-BABY" the character Mrs. Bell speaks, these words and ideas come from Dora's notes and from her memory of Rose Bell's talk during the interview. Dora's reference to the newspaper ad for 961-BABY is an artful use of Bell's own words in response to a question during the interview about who would make use of the service. Bell said, "If you can't take care of your kids, call us, and we will help you." Dora apparently thought it sounded like advertising material and imagined it so in her story. The reference to the G.E.D. also came directly from Dora's notes on Rose Bell's answer to a question. The quotations in Dora's story—"You have to help us, too. What do you know how to do?" and "Can you wash clothes? Can you cook? Can you clean?"—are indirect quotes from Rose Bell's interview when she explained the conditions for clients to receive help from her service.

Part of the process of understanding Dora's story is to know how she wove the words of a woman she admired into it. Also useful to know, in coming to understand the text, is that some of Dora's middle-school friends had already had to drop out of school because they became pregnant. We need to know, too, that her mother is a single parent who is raising Dora and her brothers, sisters, and cousins with little help. Dora's writing developed as a result of our working closely and intensively with her in small group workshops and in conferences, by helping her revise on a MacIntosh computer, by helping her make meaning for herself about things she felt were most important to write about, and by emphasizing her strengths and not her apparent deficiencies as an evolving maker of meaning for herself. With our responses to her writing, we wanted to reinforce her enthusiasm and validate her experiences in the community.[2]

As I see it, Dora, informed by many voices, composes texts and through "961-BABY" and "I Am a Cat" composes a self and a world. Her past experiences and her present study are to some extent transformed, and in that transformation she is transformed too. That change for Dora in this instance takes place through storytelling; through the stories of the people she has interviewed, including Rose Bell; through the stories of her peer, teacher, and family readers and writers who tell her own story back to her and tell their own stories to her; through the voices of characters in other texts she has read, interacting with her own emerging voices.

Bell hooks (1984), a writer who identifies herself as a black feminist, speaks of the "special vantage point our marginality gives us." She encourages black women "to criticize the dominant racist, classist, sexist hegemony as well as to envision and create a counter-hegemony" (15). She describes what this marginality is like: "Living as we did—on the edge—we developed a particular way of seeing reality. We looked both from the outside in and from the inside out. We focused our attention on the center as well as the margin. We understood both" (i). How can we come to an understanding of what it means to work with students like Dora who are, as Jay Robinson and Patricia Stock put it, "living on the margins"? (Robinson 273) Dora Simpson's story, her fiction, her fictional research into a crucial issue in her life, written as it was "from the margins," builds with experience, not neatly, not without struggle, but piece by piece with careful attention.

Student Stories and the Politics of Schooling: Multiple Perspectives, Possible Worlds

"Sensitivity to narrative provides the major link between our sense of self and our sense of others in the social world around us." (Bruner 1986, 69)

"Words that grow out of a personal narration are not always angry, but they almost always carry the possibilities of danger." (Kozol 133)

*"The basic question remains: 'Should the schools develop
young people to fit into present society as it is, or does the
school have a revolutionary mission to develop young
people who will seek to improve the society?'"* (Tyler 35)

Aside from what I have called my "primarily biographical" interpretation of Dora's story, I also see it as an example, a demonstration,
of the uses and power of storytelling. Before I talked with Dora and
my fellow teachers, one of my primary—admittedly "academic"—interests in "961-BABY" was *as a story.* As I discussed in chapter 1, I am
interested in the ways our current understanding of language works
against traditional, conventional, and widely accepted dichotomies
such as fact versus fiction, truth versus falsehood, subjectivity versus
objectivity, proof versus supposition. As I see it, certain—not all—
stories can call attention to the political nature of schooling regarding the kinds of discourse it allows or does not allow, and its view of
what counts as knowledge. If we in the educational community can
agree that there is a fixed body of knowledge in any particular discourse system, then the questions to be addressed about that discourse are ones of efficiency of transmission. If, on the other hand,
we see knowledge as a social and political transaction wherein
knowledge is created and existing notions of knowledge are contested and reshaped, then we need to question the present shape and
concerns and limits of our discourse. As I see it, all discourses are to
some extent "fictional" in the sense that they are socially and culturally constructed, and these discourses need to be open to the con-
testation and resistance that ways of knowing and learning such as
storytelling can sometimes invite. Looking at Dora's story, I think of
it as a site of struggle, one example of a constructive form of "resistance" to the content, forms, and purposes of most school writing. I
think of her story as demonstrating a way learning can—and often
should—be tied to experience. In other words, like many stories, her
story—a fiction—calls attention to widely accepted fictions of what
schooling should be about.

Story, as I see it, is the most basic means we have for organizing
our experience and making meaning with others. I realize that it is
not necessarily the case that the stories that students such as Dora
tell give us any more complete or "realistic" or "true" picture of the
world than any other form. The crisis in representation pertains
no less to stories than other forms of writing. But as Foucault and
Bakhtin in different ways helped me to see, stories, in part by pre-

serving multiple perspectives on the world, highlight or foreground the "fictional" nature of all language—the unstable, provisional nature of all discourse systems—in ways other genres do not.

I found philosopher Richard Rorty's view of narrative, and of novels in particular, consistent with this idea. Novels, Rorty says, "are a safer medium than theory for expressing one's recognition of the relativity and contingency of authority figures" (86). While it is certainly true that novels, like other forms, can and sometimes do function as propaganda, narrative, more than other forms—in part by including multiple voices—seems to "subjunctivize" reality, makes it seem more provisional, less fixed.[3] Stories like Dora's aren't arguments in the conventional sense, though arguments may in fact be imbedded in them in various ways, but they work differently than step-by-step logic. As Wendy Doniger O'Flaherty points out, "A myth says something that cannot be said in any other way, that cannot be translated into a logical or even a metaphysical statement. A myth says something that can only be said in a story" (27). Storytelling is an example of analogic thinking, which gives attention to experience. As I saw it, Dora's story could be seen in this way, drawing attention to her own lived world. Telling her story about Lynn and Rose Bell is a way of thinking that is draws analogies, makes metaphors about the way the world works. It is a way of remaking her life.

I wondered about Dora's experience in school. The Holmes Report on education clearly shows that a far different perspective than the exploratory, "subjunctive" one Rorty and O'Flaherty describe drives most schooling: "Far too many teachers give out directions, busywork, and fact-fact-fact lectures in ways that keep students intellectually passive, if not actually deepening their disregard for learning and schooling" (7).[4] Henry Giroux sees schools similarly, primarily concerned with "breaking down knowledge into discrete parts, standardized for easier management consumption, and measured through predefined forms of assessment" (124). Teachers are often what Foucault might call the "arbiters of properness" in schools, the "keepers of the gate" rather than the kind of teachers Jay Robinson and Patti Stock describe, "quite deliberately, trying to fashion in the classroom an inhabitable world for students, one in which they might safely raise such voices as they have to make meanings for themselves and others, voices that will be valued for such agency as they can manage" (J. Robinson 312). In what ways was Dora silenced in school?

I think we need to reconsider the value of storytelling and storywriting in the learning process, especially if we are to consider how we might speak with (not just to) students like Dora, and others who are "at risk," those who feel bored, powerless, disenfranchised, those who are angry, even violent. Stories are one way for both students and teachers to learn in school and about school and one possible avenue for the culture of the community, the students' various home communities, and students' ways of knowing, to intersect with the culture of schools. As Valerie Polakow says, "Stories are where we must begin. Stories are the clues which will lead us to new ways of knowing" (833). Whether or not we can fully share Polakow's optimism, there are aspects of some stories, like Dora's "961-BABY," that lead us to open our classrooms to a variety of ways of knowing that may be social, experiential, passionate, and grounded in the life worlds of our student writers. The students' stories that were created in the Dewey Center Community Writing Project, and in the classrooms and halls and homes of our students every day, point to the potential value of storytelling as a way of learning.

In my view, stories can be useful in terms of cultural and educational critique by helping us to see that "the past" is constructed in terms of particular commitments; by demonstrating some ways we might begin valuing events, details, actions, characteristics, people; by reminding us that we cannot be neutral or assume an objectivity about experience and encouraging us to connect commitments and experience. In *Literary Theory,* Terry Eagleton says, "Interests are constitutive of our knowledge, not merely prejudices which imperil it. The claim that knowledge should be 'value-free' is itself a value-judgement" (1983, 14). All learners—students, teachers, researchers—can benefit from this perspective, I think, and can learn to problematize the nature of knowledge-construction through the process of sharing stories.

Maxine Greene suggests that schools should provide "occasions for individuals to articulate the themes of their own existence" (1978, 18). One important way they can do this is through stories teachers and students share with each other and their communities. If it is truly our "concern to enable diverse persons to break through the cotton wool of daily life and to live more consciously" (185), then telling stories may be one way to begin to do that.

Having read Dora's story, I begin to add to it my own interpretation, and one of the issues I wish to focus on is its form and that form's relation to the politics of schooling and Dora's own lived experience. But in what ways does this focus reduce her story to a demonstration of the theory that I build? In affirming the power of storytelling, I have to be careful not to think of Dora's story only in terms of that issue. As Robert Coles reminds us, "What ought to be

Don't ask her age

Irene Bell
She was bron in OilCity Pennsylt.
She pants for peace. She live in the
projects for 17 years Gop Oint
She had 3 children but 1 got kill.
She say the projests had good and bad
points. She say that She wasn't
living here when he Fea base
ball. She was 19 when She came
to Detorit. She like talking about
her Son who got kill. Her Son
who was kill jump off the bridge.
She wtent to Ohiho,
She live On 70S,

June 28, 1989, journal entry.

interesting is the unfolding of a lived life rather than the confirmation such a chronicle provides for some theory" (1989, 23). One
way to avoid this kind of reduction may be to turn to other voices,
other interpretations, and share them, learn from them if possible.
One such voice is Dora's, of course. It informed and continues to inform my own evolving story, as many of my fellow teachers' voices
also did.

Talking with Dora: "I Wrote What I Wanted"

The following is an excerpt from the first audiotaped interview on
September 26, 1989, with Dora at her home near the Dewey Center,
on the subject of her story, "961-BABY."

David Schaafsma: I wonder if you could tell me a bit about yourself?

Dora: Well, there's nothing much about me, but I've got a sister and
two brothers. I go to Burton, and I'm in the seventh grade. I like
writing stories and I like reading. I don't get good grades, but I
get some good grades. I like school, and history is nice, and I'm
reading *Slaveryship* now. I have to do a book report on it.

DS [showing her a copy of her story from *Corridors*, "961-BABY"]: What did you think of your story? How did you come up with it?

D: Talking with Ms. Rose Bell. She had a group of old people helping out teenagers and their babies, who can't feed them and stuff like that, and she brought it up and we asked her about it, and she told us that she had a number, which was 961-BABY, and I thought about writing a story about it, and I made a story up.

DS: Uh-huh. How did you think of that story?

D: Because when she said she helped little kids and their babies, I thought about that it should be nice to write a story about little kids and their babies.

DS: Uh-huh. So Ms. Rose Bell came to visit and be interviewed by all of us at the Dewey Center, you heard her story, and decided to write about it. And Lynn is a name you just made up, and Don is just a name you made up. Any people you know around here that are like Lynn and Don?

D: Like Lynn, yeah, but not Don.

DS: Nobody like Don.

D: Not any more.

DS: Tell me something, Dora. Where did you get this idea for the G.E.D. in the story?

D: After she dropped out of school she was fifteen.

DS: Ms. Bell?

D [nods]: After she dropped out of school she couldn't get it, so she was just making sure—

DS: So she got the G.E.D., so she could have that high school diploma.

D: Right. And the other stuff Ms. Bell said, mostly. Like, she said, she's going to just let the people do stuff for themselves. She's not just going to do stuff for them, and they don't do anything back. So she made up jobs for them, like they are going to clean up, they have to wash and stuff like that. They would have to clean up and help around. Wash the clothes and wash dishes. And help around the place.

DS: And the rest of it you made up. Out of things you know here, and your own life, and some of it—

D: Most of it I just made up, out of my own head.

DS: So what do you think about your story, now that it is finally done and published?

D: I think it was good.

DS: It's a good story. It sure is. What did you like about it? What are you most happy about it?

D: I don't know. It turns out all right, she gets her G.E.D. and the kids start to help and all.

I had several conversations with Dora in the year following the program, conversations about her writing, her experience in school, particularly about English class, talks which took place in school and at her home. One, on December 13, 1989, took place in school on the subject of her English class in the Burton International School and its relationship to the summer program.

DS: What do you do in English?

D: In English we have different things that we do. We do sentences, lines, we're on pronouns now, and there's lots of different things.

DS: So you do a lot of grammar there. Do you do much writing?

D: No, not really, but lots of times we listen to classical music while we're doing our work, our worksheets.

DS: In the English class? That's interesting. Worksheets.

D: It's not so bad, but it's kind of boring.

DS: Did you ever write a story or anything based on the classical music?

D: No, not yet; we haven't written stories yet. I think we write next year. This year it's English class, where we're on the grammar.

I informed her that I had been talking with several teachers and students about her story, "961-BABY," which she had given me permission to do.

D: Yeah, well, next year when we have the program, I'm going to try to put more into the story, yeah, I'm going to, like, continue the story and change it around. I want to put, like, chapters into it, and stuff like that.

DS: Yeah, like make a small book out of it, short chapters? What would you add?

D: How old her boyfriend was, how old the kids were. How did her mother change after she kicked her out, what was it like with her friends, what did she do when she was in school, things like that.

DS: Some people, when I talk to them, wonder if that story has anything to do with you and your family. That person in that story is not you, obviously, you don't have any kids and things like that, but maybe like your mother. [Dora shakes her head.] You don't think so?

D: My mother wasn't sixteen when she had her kids.

DS: She was older, right? Well, you said you made it up.

D: Right, Ms. Rose, she wasn't fake and stuff like that, some of it wasn't fake. I just thought of names and things like that. It was my mind that did it, though.

DS: Right, it was in your language, you imagined it in your head, about somebody that might have run into Ms. Rose.

D: Uh-huh, and plus there's a lot of kids I know in the projects who have babies, and they don't know what to do. They dropped out of high school and they had them, and then they stay with their mother a couple of years, and they go back to high school, and they miss their friends. And it's like friends don't want to talk to them at all, because they have a baby and stuff like that.

DS: So that's why you wrote the story?

D: I don't know. I liked what Ms. Bell had to say and what she's doing for young teenaged mothers. A couple of friends of mine went to her and they are doing real well. I don't know. Maybe if they read my story, they might have some hope that they can make it, too.

Aside from my focus on Dora's story as a story, my interpretation of her writing was at first primarily "biographical." As I saw it, the text couldn't be considered separate from the complexities of her life. My own view was essentially consistent with James Boyd White's: "What is in experience intolerable can sometimes be made tolerable, if only barely so, by conversion into a story, a narrative written with a meaning of its own" (1985, 171). However, in creating my interpretation of Dora's story, I need to expand my own framework for examining her story. I need to look to the meanings, the themes Dora herself makes of her story. She tells me the story centers on Rose Bell. She says it is intended as a story of hope and inspiration for others who may be struggling to survive. In one sense, the story as Dora sees it functions as a kind of advertisement for Rose Bell's work, but in another sense it is a way of committing to the message she feels Bell is telling. She creates an ethical and social bond with Rose Bell and with a tradition of people helping people through her story, a tradition she asks others to join. Asking Dora to talk about herself and interpret her own story is crucial to helping me understand Dora and her writing. To come to an appreciation of the complexity of her life and writing, we have to make an attempt to know her and students like her.

Perhaps one way to begin to do this is to ask questions such as the ones that Joyce Ladner asks:

> What is life like in the urban Black community for the "average" girl? How does she define her roles, her behaviors, and from where does she acquire her models for fulfilling what is expected of her? Is there any significant disparity between the resources she has with which to accomplish her goals in life and the stated aspirations? Is the typical world of the teenager in American society shared by the Black girl or does she stand somewhat alone in much of her day-to-day existence? (81)

Ladner begins to answer her own questions, in part, when she says, "Life in the Black community has been conditioned by poverty, discrimination and institutional racism. It has also been shaped by African cultural survivals" (81). Through her story and through the transcripts of her conversations with me, Dora gives us some sense of the effects of poverty, discrimination, and institutional racism on people in her neighborhood, but I think she also gives some indication of what she herself has done and will do in order to survive.

Asking Dora questions, listening to her answers and getting to know her, learning more about her life, I make sense of her story to some extent in terms of her own perspective. I shape my story differently as I join her voice with mine. But, as with the issue of eating on the street, I turn to my fellow teachers' voices as well to hear their views of Dora and her writing, to learn from them if possible.

TEACHERS TELLING DORA

Though all of the teachers and many students read or heard various drafts of Dora's story during the program and shared perspectives with her on the story, Debi Goodman worked most with Dora on the text. She also has known Dora for years, having been Dora's teacher in various settings, so her reading of Dora was not surprisingly more detailed. Though the rest of the teachers worked less with Dora, and do not recount that work with as much detail as Debi does, their different interpretations nevertheless provide a rich account made of various interpretive voices. The stories that collaborative teaching provided me become voices in my enfolding story of Dora, each voice reshaping and enriching it.

961-BABY

As we got out of the car at the houstpital, I knew it was about to come. "How are you doing honey. said Don, "Just fineooooooooo" Right one time honey. You know I cannnt take care of all these kids; I said. "You don't have that many,4 is not a lot. When Don and Linne got home Lynn got th newpaper and saw a nuber which was 961-baby and ti Said: if you cant take care of you kids call and come to us." She didn't pay any mind to it. 3 days later She saw the same thing. "O.K. I will call," She said to herself and she did call. Mrs. Bell answer the phone "Hello, How may we help you. I—uh I need my G.E.D. but I gott go because I hav 3 children and lon the way. "I can help you but you have to promise that you will get your G.E.D.O.K." "O.K."
2 moths later Linne came to My Bells and said "I mdde it: from then on, She got a job when She was 29 and all her children were in school for 5 days of the week, and the whole day.

First handwritten draft of "961-BABY." Read to writers' workshop led by Toby and Debi, June 29, 1989.

Susan: Passing That Good News On

"The stories that we tell ourselves and our children function to order our world, serving to create both a foundation upon which each of us constructs our sense of reality and a filter through which we process each event that confronts us every day. The values that we cherish and wish to preserve, the behavior that we wish to censure, the fears and dread that we can barely confess in ordinary language, the aspirations and goals that we most dearly prize—all of these thingsare encoded in the stories that, in effect, we live by and through." (Gates 17)

David Schaafsma: You went to Rose Bell's session, that Dora also attended, and which was at least in part a basis for her story "961-BABY," and I know you didn't work with her much, but is there anything that you can recall about her? What comes to mind? Anything? Maybe you could talk about what you think of the story, too.

Susan Harris: The main thing that comes to mind related to Dora is her "grown-up-ness," if you will. She was more grown-up than she should have been for her age. And I'm sure that some of that came through the fact that she was responsible for the younger children. Her family situation I think caused that, and that would be true in any setting.

    Also the thing that sticks out in my mind is that, although she was talking about this girl having a baby and how she was put out and mistreated and everything, I kind of thought that she was imagining that that could be her possible plight at some point in time. I mean, the way she told about it was so vivid: how she turns to the boyfriend for help, how he refuses to help her, how she goes to this place for help, and she can't get anybody to assist her. So Ms. Bell's story figures in here, Ms. Bell being the kind of person who helps these teenaged mothers, and it kind of seems to have triggered something in her mind about what could possibly happen to a teenaged mother.

    You know, honestly, when I saw Ms. Bell for the first time, I thought to myself: bag lady, homeless person, because she had dental problems, her hair was all haggard, and a lot of the children talked about that, too. But when Ms. Bell began to speak, she was very eloquent. She was wise, she expressed great hope and optimism for her own situation. She indicated that she lived in the projects, but she was not just there, she was making use of her time, she had done all this beautiful work which she shared with the children—it was really a miraculous thing for me to see, and I'm sure this is why most of the children wrote about Ms. Bell. The beauty of this lady was just unbelievable.

I was very impressed with what Ms. Bell was saying. I wanted these children to get that kind of attitude. Because it's so easy for people to feel that there is no way out, there's no hope. Ms. Bell was a living example of a person who had just transformed her whole situation.

DS: And Dora's story?

SH: Well, Dora is passing that good news on, yes. She is showing that she is learning from this woman and teaching others. That's what we need.

We were all delighted when Rose Bell came to be interviewed on the second day of the program, but no one was more delighted than Susan. Not only did students write more on the basis of this single ninety-minute interview than any other subject, but Bell exemplified the very moral attitude Susan as a teacher wanted to cultivate. Knowing Susan's religious commitment, I was not surprised to hear her ethical interpretation of Dora's story, but I was curious to explore the relationship between storytelling and sermons in the African American tradition. Linda Goss points out that the church and its sermons "functioned in a system of cooperation where the preacher performed and the congregation responded." She sees a similarity between the kind of social relationship a sermon sets up and the social relationships involved in African American storytelling: "Cooperation and response have been key operations in African American storytelling. Those two major elements have been instrumental in holding a community of people of African heritage together when so many opposing elements challenged their physical, spiritual and intellectual survival" (Goss and Barnes 215).

Susan saw Dora as prematurely grown-up because she was the oldest daughter in a fatherless family with three younger siblings and often three cousins. Hers, like mine, was a kind of "biographical" approach to "961-BABY," her interpretation of Dora and her text grounded in her understanding of Dora's life. But Susan's view of Dora's story, and her view of Rose Bell's stories, makes clear the moral tradition of authority, the didactic nature of the storytelling: if you do the right thing and work hard, things will work out for you, and when they do you have a duty to pass that success story along to others. That is our social and ethical responsibility as storytellers, Susan seems to say, to do as Bell does with Dora, and as Dora does for her young friends, to keep retelling the stories of hope.

As I see it, Susan's story of Dora and her writing, like "961-BABY" itself, is a construction of many voices arising out of the storyteller's experience. It is the unique heteroglossia of local knowledge that she draws on to construct her world. Like Susan, each teller of stories draws from the voices she knows, weaving in her own unique way her continually evolving vision of the world. In Susan's story, the voices of her traditional Baptist family, teachers, preachers, and friends mingle with the voices of the Bible and various literary and social theorists she has read, informed by her experience raising her own children and teaching students, many of them like Dora.

Susan, like others, calls attention to her own class biases in recalling how she initially prejudged Rose Bell on the basis of her appearance. For Susan, appearances are very important; they are the practical foundation for survival. As she says, "You're not going to be the anchor person, you're not going to be in the bank dressed all sloppily, eating food in this sort of way; you're going to have to really be up to par." Lynn and Rose Bell in "961-BABY" are clearly "up to par" in the tradition of Booker T. Washington. They maintain "strong black parental standards" for moral behavior, where, as in the example of Susan's own life, observing the social conventions of the middle class remains the best means to social success in today's society. They become, like Susan herself, "role models" for constructive moral action. They, like Susan's own presentation in preparation for Family Day during the summer writing program, set an example for upholding "traditional values," values that have served her well.

Surely Susan's story is informed by working with other teachers in the program, though it's difficult to analyze from this transcript alone specifically how her colleague's versions inform her. As the teller of this tale, I can say that her voice affected my interpretation of Dora and "961-BABY" in certain ways though, as I made clear with regard to her view of eating on the street, I maintain certain commitments she doesn't seem to share with me. She helped me to acknowledge and respect the importance in the African American community of faith and religious tradition. Sometimes resistant to the notion of "models" for behavior, I came to appreciate their usefulness, especially through observing the effect Susan's own example had on our students. Susan's interpretation, consistent with her perspective on eating on the street, insisting on the importance of a con-

> Today we had a storyteller and he told us
> a story almost like Cinderlla but it was
> deffind for j to then we hear a story call
> ed Cirdervla but it had a car [mercalben]
> and it was realy funny. We Went to
> Writing in 114 and wrote in the Com po
> sition book and Now we were going to room
> 118 and read what we wrote.

June 29, 1989, journal entry after visit from storyteller Craig Roney.

Note: As Roney had done in telling various versions of "Cinderella," Dora, through "961-BABY," in a sense created a version of the story Rose Bell had told her. When I mentioned this observation to Dora several months later, she said she hadn't intended doing what Roney had done. But she did say how much she had enjoyed his storytelling. By including the entry here I am not trying to suggest a "direct" connection, but noting that she was experiencing and writing about other things at the same time she was working on "961-BABY."

cept of teacher as ethical model, enriches my own perspective: She celebrates a view of black women in a way reminiscent of novelist Margaret Alexander's:

> I think the black women, whether they were strong women or whether they were beaten or broken down, had a belief in the goodness of the future. They always wanted another world that would be better for their children than it had been for them. The black woman has deep wells of spiritual strength. She doesn't know how she's going to feed her family in the morning, but she prays and in the morning, out of thin air, she makes breakfast. (Lanker 115)

JEANETTA: THE OPPORTUNITY'S THERE

Jeanetta Cotman, like Susan Harris, had worked little with Dora. She also discussed the moral implications of Dora's having written about teenage pregnancy, in terms of Dora's own life and the life of the projects, generally. She reread the text of the story during our interview and then began talking about the general issue of women having babies out of wedlock. She discussed her belief that women who have babies out of wedlock should take more responsibility for their own actions. She said Dora's story reminded her of the many women in this society who fail to do this, while admitting that all circumstances women face may not be entirely in their control.

Jeanetta Cotman: I didn't work with Dora, so I don't really have that much to contribute. But I do feel that, after reading her story, that it is tied up with her life, with her family and with other women in the projects. You see, many women are doing this now, having babies, but that goes against my grain. I sound terrible. Maybe I shouldn't be pouring out my heart.

David Schaafsma: No, you're speaking from your heart. You're telling it the way you see it.

JC: I don't know if that's good. But I feel like you just don't have to do this, do you? And I'm not just talking about black women. White women are doing the same thing. It's not just black; it just seems that there are more of us. I feel that we have opportunities where before we didn't have opportunities. But I feel like the opportunity's there. But see, now here I go again.

   I don't know. I was brought up with a mother and father that had an education, and a grandmother, folks who had a little something. I'm talking about money, land and things. I mean, we aren't filthy rich, but we're not poor either. So maybe my way of thinking is wrong because I don't even know what these folks are talking about. I haven't been down there scratching in the dirt. Daddy sent us to college, and we worked because that's what we wanted to do. We worked to get the extra spending change. But I haven't worked my way through college. I don't know what that's all about.

DS: What about Dora's writing the story?

JC: It's all tied up with this, can't you see? It has to do with her and about all these young women having babies.

DS: What did you think of it?

JC: I thought it was good she wrote it, and Debi really helped to get a lot out of her. But compared to Camille and Julia? No. It was all right, but now something like Camille's, the dialogue, the description, that was just fantastic.[5]

DS: Do you feel you learned anything from the summer program? Do you feel like you might have changed in any way?

JC: I have become hard over the years, in some ways. You can only put up with so much stuff over the years, and it wears on you, all of this does. It really does. But I saw parents coming along on trips, I saw kids write in ways that really surprised me. So I feel I have changed from this experience. I have. But it comes slow. It takes time. I needed something to get me going again, to see how to do better. I signed up for this program, and I am changing. I have arranged my rooms in "centers" and they are doing more writing. I am not convinced this will work, but I am going to try.

Jeanetta's brief interpretation of Dora's story emphasizes yet another moral framework in which the story might be understood, one of responsibility for one's own actions. She makes it clear that, because of her middle-class upbringing, she "lacks experience" in the deprivation associated with urban poverty, but though she admits she may be changing, she finds some behavior merely wrong. While admitting that her perspective on these issues might be less "accepting" than other views, Jeanetta's interpretation advocates the necessity of individual responsibility in change. Though no one else expressed this view, we knew it was the dominant view of many people from both the black and white middle class, and an important voice in the narrative of Dora. The issue of personal responsibility and initiative in Dora's story is important for an understanding of both her text and also Rose Bell's view.

Jeanetta's insistence on "self-discipline" was an important view with regard to our understanding of eating on the street, but it was also an important view for understanding Dora and her story. Like Susan, Jeanetta betrays some of her own class bias in noting how her middle-class standards for behavior are not being observed in the inner city. But, as she says of herself in the transcript of her discussion of eating on the street in chapter 2, Jeanetta is "hard-nosed." She is a strong woman with a tough reputation as a teacher. She maintains those standards of toughness with her own children and with her students; it is by those standards that she measures Lynn, Dora, and Dora's mother.

Jeanetta's view is informed by her history—growing up in Kentucky, teaching in Detroit—shaped by particular responses to racial discrimination which had proved successful for her. One needs to take control of one's life and work hard if one wants to succeed: go to college, become a professional, move out of the inner city, make wise decisions in spite of circumstances, be *strong* in order to survive. Jeanetta and her family had survived, and more. As Jeanetta had felt about April, the "smart" student in her class who had failed to work

961-Baby
Dora Simpson

Once there was a girl who was having a baby. "As we get out of the car at the hospital. I knew it was about to come, " said Linne. "How are you doing honey," said Don. "Just fine ,oooooooo!' "Right on time honey. " " I cann't take care of all of these kids. "I said 'You don't have that many , 4 is not alot ." When Don and Linne got home Linne look in the newpaper and it said :" If you cann't take care of your children call us at 961-BABY. She didn't pay no mind to it . 3 days later she saw the same thing in the paper. "O.! I will just call. " She called, Ms. Bell answered the phone, "961-BABY,How may we help you.""I uh have 4 children and 1 on the way, I want to get my G.E.D. but I cann't get it because I have to take of all my children. " We can help but you have topromise that you will get you G.E.D. o.k." "O.K."2 months later she got her G.E.D,"I READ IT."

THE END

First typed draft of "961-BABY," completed June 30, 1989.

"up to her capacity," she also found Lynn from "961-BABY" to some extent responsible for her fate.

I continue to feel that social and cultural factors are important when evaluating situations like Lynn's. I continue to believe that issues of race, class, and gender in part construct Dora's story in important ways. Still, Jeanetta's emphasis on personal responsibility reminds me that neither Dora nor Lynn are simply determined by circumstances. As I discuss in chapter 1, meaning in discourse systems is always variable, always open to change, and individual expression in the dialogic acts of interpretation contributes to those changes. Dora has intentions; she has a will that contributes to the construction of her life. Jeanetta's interpretation was a voice of caution about what the happy ending "961-BABY" might mean with regard to Dora's life. Dora and others like her have to struggle to survive, and the circumstances work against that survival in spite of their persistence.

I talked for several hours with George Cooper on a drive from Washington, D.C., to Detroit on November 24, 1989. We discussed the summer writing program, specifically focusing—as I did with others—on Dora and the issue of eating on the street. At one point, he talked about the time he first began to know Dora, which was during the walk to the Detroit Cultural Center area for the Children's Day celebration:

George Cooper: So along this trip to the Cultural Center, I'm getting friendlier and friendlier with the kids. And Dora is coming out more and more as a lively, giggly person. And she in fact got closest to me, in a way, on the way home, talking and laughing with me. I wanted to respond by kidding Dora. But I'm talking to them: "What do you think you might write about all this?" And I'm trying to get them in touch with the idea that they might write about how much they hated it and write about how hot it was and how tired they were, and it was at that time that Dora came over and was actually interested in the idea of writing about not liking something, something boring or awful. And there was a spark, I don't know that she ever did anything with it, but there was a spark of enthusiasm in her voice that day, in the kind of go-around we had about not liking the trip.

    Now it might be interesting to contrast that version of Dora, someone I thought was having a good time, who was very much in the middle of the pictures I was taking, with her cousin Tameka who during this whole trip refused to have her picture taken. That whole day she remained rather sullen. That's not to say she didn't laugh or giggle with her friends, but she wasn't as outgoing. The trip home for her was more like the trip there. And she certainly was not a person with whom I could get close. She seemed standoffish and much more distant than Dora did. By the time we got back, though, I had made friends with Dora.

I read Dora's story aloud in the car and asked George to comment on it.

GC: Good story. Though I didn't work with her much on it, as I recall. I helped her with a few things during conferences, I'm sure, but it was mostly encouragement, I think, and asking questions to clear up a few things. When I talk to kids at U of M about writing stories, you want the stories to have a point. Because at college we're trying to teach academic writing. And yet students at the age of seventeen or eighteen when they come to the university are still not practiced or experienced enough writers to fully manage the academic discourse. They're not fluent enough in the language of academic writing, so I think that by telling stories or using narratives they can become more fluent in the art of using language and gain confidence and begin to nuance things with their writing and be able to make a point. Then they can take those skills and adapt them into the more academic structures, like in a formal argument.

So, stories like Dora's are in line with academic thinking, I think, and I try to get my kids in college courses to do that. Some kids will tell narratives, and they'll just start at the beginning and they'll tell it straight through to the end, almost, if it's possible, in one voice, in one tone, from one perspective. And I find that fascinating. Dora's story, has, on the other hand— and this is a story told by an eleven year old—has a lot of different perspectives in it. Notice where it begins. You know, right in the middle of things: "Lynn was having a baby." And as she gets out of the car at the hospital—see, she's getting out of the car, she's in the middle of an action. She sets it down— "I can't take it any more, okay?" I mean, suddenly it sounds like Ernest Hemingway has entered into here; there's a spareness that is almost foreign to my sense that Dora could have written it. So within the first four or five sentences, she has told us something about Don, about his lack of response, by saying very little. Don didn't answer. And so there's a kind of tension introduced already.

I think that this is the same Dora that I mentioned earlier, who on the trip to the Cultural Center was one of the people who seemed more sensitive. She showed her emotions, she frolicked more, she laughed, and on the way home she wanted companionship in a way that she hadn't been getting from her friends, so that she would come to me. I think there's a sensitivity and a presence of perspectives in this piece of work that shows a lot of sophistication that might not be found in other pieces of writing; it may not have appeared in writing right away from her, but it's present in this story now. So, I think it's rather good. You know, it's even present in the choosing of the title, "961-BABY." I have to give her credit for finding significance in that phone number, so that it does represent the overall cause that Rose Bell is working for.

David Schaafsma: You were there when Rose Bell spoke, and Dora was there.

GC: Yeah. It's significant that she works in Rose Bell's ideas and imagines them in connection with real human lives. She does that very well. There is a very strong sense of morality in that, in Ms. Bell doing that kind of work with people. You know, her view that you have to work for what you get. Now, I don't know when that was impressed on Dora. Whether it was through the interview, or whether it was at home, or what. But in the story it begins with Ms. Bell.

DS: How much of her personal life do you know?

GC: I know the stories the other teachers told me about the death of her aunt and how she had done in school. I met her mother, and I met the kids, her younger siblings. I think that is useful to know that about her. But it's not absolutely necessary. I mean, I think it's important to know people's backgrounds when you work with them, but I don't feel like I know her well enough to say that these multiple voices that I'm finding in here come from personal experience. I mean, they come from somewhere, and I think they're rich. Maybe for every teacher it's enough to recognize that they're there.

We compared Dora and Tameka, observed how differently Tameka and Dora seemed to meet the world, and also observed how much more interesting Dora's story seemed to us in terms of both complexity and subtlety. I made the point that I thought Tameka's story[6] was clearly less "developed" than Dora's and others' stories, and George responded:

> I would have said that Tameka's story was less developed than Dora's, yes. It's interesting because both of them live in the same basic circumstances, but they are very different. And I would be reluctant to say that knowing both of them, that their stories, that the differences in their stories, is the result of their two different personalities. I mean, I painted Dora as kind of a more sensitive, maybe more complex person. Tameka seemed to me to be kind of sullen and less interested in things, and yet I would be reluctant to say that Tameka's story, with its relatively lesser complexity, is the result of her personality, necessarily. How can you know what of that has to do with the fact that they live in separate houses? Tameka with her grandmother, Dora with her mother. I

don't know. So I think that looking into their backgrounds and their living environments is important, but I don't know how much you can finally argue from it. You can make observations and try to be sensitive to it.

When I read Dora's "I Am" poem aloud, George responded in this way:

> That's great. That's a great poem, I think. Because in the mention of dicing there—she's like a cat, too. But dicing also comes from, you know, this is a cartoon image of the cat going to the dog, *phtttt*, and there goes the dog's face into evenly cut slices. But it also seems, you know, we're finding this other thing to connect with dicing. Its connection to her personality. You can't avoid that here. She does it for you directly in a way she doesn't in the story.

As with the other teachers, I had several conversations with George about the summer and particularly about Dora and eating on the street. On one of these occasions, November 27, 1989, George took a second, closer look at Dora's writing:

GC: Well, looking at the very first draft of this [see p.167], which I imagine was typed out on the computer, it's kind of a whole story that is further developed through revisions, and I see a lot of the way in which Debi works in this, by asking questions at the right place and the right time, and what Debi does is help Dora fill in missing things from the text.

DS: Let me ask you a question. Dana suggests that the questions that Debi asks of Dora, and the suggestions she makes for further revisions, actually do damage to the text.

GC: I'd say no. I don't think that there's damage done. There's an immediacy to this first draft that is kind of thrilling, yeah. It's almost like poetry, it's so thrilling, it's so immediate. But I also feel—

DS: And Dana says the early draft allows the reader a lot of room for creation in a way that I thought you would appreciate, because you repeatedly like that kind of thing. You like the idea of making room for the reader in the text.

GC: Sure, I do. But it's a question of degree. You see, if you read the first couple of sentences of the first version here, let me read— "Once there was a girl who was having a baby. 'As we got out of

the car at the hospital, I knew it was about to come,' said Linne."
I meant to read further, but let me just stop and comment on
it. I remember earlier, saying, "Well, this thing starts in the
middle. It starts with action." It's not something that had been
revised into it, it's something that Dora, I think, had a sense of
from the beginning. It is a more or less kind of storybook
opening. " 'As we got out of the car at the hospital, I knew it was
about to come,' said Linne. " 'How are you doing, honey,' said
Don. 'Just fine, oooooo!' 'Right on time, honey.' 'I can't take care
of all these kids,' I said. 'We don't have that many, four is not a lot.'
When Don and Linne got home, Linne look in the newspaper,
and it said, 'If you cannot take care of your children, call us at
961-BABY.' "

Well, that is immediate, there's a lot happening, it's exciting,
and given what you said about the way I like to read things. I
do like there to be openness, but I think that this is too open.
The gaps between these sentences are just too large. You know,
the shifts in perspective are too great. So I would say there
needs to be some kind of revision here. Some thought has to be
given to what happens in between these sentences, and what mo-
tivates them.

DS: It needs elaboration.

GC: It needs elaboration.

DS: Dana said, "That's brilliant, even if she didn't consciously know
it, to say a girl was having a baby, as opposed to a woman, and not
to name her was brilliant. And then to change it to 'Lynn was having a baby' deadened it." And I kind of agreed with what she said.

GC: I can see the point.

DS: And that change in itself, suggested by a well-meaning teacher,
which Debi surely is, not wanting Dora to have it sound too stereotypical, harmed the story.

GC: I can see Dana's point, but I agree with Debi here. And the story
as a whole needed elaboration. I think that, from what I see
here, Debi played a good role in helping this story come out.
And there's so much more about Ms. Bell that comes out in the
final draft.

DS: I agree. And more about her relationship with Don.

GC: Right.

DS: And more about her relationship to the children and violence
and more hope, in getting the G.E.D., in getting the help through

the day-care center and getting a job and in working with her own mother. There's more detail added, and it's useful.

George's perspective on Dora's story is like Susan's—a kind of celebration—but, unlike Susan's emphasis on the story's positive moral theme, George's emphasis is on how developing a positive relationship with Dora predisposed him to look for strengths in her text. While acknowledging the presence of a strong ethical content in her writing and its relationship to Rose Bell's talk, George emphasized other aspects of Dora and her writing in his interpretation. While admitting that a focus on the social contexts of her writing might be useful, he denied it was a necessity in appreciating either the virtues of her writing or her person.

While Jeanetta's voice provides my story with a useful note of caution and realism, George celebrates the strengths in Dora: her "spark of enthusiasm" and her sensitivity and the strengths in Dora's story, its clear "point," its coherence, its subtlety and restraint, and "the presence of perspectives." He praises Dora's text for its sophistication, comparing it at one point to the work of Ernest Hemingway in its "spareness." He emphasizes the strengths, not the deficiencies, that he sees in "961-BABY."

George's perspective on Dora and her texts is consistent with his perspective on eating on the street. His approach to teaching and learning is a positive one, validating students' ways of knowing, respecting and advocating their interests. Consistent with his own experience as a student and his experience as a college teacher, George shows that he is more interested in students' needs than institutional demands; he notes Dora's investment in her writing, her engagement with a subject she truly cares about. At the same time, he demonstrates how Dora's story fulfills many of the expectations he has for college students' academic writing.

Still, George doesn't celebrate her work uncritically. He examines the story in various drafts and notes its need in its early drafts for "elaboration," greater detail, and clarity. While acknowledging his preference for works that are "open" and ambiguous, he makes distinctions between a work that is incomplete—like Dora's early draft of her story, where "the gaps between these sentences are just too large" and "the shifts in perspective are too great," and work that is more complete, yet spare, such as Dora's final draft. He admires the way the story grew, especially with Debi's close attention to working with Dora. His voice reminds us that improvement is always possible with student's writing, and he is convincing.

961-Baby
Dora Simpson

Once there was a girl who was having a baby .

" As we get out of the car at the hospital, I knewit was about to come, " said Linne .

"How are you doning , "Don said.

"Just fine OOO------.   "

Linne was 15 and have 4 kids and 1 on the way . She drop out of school

---

Second typed draft, one page, completed July 5, 1989.

DANA: APPRECIATING "961-BABY" AS LITERATURE

Dana Davidson's interpretation of Dora's story emphasizes the virtues of Dora's individual accomplishments as a writer without Debi's help as a teacher. While she admits she didn't know Dora very well and didn't work much with her writing, Dana tells a story of Dora's writing that is focused primarily on Dora's text itself; Dana celebrates Dora's stretrengths as a writer in a similar though slightly different way than George did. In our talk, I began by asking her what she thought of Dora's story:

Dana Davidson: As I'm looking through it, I thought the story was more sophisticated the way Dora first had it. But she probably didn't know. But maybe she did.

David Schaafsma: You mean in an early draft?

DD: Right, this first draft [see p.167], like when she said, "Once there was a girl who was having a baby." That is like, if you think about it as literature, that is a deep line! I could teach this to older kids if they didn't know who Dora was. That's a deep line. She probably doesn't even know it. There is also the use of conversation to tell a story without telling it. Many kids don't know how to do that. Further down she has, "On the way home, Don didn't think about what Linne said." And that's something that an eleven year old would know about, but maybe not know enough about writing to put in a story. It shows she's conscious of other levels—

that's good! The previous lines were, "She dropped out of high school at the age of fifteen, at sixteen she got pregnant. Her mom put her out. Her mom was very sad that she had to put out her only child." Kids don't usually think about that, from the parent's perspective, do they?

And though Debi does help her expand it, I think she should have left it like it was. It was a great story from the beginning. It's extremely sophisticated for a twelve year old. It seems to me most people who can't write well—and that includes myself, at least in a creative sense—would add Don talking in places where it might not be as dramatically effective. But Dora adds: " 'You know, you only have four and one on the way,' Don said." It's much more powerful to imagine their relationship and Don's attitude about it with that one line. Very sophisticated writers do that sort of thing. And at twelve years old she thought like that! She for some reason felt that she could say that line and get across all the ideas that she was thinking, which was probably that Don was neglectful, and so forth. She's teaching me a lot as a writer about being subtle and restrained. The later drafts definitely show a stronger writer in the sense that, "I can work with sentences, I can be grammatically correct, I know what I'm supposed to do." But Dora right from the start shows herself as a person who knows how to communicate things through writing just like that. She just assumes that her reader is sophisticated enough to get what she says.

DS: What do you think of the close way Debi worked with Dora?

DD: What Debi did was teach writing, and she does that well: "This is how you would write a paper." To add details and clarity. Now, don't get me wrong—I respect Debi and I learned a lot from her and all of you so much about working with students as more of a facilitator than as a teacher, in the usual sense of the word. But I think the way you teach writing to create stories is a harder task because you never know when you're changing what the kid intuitively knows. You may be messing with very subtle things, when you aren't a creative writer yourself. In that sense, I think the piece sort of lost out. I think the story was great at first.

DS: And the details that were added in a way take away from the creativity of the reader. Now you think it tells a little bit more than you would need to know.

DD: Yes, although Camille and Julia are good writers and creators of stories, so they combine the two in a way that most readers are used to hearing stories created. They had it all combined. Dora, maybe because she didn't know how to use the language so well, or because she did, I'm not sure, was very spare. You see, you can't tell how much of this was conscious on Dora's part. Maybe I'm reading too much into it. But what she did would be effective to people who know various types of literature. So it would have been effective to me to leave it pretty much as she first wrote it. It's like you find someone who can run with no training. You say that person is naturally talented. Someone who could do this, to me, seems to be an intuitive creator of story.

DS: Well, I don't know what Debi's working with her over the years might have done, as far as what you call intuition goes.

DD: But even if that is true, this is a twelve year old doing this. She is a good writer, with mature perceptions about people, and some people might think she is not so good because they don't understand how beautiful her writing is, in places. I could have taken this story to the university and analyzed it for an hour for my professors and amazed them with its power and grace. Its intelligence!

DS: I'm wondering if what you call her maturity has anything to do with her living circumstances.

DD: It may, or it may not. The thing with people that aren't poor that watch poor people grow up is that they assume that that matures them quickly. It doesn't necessarily. My grandmother was not well off, and my mother never cleaned a day in her life. My mother was still very sheltered. So, Dora could be living in that situation and still not know how men and women think. So you don't want to make assumptions about how poverty affects people. It affects them in different ways. And that can happen in any socioeconomic situation. I guess what I'm trying to say is her SES may not have instigated these ideas. I guess her mother has four children, and many of the kids are having babies, and Ms. Bell talked about it, and it is good to be aware of where these ideas come from and to be sensitive to that, but I look more at the writing and how Dora as an individual writer has accomplished this. It's easy to lose sight of that. Exposure to poverty is one thing, but articulation of insight is another thing, and they may not be closely related. I mean, I'm sensitive, I'm deep, I see the world happening, but when I try to write a story it never says what I am really doing and feeling. Why is that?

DS: You said that Julia and Camille have something that Dora doesn't have. They both have a sense of what it takes to succeed in school. Do you think it would be good to help Dora get what they have?

DD: Not necessarily. What Camille and Julia have is wonderful, and it works for them. What's the matter with variety? Let Dora do what she's going to do, as long as she does it well. Actually, that's what we appreciate now. That's the kind of fiction coming out now. Like Margaret Atwood. And Toni Morrison. Schools have to catch up to our best writers, who are doing new things. But when Dora does that they will say it's poor construction.

Dana said she "doesn't know about Dora as a student." She didn't attend the Rose Bell interview with Dora and didn't work with her on the story. She doesn't speak of "961-BABY" in terms of Dora's living circumstances or Rose Bell, as Jeanetta and Susan do. She also doesn't speak of it as George does at one point, as writing useful in a transition to academic writing. Dana tries to think of the story's virtues on its own terms, as a story. She disagrees with all other teachers about whether the story has improved through subsequent drafts by our helping Dora work on greater elaboration, detail, and clarity. She questions our assumptions about quality and raises issues of individual differences in "taste" by, like George, championing the story's "subtlety and restraint," especially in the early draft.

Also like George, Dana refuses to draw necessary connections between Dora's socioeconomic circumstances and either the form or content of her writing. As she said, "Exposure to poverty is one thing, but articulation of insight is another thing, and they may not be closely related." With George she seems to explore an approach to students and texts which values individual student differences while at the same time asserts the importance of racial and cultural identity. Her stance on these issues seems consistent with her questioning the presumed authority of the "Teacher" in the learning process. Though she is aware, for instance, that a majority of women in her community do not wear their hair in a "natural" style, she insists on her right to be herself and wear her hair in this fashion when she feels it is appropriate. Dana saw the summer program as an opportunity to explore the boundaries of received notions about teacher-student relationships. Her stance on wearing her hair in a particular way, like her stance on individual writing and learning styles, is tied to issues of authority, individuality, and cultural pride.

Dana contributes her voice to the celebration of Dora as author by calling her an "intuitive creator of story," and referring to "961-BABY" as literature. She calls attention to the "power," "grace," and "intelligence" of the story and she notes the "sophistication" and restraint in Dora's use of dialogue and the "variety of perspectives," "levels," and "dimensions" in early drafts of her story which others have noted in later drafts. As she says, "Kids don't usually think about that, from the parent's perspective, do they?"

Dana emphasized appreciating the work of the imagination in stories like Dora's, which she sees as different than other kinds of writing. She claims that, with most conventional academic writing, there are more shared criteria for evaluation, and Dana suggests we may have been applying academic standards in our advice to Dora. We often held up the more academically successful students such as Camille and Julia as examples of what we would like all students to attain, but Dana works against our certainty by asserting Dora's different strengths. She points to contemporary literary innovation in the fiction of Margaret Atwood and Toni Morrison to be used as examples in evaluating stories such as Dora's and suggests that we examine minimalist fiction in order to appreciate the strengths of early drafts of "961-BABY."

Dana also asks that we broaden our criterion for what constitutes an acceptable story in school; as she says, "What's the matter with variety?" She notes that we seem to have different—less generous—standards for evaluating student writing than our standards for professional writing. Dana's view of Dora's difference is consistent with her own (somewhat facetiously stated) view of herself: "I am who I am. I'm strong, I'm intelligent, I'm a woman, I know what I'm about, *I'm black.* I'm black, and I don't care what you think, you know?" Dana did, of course, care what others thought of her and, like all of us, learned from others in the program. Her voice in our story of interpretation is an argument for the inclusion of different ways of writing and knowing in the academy and a challenge to our notions of what constitutes "good writing." Though many of us shared this perspective generally, Dana's story of Dora's text helps to remind us of this important fact.

TOBY: READING AS A READER

I talked with Toby Curry about Dora, and related issues of urban literacy, on October 13, 1989:

David Schaafsma: How much did you work with Dora?

Toby Curry: I didn't work with her that much at all during the program. Who did—Debi?

DS: Debi did, mostly. Debi has the most experience with her, so she'll

961-Baby

Dora Simpson

Once there was a girl who was having a baby .

Didn't space (handwritten note)

" As we get out of the car at the hospital, I knew it was about to come " said Linne .

"How are you doing," Don said.

Don't need need (handwritten note)

"Just fine O_____. "

(Linne was 15 and have 4 kids and 1 on the way . She drop out of High school at the age of 15, when she was 16 she go pregnant. Her mom put her out when she fond out that she deop out o school. Her mom was very sad that she had put out her only child.)

"Righ on time honey. "

"You know I cann't take care of all these children. "

On the way home (Linne stayed at the hospital also (Don didn't think about what Linne said.

OOO

3 days later Linne came home whith a new baby now she have 5 children , that she cann't take care of. She look in th the New-paper and saw a add that said ; IIf you cann't take care o call us, and we will help you,961 BABY. so she called. Mrs. Bell answered the phone, "Hello, how may we help you?"

"I need my G.E.D. but I cin't get it because I have five children,"

"I can help you but yhou have to promise to get your G.E.D , OK?"

"OK."

Mrs. then asked, "What do you know how to do?

Linne said, "Nothing."

Third typed draft, one page, completed July 5, 1989.

have a totally different perspective because of that. Which is interesting in itself. How her perspective changes with having worked with her more.

TC: Yeah, she was in Debi's class, too. I read all her drafts of "961-BABY." I guess maybe I did help her with a few things in conferences. I mainly just read through as a reader, any reader, and told her my response each time. I encouraged her to take notes. I led a couple of writing workshop sessions in which she was a participant, and many students responded to her writing and gave her suggestions. That was the value of the program for most of the students, the collaborative learning. We were really able to develop a community of writers, and I know for a fact Dora benefitted from those because I was there for them.

Let's see. I know her family. And I had her older cousin in my room. And Dora and Tameka were in my volleyball club at Burton last year, so I saw them last year. And I saw them perceived by others as people who came from the projects.

DS: Why was that? Do you know why?

TC: I think it was like a middle-class thing. There were a lot of middle-class kids at Burton, of all races, and they just weren't quite as perceptive, you know, as accepting of the kids from the projects, kids like Dora maybe.

DS: So this stigma attaches to them . . .

TC: Perhaps, yeah. Although we had kids at Burton from the Corridor, you know, a lot of them were living in that area. I just know she comes from this kind of background, where there was some violence in the family, like her aunt's death, and you have to take that into account when you're dealing with these kids. For instance, I don't know if there's ever been a father in the family. Lanette has been supportive of the school.

DS: Burton International School.

TC: Right. She cares for her kids and must perceive the school as a "step up" from other area schools because she got her kids in there and kept them in.

DS: Yeah, she worked very hard to get them there. I wondered about that whole family, that whole matrix, to what extent it might have influenced her writing.

TC: Well, it's similar. And her mother's name is Lanette, where in the story it is Lynn. And she was raised in this kind of home setting, you know, with violence all around.

[Toby read "I Am a Cat" and remarked on its relationship to her life.] Here's that violent connection with the knife, "I'll dice you to pieces." If life is tough to you, be tough. It's like the violence in the community and the violence in the subculture, you know. It's there and you have to deal with it somehow. I mean, that's a very violent image, "I'll dice you to pieces."

DS: Well, having talked about the poem, how do you interpret "961-BABY"?

TC: Well, I liked the fact that she sees something wrong with child abuse and someone that's not prepared to take care of children and having babies, and she goes for help. And I like the way that she has Ms. Bell say that you can't get something for nothing, you have to help. I like the way she has the kids learning to cooperate, and they start helping their mom around the house. And then it's funny because the mother decides to help. And there's another positive thing, you know, at the end, she makes it, you know. So, I like that, that she's thought it through, she's learned from Ms. Bell how she can survive and shows others in her story.

DS: What did you learn from Debi?

TC: Well, what I learned from working with Debi was taking a close look at the language, line by line, in a conference. I mean, I did look at different things in the writing, but what I liked was the way she would ask kids, "Why did you decide to do that?" Or, "What might you do to make that clear for the reader," or "Is there any way you could tell us what was going on in that character's mind when they said that, and don't you think you ought to tell the reader that, then?" You know, that kind of thing, but just the way she showed me how to draw those things out and get them to elaborate. You make those assumptions about what the reader already knows. No, they don't know that. You have to tell them that.

DS: She did it mostly through asking questions, right?

TC: Yeah, right. Mostly through asking questions, and asking for more, talking about her intention with her, getting her to see that she was making choices, talking it over with her. Yeah, I think that format is great. I mean, what do you do, otherwise? You don't tell them what to say. If you're going to teach the kids to have ownership, you ask questions. I think it is useful to do that, asking questions, but to read as a reader, not as a teacher telling writers what to do, to give your honest response.

Toby's voice in my narrative of Dora reminds me of the various dimensions of collaboration that are present in Dora's text: the students who worked with her in workshops, the teachers who talked with her in conference, and, in a different way, Rose Bell and her own family. Her interpretation reminds me, like Jeanetta Cotman's does, of the way the forces in her life have shaped her text, placing emphasis on the way the culture of violence and poverty shape her. Whereas Dana Davidson and George Cooper denied race and class as necessary considerations in understanding Dora's story, Toby reminds us—and none of the teachers who taught in the program would disagree—that these issues are important for understanding—though not determining the future of—Dora. And for Toby, the realities of Dora's life can help us understand her story. Toby points out that, like her character, Lynn, Dora lives in an extremely violent community, and that violence is reflected in her story. She makes it clear that African Americans like Dora are generally treated less well than whites in Detroit, and in the inner city, "underclass" kids that live in the projects are often treated less well by classmates who live in other, perhaps "better" areas.

In her remarks in chapter 2, about "eating on the street" and teaching generally, Toby asserts a "color-blind" perspective on her students; for example, she said,"Well, this is my view: I do what I do for every kid. I don't care if they're black. I just came out of teaching with this multicultural, multiethnic, multilingual population at Burton, and I hadn't focused just on the black kids. There's appropriate and inappropriate behavior, like on a field trip or anything." Toby demonstrates a view about language in some respects similar to Jeanetta Cotman's, a view that asserts the need for teachers to help students of all cultures to an understanding of the expectations of a standard English world. When she examines Dora's story, however, she makes it clear that she is very aware that, in Dora's world, race and class are important issues for understanding and learning from Dora.

Still, in her focus on Dora's story, Toby seems to continue to assert some aspects of her "color-blind" position. Where Dana Davidson focused more on stylistic considerations, Toby, like Susan Harris, examines the thematically positive aspects of "961-BABY." For example, she says of Dora's story that she likes her apparent stand against child abuse and "the way that she has Ms. Bell say that you can't get something for nothing, you have to help." She likes the emphasis on cooperation, "And there's another positive thing, you know, at the end, she makes it, you know." Very much like Susan, Toby says that she admires the fact that "she's learned from Ms. Bell how she can survive and shows others in her story." Toby admires the way Dora learned important moral lessons through retelling the story of Rose Bell; she makes it clear she would want any student, regardless of color, to adopt such principles. In noting features of Dora's story in this way, Toby also emphasizes the dimension of personal growth that writing can have, something that sometimes can get neglected in a study of writing's social dimensions.

Toby appreciates the careful way of working with students which Debi's story explicates, as a reader who asks questions, makes honest observations, and helps students to become more conscious of the choices they must make as writers. She also makes it clear, however, that even her many years as an inner-city teacher have not given her "all the answers" to the issues; many remain unresolved, and she demonstrates her eagerness to learn more from others. This openness to other possibilities inspires me to remain open to the perspectives of my colleagues, even when my philosophical and political commitments would seem to radically differ.

One of the reasons I wanted to work in Detroit was my sense that Toby and I shared similar values. I felt in a short time that I had gotten to know her as well as anyone in the program, except George Cooper, who had been my friend for years. I didn't come into the program agreeing with Toby about all things; for instance, I had a different view of "discipline" and authority, and when I left the program that summer, I still didn't share her "color-blind" perspective on teaching and learning. Yet through the program, in part through the stories she told that revealed her commitment to and love for students, I came to respect "Mother Curry's" passionate perspective and incorporated it into my own story of the multicultural classroom we both shared.

Debi Telling Dora: The Role of a Helper

David Schaafsma: Tell me about Dora. What do you know about her?

Debi Goodman: I met Dora when she was either in first or second grade. I think I met her when she was in second grade. I met her and Tameka at the same time. I was traveling around Burton as a reading resource person. Dora was a very bossy little girl. She liked to boss other kids around. I didn't really like her when she was little. She was one of these kids that was always telling on other children and always telling other kids what to do.

961-Baby

Dora Simpson

Lynn was having a baby . As she get out of the car she look like she *at the hospital* had a pillow under her coat. She said to Don "I cann't take it any more, O.K. "

"O.K." *Don didn't answer*

"I knew it was about to come, " said Linne .

"How are you doning', "Don said. *doing? asked*

"Just fine- O hhhhh! "
    {Lynn was ~~15~~ 23 and *had* have 4 kids and 1 on the way . She *four one* drop *dropped* out of High school at the age of 15, when she was 16 she got pregnant. Her mom put her out when she fond out that she deop out of school. Her mom was very sad that she had put out her only child. }

"Righ on time honey. " *Right*

"You know I cann't take care of all these children. "

"You only have 4 , and 1 on the way," Don said.
Lynn walked in to emergency and Don left.
On the way home {~~Lynn stayed at the hospital also~~} Don didn't think *Don drove away* about what Lynn said.

                  OOO
~~3~~ *Three* days later Lynn came home whith a new baby now she ~~have 5~~ *had five* ~~children , that she cann't take care of.~~ *with* She look in the the New- *looked* paper and saw a add that said ; If you cann't take care of call us, and we will help you,961 BABY. So she called. Mrs. Bell answered the *your children* phone, "Hello, how may we help you?"

    "I need my ~~G.E.D. but I can't get it because~~ I have five *help with my children.* children,"

    "I can help you but. ~~you~~ have to promise to get your G.E.D., *You* OK?"

Fourth typed draft, first of two pages, completed July 7, 1989.

It was very hard to get
things done around the house,
the seven year old wouldn't obey
and wouldn't help her. The two
year old threw paper and milk.
The baby would holler. The
four and five year olds were always
fighting.
     Lynn felt exhausted. She would
go outside, get a stick and hit
the kids. Then she felt bad. She
didn't want to hit her children.

Fourth typed draft, marginal comments for page 1 transcribed by Debi Goodman.

2   Organization
     "OK." "I'll try
          Bell   you have to help us, too."
Mrs. then asked, "What do you know how to do?"

Lynn said, "Nothing."

"Can you wash clothes? Can you cook? Can you clean?

Lynn said, "Yes."

                        years
          Then two months later, Lynn come to Mrs. Bell and said, "I
                                        came
made it."

THE END

Fourth typed draft, second of two pages.

Mrs. Bell found ~~nursery~~ day care for Lynn's kids. The teacher helped Lynn and the children learn to cooperate. The kids started to obey and help. Lynn got the rest that she needed.

Lynn called her mother and told her mother ~~what~~ she was doing. Flynn's mother helped her with the kids too. Lynn went to school in the mornings.

Fourth typed draft, marginal comments for page 2 transcribed by Debi Goodman.

And I don't know what your impression of her was this summer, but certainly when you compare her with Tameka, Tameka is more the kind of a kid that fits into the woodwork, and Dora sort of stands out as being a little bit different, like more of a ghetto kid, or more of a needy child. Understand that they're going to Burton, so they're in a middle-class setting with a lot of middle-class and lower-class kids mixed together, where they have an opportunity to learn from peers to appear middle-class, which is what Tameka did. The other thing about the two of them is that, when they were in fifth grade, I had Dora in my morning class and Tameka in my afternoon class.

So I saw Dora coming along. When she was in third grade, she was in my reading lab, which means she was at least a year behind in reading, and I published books for her when she was little. That's something I did as a relief teacher and as a reading teacher, I went in and had kids write, and they would publish little books about things they liked. So that if anybody taught her writing, that was me, all the way along. What I did when I went in as a relief teacher was I taught writing to the kids.

DS: You got to know the family some?

DG: Oh, yes. Ruby is the grandmother, and she's often ill, but she's the matriarch of the family. And then there's an uncle, a young uncle, who's in and out of the picture. I think now he has a baby that Lanette is raising. And Lanette is often raising other children's babies and taking care of them. Lanette is the caretaker of the whole family. You know, she takes care of all the babies. Which gives you a picture of why Dora tends to be so bossy. She's always had a house filled with babies.

But Lanette is very involved in the school: she takes the kids to the library, she always came up to school for the book fair, she volunteered to come and watch the kids during folk dancing, and she would do anything that I ever asked her to do. Lanette was always there. She'd bring two or three babies along. She always had some kid in a stroller. I don't know who all these babies are, but there's always somebody in a stroller.

Dora was one of these kids that was a little different, and kids weren't that good friends with her. She was not on the inside group, you know that. Now Dora worked pretty hard in my room, and she tried, she did pretty well, she's the kind of kid that did well in my room, because if a kid works hard in my room, they pretty much get graded for effort. So, she worked real hard, and she did all the assigned work at her own ability level, which was somewhat slow at the reading and somewhat slow at the writing. She was still probably near the bottom of her class in many ways. But I think she was one of the kids that probably picked up a lot during the year because she worked hard. You know what I'm saying, she grew. And in the summer program Dora really blossomed.

She eventually she became very involved. She participated in that book committee and came up with a lot of interesting ideas. And in writing conferences she often was very insightful. She also took no flak from kids. There was that one situation in the summer program where she felt a kid had plagiarized something and she pointed it out, yet very politely. Were you there?

DS: I don't recall. What was that?

DG: I think one of the kids had plagiarized a poem or something. And she pointed it out. She can be very assertive, as you know. But my mom always said that the best strengths are your greatest weaknesses, and your greatest weaknesses are your best strengths. And of course, the other side of being bossy is being helpful, you know, and I still like that, that Dora had matured from being bossy to being able to use some of that sort of insightful and caring energy in a helpful way. I mean, bossiness to some extent is a way of caring, of being able to relate and care about other people, and this summer I didn't feel that she was bossy in a way that she was when she was in second grade and third grade, and even in fifth grade it was still an issue. But I felt that she cared about and got involved in discussions with other kids with what they were doing and often spoke up in a very strong voice, with suggestions for kids in conferences. But I think she learned from the summer, from being in workshop every day, how to be a more effective reader and writer.

We talked about Dora's story, as it evolved from the notes Dora had taken during the interview with Rose Bell on the first Tuesday of the program. These notes formed the basis, or the impetus, for a draft which Dora wrote out in her journal and began to type out on computer the next day. She encountered her first readers and listeners in a writing workshop session led by Toby and Debi on Thursday, a session which I attended:

DG: Dora read it to the group, people liked it, she was pretty happy with it, and she was pretty set that she wasn't going to do too much changing. And people had some different suggestions. I think mostly we responded by saying we thought it had a lot of possibility. The first draft is mostly dialogue,[7] and I'm sure we talked to her about putting in some detail or explanation that she might want to have.

There was some confusion in the original version over the sequence of her getting pregnant and instantly having a baby, and initially it was like she called 961-BABY and said "I'm pregnant" instead of "I just had a baby"; there was some actual confusion in this story, where it didn't follow and it didn't quite make sense. And there was this guy, Don, who right up to the very last version of the story just sort of disappeared from the story and never showed up again. And I think I suggested even in that initial conference that she put in more details about what it was like. Like this whole section now, where she says Lynn had five children, it was hard to get things done. This wasn't in there at all. There was no detail about what Lynn's life would have been like, and I'm pretty sure that I said to her even then, "you know, Dora, you know a lot about what it's like to have little babies around. Why don't you describe what Lynn's house was like, what the kids were like, what would they do?" I'm pretty sure that I made that initial suggestion, but she didn't really pick up on it right away. She did go and make some changes herself.

When she first typed the story in, the first draft was one paragraph. Well, in the second revision conference, we talked about some of the logistical problems: "OK, she's having a baby, she gets to the hospital, what does she say, what does he say? Why does he say this?" You know, just very specific questions following it up bit by bit. You know, "What if this happened, what if that happened?" I used this method with a lot of the kids. I started to use the method of extending language experience into revision, where she had written and typed up the first draft. But I served as a scribe to record the revision, freeing her up to revise, in a sense, especially with this tightly written task. But I would ask, "OK, what happened there and what was that about?" and "OK, how do you want to say that?" All right, and then I wrote it down, and put the arrow where it would go.

The paragraph about the five children I think I was a little pushy about, "OK, what was it like? What did the kids act like?" and she came up with these lines: "The seven year old wouldn't obey her and wouldn't help her. The two year old threw paper and milk. The baby would holler. The four and five year olds were always fighting." You know, getting her to be more specific about the kids. And so I elicited, you know, "Tell me more about them." I directed the revision to the extent that I knew which aspects maybe could be expanded more, and then I served as a scribe for her.

I remember that one of the last things that we talked about was, I kept saying, "What happened to Don? Where did he go?" And we agreed that right here when Lynn came home, there should be a sentence about him. And that when Dora went up to the computer, she would write that sentence. So this sentence here, "Lynn walked in the bedroom and found Don's clothes were gone," which I just love, just love that sentence. She could have said Don left her. But it's this way, it's so specific, and that sentence came out of her head, totally away from me, while she was working on the computer, just with the notion that something happened to Don. I gave her the push, sure, but she put that sentence there herself. I loved this sentence when she came back and read the final version.

One of my understandings is that you want to work with the kids where they are, and stretch them a little bit. You allow kids to do as much as they can on their own, and the adult drops off with any assistance when the child is able to do something themselves, but that's always a fine line. But by keeping the discussion at the conceptual level and not really focusing on proofreading the story, I feel that I was able to do something for Dora that she was not able to do completely for herself, and to help her conceptualize revision with me.

And I also think that in many ways kids have to know that real writers have editors, and there are certain things that you have to contend with. But I feel like basically her language was accepted, and she made the decision. I never suggested the change in her language unless it was a factual change. The focus was always on the story and the message, making it clear and providing detail, and I think that Dora was always treated as a writer. I wasn't in the role of an expert, just a helper. Supporting her until she was able to do things for herself in revision, which is a very difficult thing to do. And to really think the story, and later each word, through.

I think a lot of times what you get from young writers is a skeleton. Of course, sometimes you get too much, as in what Don Graves calls the "bed to bed" stories, where students try to record everything from "when I wake up until I go to bed," but in Dora's case what she had was too little, an outline with too little detail. And by asking her for more detail and prompting her, I certainly chose in some sense where I wanted more detail, but I think it made her piece much stronger.

I don't think you have to force kids. I just think you have to have this expectation that they're going to polish their writing, that they're going to work on it. I grew up as a writer, so maybe that helps me help kids think like writers. But it is hard if you've never used conferences, if you have never organized writing workshops with your kids; it is slow progress to be patient for them to grow and become self-disciplined. It is hard to really focus on it and keep at it, but it can really pay off.

Debi's story makes it clear that there is a way of reading Dora and her text, a way of working with her and similar students that neither simply and uncritically "celebrates" nor appropriates her intentions. This way of working is consistent with Lev Vygotsky's approach: "What the child can do in cooperation today he can do alone tomorrow. Therefore, the only good kind of instruction is that which marches ahead of development" (188). In suggesting that a fifth grader's needs for instruction might be quite different than an eleventh grader's needs, Debi shows that she believes that teaching must take into account development. Vygotsky's approach is also developmental, insisting as Debi does that socially meaningful activity is necessary in the child's progression from elementary to higher mental functions. "Socially meaningful activity" in this case refers not only to the task itself, but also to the social process that takes place when people learn from each other.

Debi tells the story of the seasoned whole language teacher working productively with one student, giving us an idea of the process of one story's construction as it evolves. She underscores the usefulness of teachers developing personal relationships with their students and coming to an understanding of the complexity of their lives by working with and interpreting a student's text in a way that is sensitive to personal circumstances. Debi's story reinforces Toby Curry's notion of Dora as a victim of other people's perceptions of her as "ghetto kid." Debi gets to know students and gets involved in their lives; she knows more about Dora, for instance, than the facts in the school file charts. She knows the family well; she details Dora's relationship with her mother and cousin Tameka, providing insight into working with Dora in a way that builds on her strengths without ignoring her weaknesses. For instance, Debi discusses what we had come to recognize as Dora's "bossiness" and helps us to see it in a new light: "The other side of being bossy is being helpful, you know, and I still like that, that Dora had matured from being bossy to being able to use some of that sort of insightful and caring energy in a helpful way. I mean bossiness to some extent is a way of caring." At one point she helps us see Dora's behavior in terms of her family responsibilities—having to help take care of her brothers, sisters, and cousins—and also as part of the process of growing and developing through working with others. Debi helps us see that what we might have judged as "bossiness" on the literal level is far more complicated than what we may have initially thought. Knowing what we know, we are able to "read deeper" into Dora.

Debi says she is "pushy" in her promotion of the development of "961-BABY" as "realistic fiction," as Dana Davidson also observed. While one might discuss the issue of the amount of control and authority which Debi seemed to exert over Dora's text in the process of questioning and "dictation," I agree with her perspective on working with students generally, her emphasis on working with student intentions and strengths. Debi focuses on working with larger issues like purpose and audience without neglecting issues of clarity. She doesn't focus on surface features of texts, but demonstrates that she cares about details. Dora knows, when Debi is through talking with her, that Debi cares very much about her writing. She has high standards for quality, yet as someone devoted to readeading in terms of "miscue analysis," she doesn't read Dora's writing primarily in terms of its "deficits." As I pointed out in chapter 4, I think Debi emphasizes teaching students by letting students "write what they want" and then works on that writing with them. Debi also illustrates, through her stories about Dora, how particular ways of working with students can also lead us to learn from them about how to work with them and value their ways of knowing.

As with Jeanetta Cotman and Toby Curry, Debi is an experienced teacher who has taught for many years in Detroit's inner city. She is tireless, devoting endless hours to working with her students. She helps one to resist easy generalizations about the nature of supposedly "at risk" children.

LEARNING FROM DORA

In my view, each of Dora's texts, and each revision, is a version of her life, a self she creates to help her make sense of it. But in talking with her and others about those texts, I learn from them and construct a far richer story for myself than I could have alone. In my story of the interpretation of Dora's "961-BABY," as in my story of the interpretation of eating on the street, I have found that, while I may have disagreed with some of my colleagues, all of their stories, all of their voices, enrich my understanding of Dora and her texts. Like Dora, like the teachers I have worked with, I tell stories to explore issues that are important to me, stories that necessarily draw on others' voices. Many cultural voices are needed to "novelize" our various understandings of teaching literacy in a multicultural society. And while each voice provides some helpful information or takes a useful perspective on that information for me, no voice takes on an air of certainty. I initially took an almost exclusively biographical approach to Dora and her writing, and I retained that approach to some extent, but I learned a great deal from others about other important ways of seeing her and her texts. There is evidence in the telling of these stories that others, too, have learned from each others' stories.[8]

961-Baby

Dora Simpson

Lynn was having a baby . As she get out of the car at the hospital, she look like she had apillow under her coat. She said to Don ,"I can't take it any more, O.K. "

Don didn't answer.   ʌ *THAT DON'T SOUND QUITE RIGHT*

"I knew it was about to come, " said Lynn.

"How are you doing," Don asked.

"Just fine- Ohhhhh. "

Lynn was 23 and had four kids and one on the way . She dropped out of high school at the age of 15. When she was 16 ,she got pregnant. Her mom put her out when she found out that she dropped out of school. Her mom was very sad that she had put out her only child.

"Right on time honey. "

"You know I can't take care of all these children. "

"You only have four, and one on the way," Don said.

Lynn walked in to emergency and Don left. On the way home, Don didn't think about what Lynn said.

OOO

Three days later Lynn came home with a new baby. Lynn walk s in the bedroom, and finds Don clothes was gone.

Now she had five children. It was very hard to get things done around the house. The seven year old wouldn't obey her and wouldn't help her. The two year old threw paper and milk. The baby would holler. The four and five year olds were always fighting.

Lynn felt exhausted. She would go outside and get a stick and hit the kids. Then she felt bad. She didn't want to hit her children.

Fifth typed draft, first of two pages, completed July 10, 1989.

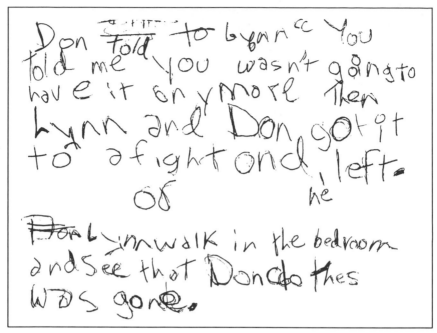

Fifth typed draft, marginal comments for page 1 written by Dora.

I have presumed from the beginning that, in the process of trying to understand and, to know Dora, I would gain insights that would help me to better teach her and students like her. But as her teacher, to what extent can I now with confidence say that I know enough about her to direct her learning in productive ways? And as a researcher, to what extent can I now speak for her? Michael Polanyi speaks of "the irreducible indeterminacy inherent in the meaning of all descriptions" (95). In other words, Dora isn't completely knowable.

Adrienne Rich looks at it this way: *"You cannot speak for me. I cannot speak for us.* Two thoughts: there is no liberation that only knows how to say "I." There is no collective movement that speaks for all of us all the way through. And so even ordinary pronouns become a political problem" (19). Elizabeth Ellsworth, in a similar vein, asks, "What diversity do we silence in the name of 'liberation' pedagogy?" (299). She says,

> As a white middle-class woman, with regard to the issue of working with and representing diverse people in her scholarship and

2   Organization

She looked in the newspaper and saw an add that said , "If you can't take care of your kids, call us, and we will help you; 961 EABY. " So she called. Mrs. Bell answered the phone, "Hello, how may we help you?"

"I need help with my children.'"

"I can help you but you have to promise to get your G.E.D., OK?"

"I'll try."

Mrs. Bell then asked, "You have to help us too. What do you know how to do?"

Lynn said, "Nothing."

"Can you wash clothes? Can you cook? Can you clean?

"Yes," said Lynn.

Mrs. Bell found daycare for Lynn's kids. The teacher helped Lynn and the children learned to cooperate. The kids started to obey and help. Lynn got the rest that she needed.

Lynn could ge to school in the morning.

at the daycare

Lynn called her mother and told her mother what she was doing. Lynn's mother helped her with the kids too. Lynn went to school in the morning.

Then two years later, Lynn came to Mrs. Bell and said, "I made it."

THE END

Fifth typed draft, second of two pages.

teaching, I have not and can never participate unproblematically in the collective process of self-definition, naming of oppression, and struggles for visibility in the face of marginalization engaged in by students whose class, race, gender and other positions I do not share. (309–10)

As a white, middle-class male who chose to work with and write about a lower-class black girl, I think of what Robin Morgan wrote: "I haven't the faintest notion what possible revolutionary role white heterosexual men could fill" (218). But, given that I have a commitment to such a role and ultimately want, with others, to learn better ways to work with students such as Dora, I must turn to teachers like the ones I worked with in the Dewey program, and teachers like Lisa Delpit, who suggests: "Those who are most skillful at educating Black and poor children do not allow themselves to be placed in 'skills' or 'process' boxes. They understand the need for both approaches, the need to help students to establish their own voices, but to coach those voices to produce notes that will be heard clearly in the larger society" (100).

Acknowledging our limitations, yet drawing on the strengths of our various perspectives, those of us who choose to may learn from our students how to be flexible enough to teach them. But in working with and writing about students, we must preserve a sense of the complexity of doing so.

It seems to me now that Dora may be interpreted in almost infinite ways: as a survivor, a "tower of strength," or, perhaps, as a struggling eleven-year-old child. Some may see her as a "Third World Black Woman," as bell hooks might say, an "adult" in many respects, with the toughness and viciousness needed to "get over." As Dora says of herself in her poem, she is "cute" but can also "dice you to pieces" if she needs to. But like all students, she is irreducible, finally, to statistics or metaphor or stereotype. She is Dora, changing to some extent every day in a world that says "Who told you anybody wants to hear from you? You ain't nothing but a black woman." Perhaps only a story can give some sense of her complexity.[9]

COLLABORATIVE MYTH MAKING: TEACHING AND LEARNING WITH GEORGE, TOBY, DEBI, DANA, SUSAN, AND JEANETTA

"Communities are texts in the process of formation."
(J. Robinson 15)

"The object of understanding human events is to sense the alternatives of human possibility." (Bruner 1986, 53)

Wendy Doniger O'Flaherty, in *Other People's Myths,* says, "All truths being multiple, it is not surprising that the true version of any story is also multiple" (64). As an example, she describes *The Mahabharata,* the great Indian epic, as an oral (and written) "work in progress" because each reader retells the classic Indian myth in every generation. As O'Flaherty points out, all versions of the myth, all variants, are part of the myth, necessary to its growth and nature. This collaborative process of myth making is like history itself which grows, not in "tree-like" fashion, but in more "fluid" ways. Multiple perspectives on events, then, are important for our learning about those events. Craig Roney helped us make this point in the writing program with his emphasis on the importance of retellings: his telling of four different versions of "Cinderella"; his explanation of their difference in terms of cultural context; and his encouragement of student versions, some of which were published in *Corridors.* We get to know more about the mind and world of each teller with these versions, but we also gain a richer understanding of the "myth" of "Cinderella."

One of the reasons multiple versions of events are important is because they tell us more about the nature of tellers and storytelling. As Glassie reminds us, "Stories can't be spoken of as things apart from their tellers" (37). Every version is constructed by individual human actors in particular settings, and each version not only reflects those particular contexts, but is saturated with the heteroglossia of voices from those settings. Each teller's way of telling a story gives us a glimpse into her or his way of seeing the world. The stories help us see the ways individual storytellers construe and construct the world in telling their tales. The way we construe/construct depicts learning theories that can help us understand how differently individuals come to know and gives us an indication of the variety of ways of knowing.

Of course, the very experience of encountering a myth of another culture (such as I experienced about "eating on the street," for instance), or another version of a story, can sometimes cause enormous difficulties in cultural encounters. For instance, linguist Alton "Pete" Becker describes an occasion where Western journalists interviewed a leading Balinese dancer on the nature of his work and art. They asked him questions from their own cultural perspective about "whom he had studied with," how often he "practiced," and what he hoped to do when he was an "adult," all questions which are irrelevant in Balinese art and culture. As O'Flaherty points out, "It is often difficult to see, let alone accept, the treasure that is offered to us by other people's mythologies" (75). When you examine others' myths, you also to some extent must begin to examine your own and begin to see the mythical or constructed nature of what you believe and experience as truth. People working in a multicultural setting—such as we were in our summer program—people intent on not silencing each other's voices and working together on common goals of learning and teaching, both transform and are transformed to some extent in the act of sharing stories. This is a view of myth making and of history as communion, not just communication (O'Flaherty 148), a kind of collaboration that does not eliminate conflict, that makes use of differences for growth.

Such was our intent in our collaboratively designed Dewey program: to create conditions for teachers and students to learn from and with each other, with the aim of exploring the extent to which we might be able to "democratize" education within our learning community. Though compromise and cooperation were an important aspect of our teacher collaboration—we certainly were convinced of some aspects of each other's perspectives and acted on them—conflict was also an important part of our learning experience. We tried to provide opportunities for ourselves to discuss our differences of opinion. When John Dewey speaks of wanting to constitute the social interaction of the learners as the "normal source of order" (1938, 630), he is describing changing the normal educational process and shifting its priorities. Paolo Freire's goal, similarly, is to recover historical agency through the dialogue of teachers and students as subjects "who meet to name the world in order to transform it" (1970, 97), which is a view of collaboration for the purpose of praxis. This view is consistent with the social perspective on narrative and learning which Bakhtin espouses, an agonistic view of collaboration that preserves—even embraces—the notion of conflict at the heart of the learning process. This perspective on collaboration is ultimately a challenge to the notion of "objective" authority rather than a tool to preserve the status quo.

Bill Karris discusses collaboration in a similar way: collaboration as a way of coming to consensus, a way of eliminating differences, follows a "Rogerian" perspective, the ideals of which are primarily compromise and cooperation. Karris notes that the "privileging of compromise" in the attempt to eliminate conflicts can be restrictive: "To allow predetermined principles to exclude or restrict the generation of new and inventive solutions to problems runs counter to the epistemic nature and value of rhetoric" (114). What he calls the epistemic view works against the possibility of "efficiency" as a goal for the construction of knowledge, and perhaps even precludes its possibility. As Karris sees it, "conflict over ideas can be a positive development in the collaborative process" (122). Growth takes place through agonistic development, and a vocal opposition is necessary. This is consistent with a view of culture as struggle, like Bakhtin's, one that preserves deeply rooted contradictions and tensions, strong opinions, and conflicting voices.

Barbara Meyerhoff helps us understand the conflictual nature of "community-building" in *Number Our Days*, the story of Aliyah, a Jewish retirement community. She speaks of the highly argumentative nature of the residents' conversations, and storytelling in particular, which she sees as "efforts at ordering, sorting, explaining—rendering coherent their long lives, finding integrating ideas and characteristics that helped them know themselves" primarily through a "revitalization of the past" (34). Storytelling, she points out, is a passion for these people, absolutely central to their culture: "In the ritual (of storytelling), they exercised their basic human prerogative, the right to indicate who they are to the world, to interpret themselves to themselves instead of following accident, history, and reality to make that interpretation for them" (107). Further, she notes it was a community "sewn together by internal conflict, whose members were building and conserving their conceptions using grievance and dissension" (187). Anger welded them together, in a sense, an anger rooted in deeply felt commitments.

Stories can help make sense of the past and be a source of strength and cohesion; the very common concerns of the community can help to bind its members together. Thus, stories about the past can be seen as "culture-preserving." One need of the people of Aliyah, Myerhoff demonstrates, like the people in Glassie's Ballymenone, is to imagine a way to live in relative harmony. Like any community, they need to find a way to "come to terms with" differences and learn from each other, and oral storytelling has been useful for that purpose. To this end, Glassie says, "The story form has been one of the most powerful and effective sustainers of culture across the world. Its great power lies in its ability to fix affective responses to the messages it contains and to bind what is to be remembered with emotional associations" (455).

Certainly, stories such as Dora's or Susan's or Rose Bell's are a testimony to this kind of cultural "sustenance." They are culture-sustaining in that they address moral traditions of social responsibility long recognized in their communities. In her best moments, Susan Harris uses her inspirational stories, as teachers teaching for change do, to reshape culture, to redefine culture in the very act of changing it, supporting particular ways of teaching that work against the dominant, status quo pedagogies.

Storytelling as a means of community building was an important aspect of our work in the Dewey program. In the process of sharing stories about children, our car repair bills, our pasts on the football field, we became friends. We often laughed at the stories we told about ourselves and grew to respect each other for our stories documenting commitments to kids. There certainly was a psychological sense of empowerment we could claim in our rare opportunity to work together and share common concerns. But that binding did not take place only in terms of commonalities; it also took place in terms of differences, differences that were certainly altered, but not erased, differences that became an important source of learning for all of us.

An important aspect of our collaborative myth making, with regard to the preservation and celebration of difference, is its orality. The teacher stories I have shared here were spoken, and that very fact, which reinforces their very provisional and contextual nature, helps us to see the agonism at the heart of the collaborative process. As Kieran Egan (1987) points out, "Oral cultures engage the emotions of their members by making the culturally important messages event-laden, by presenting characters and their emotions in conflict in developing narratives—in short, by building the messages into stories" (455). Glassie sees this, too, in his work with Irish storytellers: "Stories embody argument over important ideas and push toward the frontiers of culture to provide the outsider as well as the insider with a means for constructing the culture in its own terms" (291). He goes on to say that the stories told in Irish "ceilis" do not just merely confirm the ideological unity of the people present; rather, "use social unity to raise the truth that confines ideology and calls doctrine into question" (298). Stories, Glassie is saying, can be told to build unity and heal wounds, but they can also be important in exploration, in learning. The stories I tell in this chapter about Dora, and in previous chapters about eating on the street are ones in which conflicting voices are preserved and where closure is obviously not achieved.

Among those of us who taught in the Dewey program, there was a certain resistance to writing about our experiences, though we encouraged ourselves to do so. This may have been partly due to the fact that many of us preferred to talk, but it may also have been due to the fact that, as Walter Ong puts it, "Writing fosters abstractions that disengage knowledge from the arena where humans struggle with one another" (43–44). Writing can be used to cool conflicts more easily than talk, can isolate factors and abstract issues. Writing seems to fix meaning in a way that conversation doesn't, and we wanted to use all of our time to talk issues out.[10] In conversation, we seemed to shape and reshape our ideas more quickly; we seemed more willing to be creative, take risks. More was accomplished in the very provisional world of talk than might have been accomplished in writing (though we all did agree to write about the program later). The tensions of everyday struggles were felt face to face in the primarily oral environment of collaborative teaching, and these tensions were, importantly, not quickly resolved.

We were a strong-willed group of teachers with strong, and we knew, sometimes divergent opinions. Though we shared a desire and an enthusiasm for teaching together in the program and developed a close friendship, we also did not avoid "touchy" issues in our frequent talks together. We used the opportunity to discuss important matters pertaining to our passionate interest in urban literacy and our love of teaching this particular group of children. We took daily opportunities to share stories about our students, stories rich in our several experiences, some of them more obviously "community building" in many positive ways, stories that stressed our commonalities and shared interests, but also some that were painful and conflicting, that contributed in equally important ways to building our community.

Collaborative learning is messy—not neat and linear—complicated and enriched as it is by the stories of experience. The story of our teaching collaboration, unlike most carefully written stories, has no fixed beginning or ending. It is a slow and apparently "inefficient" process of construction with inevitable starts and stops and sometimes outright failures to understand or agree. The talk is tentative, a form of thinking-in-process, ephemeral, constantly changing. In the summer program, we were dealing with complex, cumulative, often contradictory processes, with many interests represented, and these interests are often conflicting and always changing. We negotiated these complexities partly through an exchange of stories on issues about which we cared.

The Dewey story about literacy in a multicultural classroom depends on the stories of cultural conflict about such issues as eating on the street and students such as Dora. Multiple perspectives are needed to inform and construct this story, and negotiating these cultural conflicts together in *conversation,* where they could best be addressed, was crucial to our learning about these issues. These shared stories are not "relative," or aimless, but committed—toward Dora and other students, toward preserving the best of culture and community, and producing, to some extent, necessary changes. This larger story, comprised of our collective stories, is an act of imagination that is committed to change, to praxis, to social justice.

REFLECTIONS ON CURRICULUM AS STORYTELLING

THE SUMMER STORY
Thadd McGaffey

Thadd wrote for the first forty minutes or so and got his story completed.

Thadd was relieved to have that burden off of his shoulders. "Ahhh, now I can have some fun," he said. The rest of the day Thadd had a lot of fun at the Dewey Center and at home.

Thadd got a lot more out of this than he had expected. He got a lot of new friends: Julie, Kate, Eboney, Amyra, and all of the teachers, Debi, Toby, Dave, George, Dana, Susan, Markus and Mrs. Cotman. And Thadd hopes to be back with all his new friends again next year and all through the next year.

"Learning to tell stories about one's every day experience is one means of crossing the threshold of awareness. They are a means of gaining an interpretive sense of our experience that can be called narrative understanding. . . . Why is telling stories as a mode of inquiry especially appropriate for experienced teachers as a means of staff development? Because a narrative understanding of classroom events can become a way of making visible the invisible routines of the enacted curriculum. By this transformation, the enacted curriculum as experienced by students can be seen more clearly and fully. It becomes available for deliberation and for redesign, if and when that is appropriate." (Erickson 135–36)

"Teacher education has rarely occupied a critical space, public or political, within contemporary culture, where the meaning of the social could be recovered and restated so that teachers' and students' cultural histories, personal

*narratives, and collective will could be permitted to coa-
lesce around the development of a democratic counter-
public sphere."* (Giroux 160)

*"Neither the discourse nor the discursive practices of edu-
cation originate in the ordinary language and experience
of students and teachers."* (Stock 1987, 4)

In the relative safety and comfort of Madison, Wisconsin, I read the paper and am daily made aware that what Jonathon Kozol calls "savage inequalities" certainly exist in this country; perhaps nowhere is that fact more evident than in Detroit. One in every five children in the United States lives in poverty—an estimated twelve million children, according to the Childrens' Defense Fund. The economic conditions have almost certainly worsened since 1989 in the area where Dora lives. Deep cuts made by Michigan Governor John Engler's administration in social services have been most cruelly felt in Cass Corridor. And schools—including the criminally under-funded schools in the inner cities—occupy a dominant role in the existence of unequal power relations in our society. I firmly believe that, as educators and as citizens we have to take action to change these conditions; we have to take action to rectify racial, class, and gender inequities. Telling stories will not be enough. Within schools, for instance, there seem to be relatively stable structures that we can identify and act to change. Part of the process can usefully begin with an exchange, open to differences and possibilities, between partici-pants in the process. The voices of teachers, students, parents, and administrators must be heard in the decision-making process.

As Harold Rosen says, "within schools there is movement, con-flict, imperfect control which makes it possible, inside limits which are always shifting and need therefore to be discovered in practice, to contest the terrain" (18). The "reality" of schooling can be usefully seen as a kind of text, I think, subject to multiple interpretations, mul-tiple readings, multiple uses. The stories of students and teachers, critical and constructive, can be part of the "movement" and "con-flict" that can rupture and reshape schooling. Ian Reid calls these sto-ries of contradiction forms of "micropower" that may work to modify larger "macropower" structures that create inequities. But in the pro-cess of encouraging such stories we need a politics of open-endedness—dispensing with fixed hierarchical assumptions—as part of a rethinking of the educational and social enterprise. Gayatri

Spivak calls this openness "a weave of knowing and not knowing which is what knowing is" (1990, 78).

Maxine Greene says that "students must be enabled to encounter curriculum as possibility" (1978, 18); but it is clearly not only students that need to be enabled. Another way to think of encountering "curriculum as possibility" is to conceive of the shaping of theories and curriculum as acts of storytelling. The possible value of storytelling is something those of us who are teachers must consider for ourselves as we try to learn from each other and our students and as we depict the learning that goes on in our classrooms for others. Fictions, "moves made in the imagination, moves explored and enacted in language—are vitally important in helping us work with our students" (J. Robinson 227). Those of us who are exploring a variety of qualitative methodologies, for instance, are beginning to discover the virtue of telling stories or conducting narrative inquiry about—and sometimes with—students and fellow teachers.[11] Many of these stories depend on the multiple and occasionally contradictory voices of students and teachers exchanged in the process.

But is curriculum seen as "acts of storytelling," especially stories that depend on a multiplicity of voices, an apolitical conception?[12] In other words, is saying "yes" to many perspectives the same as having no perspective at all? Is there a way to negotiate a curriculum in such a way that competing voices, and differences, are to some extent included? Can one adopt a "progressive" stance, as some of us tried to do in Detroit, in the midst of conflicting stances? Patti Lather, speaking of a praxis-oriented research paradigm, says, with applications, I think, to curriculum making: "A key issue revolves around this central challenge: how to maximize self as mediator between people's self-understandings and the need for ideology critique and transformative action without becoming impositional" (1991, 64). For those of us interested in making fundamental changes in schools, Lather suggests that we "transform our own practices so that our empirical and pedagogical work can be less toward positioning ourselves as masters of truth and justice and more toward creating a space where those directly involved can act and speak on their own behalf" (1991, 164). Making space for multiple voices in the construction of curricula does not necessarily mean an end to "liberatory struggle"; in some ways, it is the most appropriate beginning for that struggle.

Myles Horton and Paolo Freire (1991) wrestle with a similar issue. As Horton suggests, "How is it possible for us to work in a community without feeling the spirit of the culture that has been there for many years, without trying to understand the soul of the culture?

We cannot interfere in this culture. Without understanding the soul of the culture we just invade the culture" (131). And how is it that we can "feel the spirit" of a culture without invading it? Horton says "one of the virtues we have to create in ourselves as progressive educators is the virtue of humility" (195). To be humble we have to listen, watch, and make sure that we don't impose our conceptions of the world on those we might hope to "liberate" through our imposition.

"We make the road by walking," Horton says, and not by prede-termined plans and fixed principles. He makes a distinction between being an educator and an organizer. Being an organizer is goal-directed, technical; organizing implies that there's a specific, limited goal that needs to be achieved, and the purpose is to achieve that goal. Being an educator, on the other hand, has to do more with lis-tening, questioning, and developing relationships with those who are your colearners. Within an organizing framework, Horton says, "I was interested in going as far as I could in helping people develop the capacity to make decisions and to take responsibility, which I think is the role of an educator" (125). In our work in Detroit, those of us who saw ourselves as progressive educators tried to find our way in the practice of collaborative teaching and curriculum planning by making our commitments clear without attempting to impose them on anyone. We found that one of the best ways to develop curriculum was to provide an occasion for conversation to take place, where we could plan together with students how to help them learn to write, where an exchange of stories about teaching could take place.

Kieran Egan sees how teaching itself may be likened more use-fully to acts of storytelling than other metaphors. This perspective, which works against the mechanistic conception of "lesson plans" consistent with "behavioral objectives" and "scope and sequence" planning, both validates and celebrates the importance of students' and teachers' storied ways of learning and seeing the universe. Seeing "lessons as good stories to be told rather than sets of objectives to be attained" (1986, 2) is more organic and meaning centered and em-phasizes the imagination and feelings as tools in learning. Although Egan has a tendency to think of stories in terms of binary moral op-positions, he also sees that stories tend to preserve the meaningful and significant in coherent pattern, and that this may be a useful way of thinking of the process of teaching and learning. He sees that teachers are professional "storytellers of knowledge" (109), and has an image of the "teacher as the teller of our myths" (113). While he neglects students' contributions to this classroom storymaking, and fails to call attention to students' own capacities as storytellers in the

shaping of knowledge, he does view teaching in terms of value making and experience. Egan's conception of teaching as storytelling has
much to offer to the notion of curriculum as storytelling.

This view of the uses of storytelling seen as a way of learning how
to change or develop theories about teaching works against the conception of teaching fostered by most teacher education programs
that perpetuate a reductive view of knowledge and a passive view of
curriculum building and pedagogy. As Ken Zeichner says, "Teacher
education programs are mostly concerned with procedures and organizational arrangements for the purpose of efficiently helping students realize tacit and often unexamined ends" (120). Within this
model, "the prospective teacher is viewed primarily as a passive re-
cipient of this professional knowledge and plays little part in defining
the substance and direction of his teacher preparation program"
(117). Teacher education seen only as technical expertise, as a means
of filling in blanks, perpetuates a view of knowledge as given and perpetuates a view of learners as passive recipients of that knowledge.

"Teacher-proof" curriculum packages are consistent with particular kinds of predesigned classroom research. Ira Shor (1987) states
an alternative perspective on teacher education programs: "The most
important value [in teacher education] is participatory learning that
mobilizes critical thought and democratic debate" (26). In teacher
education programs and, more specifically, in the shaping of curriculum and building of theories that should take place in teacher education programs, we might think of "facts" as embedded in fictions:
they only take on significance in relation to other items in a meaningful pattern; all knowledge is really story in this respect, connected
to life, to practice, related to learners' lives. Knowledge, and the acts
of constructing knowledge—this fictionalizing—continually demands critical examination, and teachers have to be actively involved
in the shaping.

What is the prevailing view of knowledge in many teacher education programs, and in most schools? How is knowledge constructed, and how should it be constructed to be more consistent
with emancipatory ideals? If the research program that informs
teacher education programs is conceived conceptually as grand narratives that derive from positivist perspectives on language, perspectives that devalue everyday experience and eliminate alternative
beliefs in the goal of efficiency, what stories might better inform its
practices? Knowledge conceived of as socially and politically constructed underscores the value of collaboration in learning. If we can
begin to view teaching as a fundamentally social relationship, char-

acterized by mutual dependence, social interaction, and conflict; if we begin to view education itself as a cultural forum, as the construction of, and not the transmission of knowledge, then it may be useful to think of teaching and learning more in terms of acts of storytelling. Another way to think of the uses of storytelling for learning about the classroom is to consider how teachers who collaborate teach each other through telling stories about their separate and shared teaching experiences. The curriculum that we shaped and the theories of language learning that we developed in the Dewey Center program were composed through our classroom storytelling, and the curricula that we shaped in the following year were also in part shaped by those stories and by the stories of still others.

By working together in Detroit in the Dewey Center Community Writing Project, we as teachers were concerned with the political and epistemological implications of our curriculum. As opposed to a static, closed system, we attempted to establish a more dynamic, social view of knowledge acquisition for the purpose of student and teacher empowerment; we developed a curriculum through storytelling.

The curriculum that we developed was not simply a matter of exchanging teacher stories, however; it was composed with students. As Patricia Stock writes, "Unless and until students appropriate teachers' instructional plans and translate those plans into their own terms, into their own intellectual projects, teachers' plans become just that." Curriculum, Stock explains, "inheres in those intellectual projects that teachers and students undertake individually and together in the presence of one another on grounds they construct dialogically, on grounds they construct with the language they shape for one another in order that they may bring their past experiences and their images of the future to bear upon their present concerns" ("Dialogic Curriculum" 4). Teachers and students construct curricula together.

Stories are not efficient; they are not at all conclusive about the construction of curricula; they are not definitive about the nature of literacy instruction; they raise more questions than they answer. Because these things are true, storytelling as a means of learning about the classroom may be the best way to preserve differences in the process of "novelizing" our various understandings of teaching literacy in a multicultural society. The novel, Milan Kundera says, "is born out of a recognition that we do not fully understand each other and need to redefine ourselves" (117). Stories, the stories of students and teachers, may be, as Paul Ricoeur says, "models for the redescription of the world," the world of the classroom and beyond.

NOTES
BIBLIOGRAPHY

NOTES

<small>Preface</small>

1. Though some readers may be interested in a detailed description of the program, that is not the purpose of the present work. I do discuss the outline of the program in some detail in chapter 1, but full and rich descriptions of similar programs exist elsewhere in, for example, Atwell, *In the Middle*; Bartholomae and Petrosky, *Facts, Artifacts and Counterfacts*; Romano, *Clearing the Way*; Paley, *The Boy Who Would Be a Helicopter*; and Freire, *Pedagogy of the Oppressed*. Though all of the programs described in such books reveal somewhat different political and epistemological assumptions, they nevertheless have in common an approach to students and teachers that attempts to validate their ways of knowing, and thus bear some resemblance to the work most of us were committed to in our work in Detroit.

2. Given that same opportunity, I did, too. My story, "Lillie Dancing," in part demonstrates that stories had been a means of personal exploration in my own life. My "Gilbert and Dave's Stories" demonstrates that this important narrative exploration of issues was also taking place in students' stories. In both pieces I focused on personal—and not social—uses of narrative.

3. Though it is not the story I set out to explore about the process in which students were *daily* constructed through teachers' stories, I do think the stories the teachers tell throughout this book, particularly those focusing on Dora in chapter 6, do indicate how such a process might have taken place.

4. This issue raises for me several rather complicated concerns. All the conversations took place informally, yet words, even words spoken between friends, take on a kind of "fixed" character in writing. Almost all the teachers who saw the original transcripts were struck by the way spoken words seem to take on lives of their own in print. As a result, one teacher requested anonymity.

5. For those interested in the teaching of literacy, see Willinsky, *The New Literacy*; Robinson, *Conversations on the Written Word*; Kozol, *Illiterate America*; Fishman, *Amish Literacy*; Shor, *Critical Teaching and Everyday Life*; Lunsford et al., *The Right to Literacy*; and Kintgen et al., *Perspectives on Literacy*. Among various excellent sources about multicultural education, I would suggest Hidalgo et al., *Facing Racism in Education*; Rose, *Lives on the Boundary*; Moraga and Anzaldua, *This Bridge Called My Back*; and Paley, *White Teacher*.

CHAPTER 1. IMAGINING EMPOWERMENT: TELLING STORIES IN WRITING PROGRAMS

1. From 1985 until the present, Jay Robinson has been the CEIC's director; from 1985 to 1989, Patricia Stock was its Associate Director. I also worked in Saginaw at that time with Cathy Fleischer, Kathy Dixon, and Dick Harmston on various projects.

2. Dana has since taken a job teaching at Detroit's Farwell Middle School, in another part of the inner city.

3. For a discussion of the cultural basis of various versions of Cinderella, see Robert Darnton, "Peasants Tell Tales: The Meanings of Mother Goose," in *The Great Cat Massacre*. The work of both Darnton and Richard Price, *First-Time*, were useful for me in understanding the nature of historical "versions" of events, and I found Craig Roney's focus on the importance of each students' "retellings" of stories consistent with these works.

4. This book is still in progress, now expanded to include essays and stories about the impact of several summers' writing programs on participants' classroom teaching, and about some of the collaborative teaching and study in the Detroit public schools.

5. The complete text of Dora's story can be found in chapter 5, where I focus on various interpretations of the story.

6. I draw here on much talk and reading, most of it done in the context of graduate seminars and informal discussion groups. These seminars, such as Biff Barritt's phenomenology study group, where we spent a year reading Wittgenstein's *Philosophical Investigations,* and Jay Robinson's seminars, "Language and Literacy" and "The Rhetoric of Narrative," where we read, among other things, Vygotsky's *Thought and Language* and Bakhtin's *The Dialogic Imagination,* were a source of rich conversations that certainly informed my understandings—or misunderstandings—of these complex issues.

Though it is impossible to trace all of the ways "my voice" is informed by others, in the theoretical passage that follows, for instance, my understanding of Foucault was greatly enriched by Patricia Lambert Stock, *The Teacher as Researcher,* and through subsequent discussions with her and others. I am especially indebted in this section to my colleague, George Kamberelis, whose paper, "Intertextuality, Identity, and the Development of Voice," with its keen understanding of issues of agency in the work of Foucault and Bakhtin, inform my own thinking. The thinking that resulted from that paper—and subsequent discussions—is certainly reflected in these pages. I elaborate on this issue to acknowledge two—of many—voices that shaped my own, but also to underscore the point I try to make with the help of the work of Bakhtin near the end of this section: our "voices" are never entirely "our own."

7. Polanyi also made it clear that language is social, but in *Personal Knowledge* it seems to me he emphasizes intentionality.

8. Barry Lopez (1982) notes similarly how we "create wolves" in terms

of our local perspectives, desires, and needs; he asserts that wolves do not really exist except in terms of the myths we create about them (203).

9. John Willinsky's *The Well-Tempered Tongue: The Politics of Standard English in the High School* is a close look at the ways standard English is socially constructed in the English classes of one Canadian high school.

CHAPTER 2. JEANETTA AND TOBY: LITERACY AND HISTORY IN DETROIT

1. The Detroit River is a strait between Lake Erie and Lake St. Clair.

2. My focus on names and naming here began with my own rather surface, "outsider's" impression of the irony of finding these men's names everywhere in what has been for some time an impoverished and almost exclusively African American inner city, as well as my own belief in the power, the necessity, of naming one's own world in order to make it one's own. My brief rendering of the "histories" of Cass, Couzens, Lodge, and Jeffries—and the opening paragraphs of the historical versions section—is based on a variety of sources. Some of the information came from my memory of my own learning of Michigan history in Grand Rapids, Michigan, during my elementary school education at Oakdale Public School in the late 1950s and early 1960s. Whenever possible, as elsewhere in this chapter, I tried to consult a variety of sources for my information. In order to get a sense of the version of history students in the Detroit Public Schools—including some of the students in the Dewey program—were reading, I began my reading with *Detroit, Wayne County, and Michigan: A Story for Children,* a textbook—still used in some schools—written by a coalition of Detroit Public School teachers during the 1950s for use in the middle grades. In part due to the brevity of the "portraits," and in part because my purpose here is to emphasize a particular view of the history of race relations in Detroit, I may have falsely created the impression of a rather "unified" historical perspective in the following section. I trust that my overall purposes in this chapter will prevail: to give a sense of the commitments revealed in any historical version of events and to respect wherever possible multiple perspectives on events.

3. Though we did not discuss her experience with the 1967 riot, Jeanetta had been a resident of Detroit for less than five years when it occurred. The burning of Cass Corridor, the very area where she taught, echoes another burning, that of her father's school in Mount Sterling.

4. During this time following King's assassination, Debi Goodman doesn't recall any violence. Living in Detroit at the time, however, she recalls that Mayor Gribbs imposed "martial law," including curfews and restrictions against public gatherings on that Sunday. She remembers that a march in King's honor following a church service resulted in the arrest of many of the marchers, including some of her friends.

5. Thadd and Jason were seventh graders who caused concern for some teachers during the first week because they seemed to be writing little and

apparently encouraged some of the other boys to join them in this slow-down; however, they were also perceived as very able writers.

6. Malcolm Bingay would not be viewed primarily as a historian, of course. As a longtime journalist, he turned to writing "popular" history with *Detroit Is My Home Town.*

Chapter 3. Debi and Susan: Changing Schooling, Changing Lives

1. David Bloome, former assistant professor of education at the University of Michigan, now at the University of Massachusetts, Amherst, is a mutual friend who had done ethnographic research into writing instruction in Toby's classroom at Burton International School in Detroit.

2. The troubling fact of some of our "limited expectations" for Couzens students has its sources in notions of academic reputation and our knowledge of students' experience with writing. The majority of our students in the Dewey program attended Burton International School, many of them having been students in Debi Goodman's or Toby Curry's classes. Burton, located just a few blocks from the Dewey Center, is a magnet school with a strong academic reputation, enhanced by a strong emphasis on writing, particularly in classes. Many of the students from Burton who joined the program "already saw themselves as writers," Debi told me. Couzens had a less strong reputation in the Detroit Public School system, and teachers, including Jeanetta Cotman, admitted to us that many teachers in the school had put less emphasis on writing than they might have.

3. Bell hooks writes about the importance of speaking one's beliefs: "It is that act of speech, of talking back, that is no mere gesture of empty words, that is the expression of our movement from object to subject—the liberated voice. . . . It should be understood that the liberatory voice will necessarily confront, disturb, demand that listeners even alter ways of hearing and being" (9, 16).

4. Camille Ryan's "The Other Side of the Projects" (*Corridors* 16) focuses on a young woman, Jody Simpson, who has graduated from college and who has returned to visit Rose Bell and other residents of the projects. Jody speaks standard English in her various encounters with residents, who sometimes speak in what Susan might call a "community dialect," as in the following example: "Boy I sho' do hate to stand in that rain for the bus." "Don't be silly. I'll drive you in my car," I said. (*Corridors* 21)

Chapter 4. Dana and George: Valuing Each Student's Way of Knowing

1. I team-taught the "Professional Semester," a four-course English teacher preparation sequence in fall 1988 with Anne Ruggles Gere, Alan Howes, Colleen Fairbanks, and Laura Roop. I have written about Dana elsewhere with Colleen Fairbanks and Laura Roop, as part of a series of case studies of student teachers, in "Developing Teacher Empowerment: Case Studies of Teacher Research," a manuscript as yet unpublished.

2. In the Huron Shores Summer Writing Program, where George and I had worked, high school student representatives were part of daily planning meetings with teachers. In planning the first summer of the Dewey program, George and I wanted to include students in "teacher" meetings. All teachers agreed that this idea was consistent with our program, and it became part of our overall plan. For the first two days of the program, students were invited to the afternoon planning meetings, but teachers, feeling a need to talk about certain issues without students, agreed to regularly elicit student perspectives in large group meetings attended by students and teachers.

CHAPTER 5. DORA: COLLABORATIVE MYTH MAKING, TEACHING, AND LEARNING

1. "961-BABY" is presented here in its entirety as it appeared in *Corridors: Stories from Inner City Detroit.* Elsewhere in the chapter, various drafts are interspersed, following the analysis of my interviews with Dora and my colleagues. Though the drafts are presented chronologically, I do not intend a necessary relationship between the text of the interview and the draft that follows it. The drafts are placed throughout the chapter for aesthetic as much as any other reason, though I also want to convey the fact, as should be clear from the interview transcripts, that Dora developed her texts over several days, with the help of many readers. Attention was focused during the writing project on the process of student writing, and not just the products.

Because some teachers discuss it, I also include Dora's poem, "I Am a Cat."

2. Though it is not my primary purpose in this chapter to do a close analysis of the intertextual dimensions of "961-BABY," the texts of the interviews that follow this section should reveal the extent to which Dora has been influenced in her writing by particular teachers and peers.

3. As one reader pointed out to me, skeptical of my seemingly uncritical embrace of narrative, Nazi leader Joseph Goebbels wrote a novel. Obviously, there is no necessary humanizing function of art, whether that art is in narrative form or otherwise. I don't want to suggest that any form is necessarily liberating or antiauthoritarian, but I do want to point out that narrative seems to me to be associated with these tendencies. Paul Gee speaks of an "effacement of individual differences" that takes place in the making of "essayist" texts, the texts that dominate most schooling. And, as he points out, "Essay-text literacy . . . is connected with the forms of consciousness and the interests of the powerful in our society" (742). Whether or not one can altogether accept this view, it does seem that forms like the five-paragraph essay are consistent with the apparently efficient, neatly packaged "knowledge" that dominates so much schooling.

4. The findings of the Holmes Report are much like the reports in Theodore Sizer (1985), Ernest Boyer (1983), and John Goodlad (1984).

5. An excerpt from Camille Ryan's story, "Miss Rose Bell" can be found in chapter 1.

6. "From Detroit to Ann Arbor," Tameka Sandifer:

We walked, me, Kee-Kee, Lanette, Carolyn, Dora, and Kimberly and Justin (my cousins). We saw Farrah leaving her mother; we were all at school.

"Oops, I forgot my money," I said, so me, Farrah and her mother rushed back home, because no one was at school but Mrs. Cotman. I went to my house, unlocked the door.

"Tameka, is that you?" my grandma said.

"Yes, it is."

"So what is it?"

"I need some money."

So she gave me three dollars, then we rushed back to school. Everyone was there, but not the bus. But finally the bus was there. The bus driver did not know the way to the train station so Mrs. Cotman gave her some directions.

We were finally at the train station. We got on the train. We sat down. Carolyn was glued to her seat, me and Farrah laughing. Mrs. Curry was telling jokes, people were laughing at them; people were walking on the train, but not Carolyn. She would not move.

Finally we were in Ann Arbor; they had a lot of trees, people and everything. First we went to a football stadium and Dave said it was one of the largest ones in the world. It had eighty stairs. I only made it to seventy-five, but Farrah made it to number eighty, then we had to go.

We went to the basketball arena and went up some more stairs. We tried to find a bathroom. When we found one it was "Peau!" but Carolyn sprayed some perfume. And it was dark. She turned on her lighter; there was no light switch. Someone closed the door; we screamed; they opened it back up. Dana went to find a bathroom. I went back downstairs and started to drink some pop. Then we all left the basketball arena.

After we left the basketball arena we got on a bus and we did not even have to pay. We got off at a museum. We went inside and went in a gift shop. Things cost too much. We went upstairs, we saw old dinosaur bones and other neat stuff. We came back downstairs; finally it was time to eat. We went to a place like The Sweet House: all you can eat. I had a fruit plate, meat, corn chips with melted cheese, a lot of pop, and I had ice cream with chocolate syrup. Then we left the food bar.

We went in a classroom at the U of M. Some of us read stories and then it was time to come home. We had a great time. (*Corridors* 102)

7. See p. 167. The draft appears very much like a play.

8. As I mentioned early on, one of my initial ideas was to explore how each teacher learned from the others in the process of teaching together, to explore the intertextual dimensions of each teacher's stories. As this chapter in particular makes clear, whereas I do attempt to, among other things, illustrate the value of teachers' narratives for learning about teaching, my emphasis has been on how my colleagues' stories shaped *my* stories about eating on the street.

I plan to conduct a "follow-up" study to this one to explore the ways in which *all* of my fellow teachers' stories of experience have been informed by each others' stories in the process of collaborative teaching.

9. My written story of Dora evolved from 1989 to 1993 and is based in part on comments from teachers and Dora herself. When this book was first written, Dora was just beginning seventh grade. As it goes to press, Dora is an eleventh-grade student at Murray Wright High School. Dora saw many versions of the text and commented on them variously, though in 1989 she probably was less able to understand the possible implications of what it might mean to be represented. In the summer of 1993, I spoke with her and her mother, Lanette, by phone several times, and they gave me permission to share the following information about Dora.

I asked Dora how her first year of high school had gone, and she was positive: "Good! I like it. My grades are going up. They *keep* going up." Her mother proudly agreed: She's doing A/B work!" When I asked how she did in English class, she replied, "It was OK. We did a lot of reading of literature in there, more than writing, at least. That's what I like to do, you know, is write, but we didn't write very much."

Dora had a successful year in track, too, running the 400 meter, 800 meter, and the mile, and placed fifth in the state tournament in the 800 as a tenth grader. She plans to try out for the volleyball team in the upcoming school year.

Dora was again a participant in the Dewey Center Community Writing Project in the summer of 1990, where she published her writing in another student publication, *Reflections: Expressions from Inner City Detroit.* In the summer of 1992 she enrolled in a journalism program, so I asked her what she had done connected with writing in the summer of 1993. She replied, "I did Explorers, which is a Detroit law enforcement camp."

"So are you planning to become a Detroit policewoman?" I said.

"No, I just was interested in the program and learning more about what they do. We learned how to do 'search and seizures,' for instance. It was very interesting. But no, I am planning to become a veterinarian so I can take care of animals here in the Jeffries Homes. We have a lot of animals that need taking care of in my neighborhood, and I like animals, so I'd like to do that. They supposedly have a very good program in veterinary medicine at the University of Michigan, so I'm going to try for that."

I do not mean to suggest that one three-week summer writing program in 1989 might have changed Dora's life. Then again, as Lanette shared with me, "Who knows? Maybe it was that writing project that really got her going. I've always been involved with my kids' schooling. I keep getting my kids into these programs and seeing if they'll get interested! I took Justin and Sherman [Dora's younger brother and sister] to visit Dora this summer at Explorers, and they seemed really interested. We'll see!"

10. As I have discussed elsewhere, seeing the transcripts of the conversations was somewhat disconcerting for many teachers. That the informal conversation we had shared was now "fixed" in something like a story—instead of a form such as an essay—only slightly alleviated a certain understandable anxiety some teachers initially had. I attempt in my story to give the impression of provisionality, but the temporary, ethereal nature of talk is still lent a certain permanence here.

This anxiety about the "fixity" of writing extends to my own writing through the many months I invested in this manuscript. With each draft I shifted emphasis in particular sections, influenced by the voices I continued to read, and influenced as well by the helpful responses from those readers. My view, my intellectual perspective, inevitably shifts in certain ways and I am well aware that my views, just as my Dewey colleagues' views, will be somewhat different by the time this text is published.

11. See John VanManen who explores a variety of ways one can use stories in research. Max VanManen, in addition to validating what some people are now calling "narrative inquiry," also gives a fine introduction to "critical phenomenology," a philosophical basis for research that is grounded in both participants' lived world and critical theory. See also Nel Noddings and Carol Witherell's fine collection of stories and essays on the uses of narrative in educational research.

12. Other important contributions to the understanding of curriculum and narrative are F. Michael Connelly and D. Jean Clandinin (1988) and Janet Miller (1990). Working with a conception they call "personal practical knowledge," Connelly and Clandinin emphasize reflective practice and the knowledge and expertise teachers already have for the purpose of curriculum planning and learning about teaching. Miller and her colleagues articulate and question the contexts and assumptions that influence and and frame teaching practice as they explore the constraints and the possibilties of defining and thus empowering teachers as teacher-researchers. In both of these studies the changing and multiple voices of teachers is clearly heard.

BIBLIOGRAPHY

Agar, Michael. *The Professional Stranger.* New York: Academic Press, 1980.

Anderson, Elijah. *Streetwise: Race, Class, and Change in an Urban Community.* Chicago: University of Chicago Press, 1990.

Anson, Robert Lee. *Best Intentions: The Education and Killing of Edmund Perry.* New York: MacMillan, 1984.

Apple, Michael. *Education and Power.* Boston: Routledge and Kegan Paul, 1982.

Aronowitz, Stanley, and Henry Giroux. *Education Under Siege: The Conservative, Liberal, and Radical Debate Over Schooling.* Boston: Bergin and Harvey, 1985.

Artaud, Antonin. *The Theater and Its Double.* New York: Grove Press, 1958.

Atkinson, Paul. *The Ethnographic Imagination: Textual Constructions of Reality.* New York: Routledge and Kegan Paul, 1990.

Atwell, Nancie. *In the Middle: Writing, Reading, and Learning with Adolescents.* Portsmouth, N.H.: Heinemann, 1987.

Bakhtin, Mikhail. *The Dialogic Imagination.* Ed. Caryl Emerson and Michael Holquist. Austin: University of Texas Press, 1981.

Barritt, Loren, Hans Bleeker, Ton Beekman, and Karel Mulderij. *Researching Educational Practice.* Grand Forks, N.D.: University of North Dakota Press, 1985.

Bartholomae, David, and Anthony Petrosky. *Facts, Artifacts, and Counterfacts.* Portsmouth, N.H.: Boynton/Cook, 1987.

Becker, Alton. "Entering Another Aesthetic." Presentation, University of Michigan, March 20, 1988.

Berger, Peter L. and Thomas Luckmann. *The Social Construction of Reality: A Treatise in the Sociology of Knowledge.* New York: Doubleday, 1966.

Bingay, Malcolm, *Detroit Is My Own Home Town.* Detroit: Hamer, 1946.

Bird, Lois Bridges, ed. *Becoming a Whole Language School: The Fair Oaks Story.* Katonah, N.Y.: Richard Owen, 1989.

Booth, Wayne. "Freedom of Interpretation." In *The Politics of Interpretation,* ed. W. J. T. Mitchell, pp. 51–82. Chicago: University of Chicago Press, 1986.

Boyer, Ernest L. *High School: A Report on Secondary Education in America.* New York: Harper and Row, 1983.

Britzman, Deborah P. "Cultural Myths in the Making of a Teacher: Biography and Social Structure in Teacher Education." *Harvard Educational Review* 56 (1986):442–72.

Bruffee, Kenneth. "Collaborative Learning and the 'Conversation of Mankind.'" *College English* 46 (1984):635–52.

Bruner, Jerome. *Acts of Meaning.* Cambridge: Harvard University Press, 1990.

———. *Actual Minds, Possible Worlds.* Cambridge: Harvard University Press, 1986.

Bryant, Tim, ed. *Focus on Collaborative Learning.* Urbana, Ill.: NCTE, 1988.

Calkins, Lucy. *Lessons from a Child: On the Teaching and Learning of Writing.* Portsmouth: Heinemann, 1983.

Cass, Lewis. "The History, Traditions, Languages, Manners, Customs and Religions of Indians Living Within the United States." Pamphlet.

Cassirer, Ernest. *Language and Myth.* New York: Harper and Brothers, 1946.

Chambers, Ross. *Story and Situation: Narrative Seduction and the Power of Fiction.* Chicago: University of Chicago Press, 1984.

Chomsky, Noam. *American Power and the New Mandarins.* New York: Pantheon Books, 1969.

Clark, Michael. "Evaluating Writing in an Academic Setting." In *fforum: Essays on Theory and Practice in the Teaching of Writing;* ed. Patricia L. Stock. pp. 59–78. Portsmouth, N.H.: Boynton/Cook, 1983.

Clifford, James, and George Marcus, eds. *Writing Culture: The Poetics and Politics of Ethnography.* Berkeley and Los Angeles: University of California Press, 1988.

Coles, Robert. *The Call of Stories: Teaching and the Moral Imagination.* Boston: Houghton Mifflin, 1989.

———. *Children of Crisis: A Study of Courage and Fear.* New York: Little, Brown, 1967.

Connelly, F. Michael, and D. Jean Clandinin. *Teachers as Curriculum Planners: Narratives of Experience.* New York: Teachers College Press, 1988.

Cooper, Marilyn M., and Michael Holzman. *Writing as Social Action.* Portsmouth: Heinemann, 1989.

Cremin, Lawrence. *The Transformation of the School: Progressivism in American Education.* New York: Random House, 1961.

Daniels, Harvey A., ed. *Not Only English: Affirming America's Multilingual Heritage.* Urbana, Ill.: NCTE, 1990.

Darnton, Robert. *The Great Cat Massacre: And Other Episodes in French Cultural History.* New York: Basic Books, 1984.

Davis, Angela. "Radical Perspectives on the Empowerment of Afro-American Women: Lessons for the 1980's." *Harvard Educational Review* 58 (1988):348–53.

Delpit, Lisa D. "The Silenced Dialogue: Power and Pedagogy in Educating Other People's Children." *Harvard Educational Review* 58 (1988):280–98.

———. "Skills and Other Dilemmas of a Progressive Black Educator." *Harvard Educational Review* 56 (1986):379–85.

Derrida, Jacques. *Of Grammatology.* Trans. Gayatri Chakravorty Spivak. Baltimore: The Johns Hopkins University Press, 1976.

Detroit Public Schools. *Detroit, Wayne County, and Michigan: A Story for Children.* Detroit: The Board of Education of the City of Detroit, 1955.

"Detroit Tragedy." *Washington Post,* July 25, 1967, 7.

Dewey, John. *Democracy and Education.* New York: Collier, 1916.

——. *Experience and Education.* New York: Collier, 1938.

——. *The School and Society.* New York: Collier, 1899.

The Dewey Center Community Writing Project, 1989. *Corridors: Stories from Inner City Detroit.* Ann Arbor: The Center for Educational Improvement through Collaboration, 1989.

Didion, Joan. *The White Album.* New York: Farrar, Straus and Giroux, 1977.

Disbrow, Donald W. *Schools for an Urban Society.* Lansing, Mich.: Michigan Historical Commission, 1968.

Donaldson, Margaret. *Children's Minds.* New York: Norton, 1978.

Eagleton, Terry. *Literary Theory: An Introduction.* Minneapolis: University of Minnesota Press, 1983.

——. *Marxism and Literary Criticism.* Berkeley and Los Angeles: University of California Press, 1976.

Egan, Kieran. "Literacy and the Oral Foundations of Education." *Harvard Educational Review* 57: (1987):445–72.

——. *Teaching as Storytelling: An Approach to Teaching and Curriculum in the Elementary School.* Chicago: University of Chicago Press, 1986.

Elbow, Peter. *Writing Without Teachers.* London: Oxford University Press, 1973.

Ellsworth, Elizabeth. "Why Doesn't This Feel Empowering? Working through the Repressive Myths of Critical Pedagogy." *Harvard Educational Review* 59: (1989):297–324.

Erickson, Frederick. "Tasks in Times: Objects of Study in a Natural History of Teaching." In *Improving Teaching;* ed. K. K. Zumwalt, pp. 131–47. Alexandria, Va.: Association for Supervision and Curriculum Development, 1986.

Ezekiel, Raphael. S. *Voices from the Corner: Poverty and Racism in the Inner City.* Philadelphia: Temple University Press, 1984.

Fine, Michelle. *Framing Dropouts: Notes on the Politics of an Urban High School.* Albany: State University of New York Press, 1991.

Fine, Sidney. *Violence in the Model City: The Cavanaugh Administration, Race Relations, and the Detroit Riot of 1967.* Ann Arbor: The University of Michigan Press, 1989.

Fish, Stanley. *Is There a Text in This Class? The Authority of Interpretive Communities.* Cambridge: Harvard University Press, 1980.

Fishman, Andrea. *Amish Literacy: What and How It Means.* Portsmouth, N.H.: Heinemann, 1988.

Fordham, Signithia. "Racelessness as a Factor in Black Students' School Success: Pragmatic Strategy or Pyrrhic Victory?" *Harvard Educational Review* 58: (1988):54–84.

Foucault, Michel. *Discipline and Punish: The Birth of the Prison.* Trans. Alan Sheridan. New York: Random House, 1975.

———. "Interview with Lucette Finas." In *Michel Foucault: Power, Truth, Strategy.* ed. M. Morris and P. Patton. Sydney: Feral Publications, 1979.

———. "Questions of Method." *Ideology and Consciousness* 8 (1981):11.

———. *Madness and Civilization: A History of Insanity in the Age of Reason.* Trans. Richard Howard. New York: Random House, 1965.

———. *Power/Knowledge.* Trans. and ed. Colin Gordon. New York: Pantheon, 1980.

Freire, Paolo. *Education for Critical Consciousness.* Trans. and ed. Myra Bergman Ramos. New York: Continuum, 1973.

———. *Pedagogy of the Oppressed.* Trans. Myra Bergman Ramos. New York: Seabury, 1970.

Gadamer, Hans-Georg. *Philosophical Hermeneutics.* Trans. David E. Linge. Berkeley and Los Angeles: University of California Press, 1976.

———. *Truth and Method.* Trans. Garrett Barden. New York: Crossroads, 1960.

Gates, Henry Louis. "Narration and Cultural Memory in the African-American Tradition." In *Talk That Talk: An Anthology of African American Storytelling,* pp. 15–19. New York: Simon and Schuster, 1989.

Gee, James Paul. "Orality and Literacy: From *The Savage Mind* to *Ways With Words,*" *TESOL Quarterly* 20 (1986):719–46.

Geertz, Clifford. *The Interpretation of Cultures.* New York: Basic Books, 1973.

———. *Local Knowledge.* New York: Basic Books, 1983.

———. *Works and Lives: The Anthropologist as Author.* Stanford: Stanford University Press, 1988.

Genette, Gerard. *Narrative Discourse: An Essay in Method.* Trans. Jane Lewin. Ithaca, N.Y.: Cornell University Press, 1980.

Gere, Anne Ruggles. *Writing Groups: History, Theory, and Implications.* Carbondale, Ill.: Southern Illinois University Press, 1987.

Giroux, Henry A. *Teachers as Intellectuals: Toward a Critical Pedagogy of Learning.* Boston: Bergin and Harvey, 1988.

Glassie, Henry. *Passing the Time in Ballymenone: The Culture and History of an Ulster Community.* Philadelphia: University of Pennsylvania Press, 1982.

Golub, Jeff, ed. *Focus on Collaborative Learning: Classroom Practices in Teaching English, 1988.* Urbana, Ill.: National Council of Teachers of English, 1988.

Goodlad, John I. *A Place Called School: Promise for the Future.* New York: McGraw Hill, 1984.

Goodman, Ken. *What's Whole in Whole Language?* Portsmouth, N.H.: Heinemann, Inc. 1986.

Goss, Linda and Marian Barnes, eds. *Talk That Talk: An Anthology of African-American Storytelling.* New York: Simon and Schuster, 1989.

Goswami, Dixie and Peter R. Stillman, eds. *Reclaiming the Classroom: Teacher Research as an Agency for Change.* Upper Montclair, N.J.: Boynton-Cook, 1987.

Greene, Maxine. *The Dialectic of Freedom.* New York: Teachers College Press, 1988.

———. *Landscapes of Learning.* New York: Teachers College Press, 1978.

Gunn, Giles. *Thinking Across the American Grain: Ideology, Intellect, and the New Pragmatism.* Chicago: University of Chicago Press, 1992.

Habermas, Jurgen. *Knowledge and Human Interests.* Trans. Jeremy Shapiro. Boston: Beacon Press, 1971.

Hale-Benson, Janice E. *Black Children: Their Roots, Culture and Learning Styles.* Baltimore: Johns Hopkins UP, 1986.

Hardy, Barbara. "Towards a Poetics of Fiction: An Approach Through Narrative." In *The Cool Web: The Patterns of Children's Reading,* ed. Margaret Meek, Aidan Warlow, and Griselda Barton. New York: Atheneum, 1978.

Healy, Mary K. *Using Student Writing Response Groups in the Classroom.* Berkeley: University of California Bay Area Writing Project, 1980.

Heath, Shirley Brice. *Ways with Words: Language, Life, and Work in Communities and Classrooms.* Cambridge: Cambridge University Press, 1983.

Heidegger, Martin. *Poetry, Language and Thought.* Trans. Albert Hofstadter. New York: Harper and Row, 1971.

Hempel, Amy, "In the Cemetery Where Al Jolson Is Buried." In *Reasons to Live,* ed. Amy Hempel. New York: Knopf, 1985.

Hidalgo, Nitza M., Ceasar L. McDowell, and Emilie V. Siddle, eds. *Facing Racism in Education.* Cambridge: Harvard Educational Review, 1990.

Himley, Margaret. " 'Deep Talk' and Descriptive Knowledge." Paper/ Presented at College Conference on Composition and Communication, March, 1989, Seattle, Wash.

Holmes Group Report. *Tomorrow's Teachers.* East Lansing, Mich.: The Holmes Group, 1986.

hooks, bell. *Feminist Theory: From Margins to Center.* New York: Schocken, 1984.

———. *Talking Back: Thinking Feminist, Thinking Black.* Boston: South End Press, 1989.

Horton, Myles. *The Long Haul.* New York: Doubleday, 1990.

Horton, Myles, and Paolo Freire. *We Make the Road by Walking: Conversations on Education and Social Change.* Ed. Brenda Bell, John Gaventa, and John Peters. Philadelphia: Temple University Press, 1991.

Hughes, Langston. "Aunt Sue's Stories." In *Talk That Talk: An Anthology of African-American Storytelling;* Ed. Linda Goss and Marian Barnes. New York: Simon and Schuster, 1989, 291.

The Huron Shores Summer Writing Institute. *Breakwall.* Rogers City, Mich.: The Huron Shores Summer Writing Institute, 1990.

Jaggar, Angela, and Trika Smith-Burke, eds. *Observing the Language Learner.* Urbana, Ill.: NCTE, 1985.

Jameson, Frederic. *The Political Unconscious.* Ithaca, N.Y.: Cornell University Press, 1981.

Kail, Harvey. "Collaborative Learning in Context: The Problem with Peer Tutoring." *College English* 45 (1983):594–99.

Kamberelis, George. "Intertextuality, Identity, and the Development of Voice in Adolescent Writing." Paper presented at the International Summer Institute for Semiotic and Structural Studies. Evanston, Illinois (July, 1986).

Karris, Bill. "Conflict in Collaboration: A Burkean Perspective." *Rhetoric Review* 8 (1989):113–25.

Katzman, David M. *Before the Ghetto: Black Detroit in the Nineteenth Century.* Urbana, Ill.: University of Illinois Press, 1973.

Keenan, Marney Rich. "Faith, Hope, and Charity." *Detroit News.* November 19, 1989, pp. 3–4.

Kendall, Laurel. *The Life and Hard Times of a Korean Shaman: Of Tales and the Telling of Tales.* Honolulu: University of Hawaii Press, 1988.

Kent, Thomas. "Paralogic Hermeneutics and the Possibilities of Rhetoric." *Rhetoric Review 8* (1989):24–42.

Kintgen, Eugene R., Barry M. Kroll and Mike Rose, eds. *Perspectives on Literacy.* Carbondale: Southern Illinois University Press, 1988.

Knoblauch, Cy and Lil Brannon. *Rhetorical Traditions and the Teaching of Writing.* Upper Montclair, N.J.: Boynton/Cook, 1984.

Knowles, J. Gary. "A Beginning Teacher's Experience: Reflections on Becoming a Teacher." *Language Arts* 7 (1988):206–23.

Kohl, Herbert. *Thirty-Six Children.* New York: Signet, 1967.

Kotlowitz, Alex. *There Are No Children Here: The Story of Two Boys Growing Up in the Other America.* New York: Doubleday, 1991.

Kozol, Jonathan. *Illiterate America.* New York: Doubleday, 1985.

———. *Savage Inequalities: Children in America's Schools.* New York: Crown, 1991.

Kundera, Milan. *The Art of the Novel.* Trans. Linda Asher. New York: Grove Press. 1986.

Labov, William. *Language in the Inner City.* Philadelphia: University of Pennsylvania Press, 1972.

Ladner, Joyce. "Introduction to *Tomorrow's Tomorrow: The Black Woman.*" In *Feminism and Methodology.* Ed. Sandra Harding. pp. 74–83. Bloomington: Indiana University Press, 1987.

Langer, Suzanne K. *Philosophy in a New Key.* Cambridge: Harvard University Press, 1942.

Lanker, Brian. *I Dream a World: Portraits of Black Women Who Change America.* New York: Stewart, Tabori, and Chang, 1989.

Lather, Patti. *Getting Smart: Feminist Research and Pedagogy With/In the Postmodern.* New York: Routledge, 1991.

―――. "Research as Praxis." *Harvard Educational Review* 56 (1986): 257–77.

Lefevre, Karen Burke. *Invention as a Social Act.* Carbondale, Ill.: Southern Illinois University Press, 1987.

Lejeune, Phillipe. *On Autobiography.* Trans. Katherine Leary. Minneapolis: Minnesota University Press, 1989.

Levi-Strauss, Claude. *Myth and Meaning.* New York: Schocken Books, 1979.

Lewis, C. S. "Bluspels and Flalansferes." In *Rehabilitations and Other Essays.* Cambridge: Oxford University Press, 1939. 204–16.

Limon, Jose E. "Carnes, Carnales, and the Carnivalesque: Bakhtinian Batos, Disorder, and Narrative Discourses." Photocopy. University of California, Santa Cruz, 1987.

Lopez, Barry. *Arctic Dreams.* New York: Scribner's, 1986.

―――. *Crossing Open Ground.* New York: Scribner's, 1988.

―――. *Of Wolves and Men.* New York: Scribner's, 1982.

Lunsford, Andrea A., Helen Moglen, and James Slevin, eds. *The Right to Literacy.* New York: Modern Language Association, 1990.

Lyotard, Jean-Francois. *The Postmodern Condition: A Report on Knowledge.* Trans. Geoff Bennington and Brian Massumi. Minneapolis: University of Minnesota Press, 1984.

Macrorie, Ken. *Uptaught.* New York: Hayden, 1970.

Maeroff, Gene I. *The Empowerment of Teachers: Overcoming the Crisis of Confidence.* New York: Teachers College Press, 1988.

Malinowski, Bronislaw. *A Diary in the Strict Sense of the Term.* Trans. Norman Guterman. Stanford: Stanford University Press, 1989.

Martin, Wallace. *Recent Theories of Narrative.* Ithaca, N.Y.: Cornell University Press, 1986.

Mayhew, Katherine Camp, and Ann Camp Edwards. *The Dewey School.* New York: Collier, 1936.

Meyerhoff, Barbara. *Number Our Days.* New York: Simon and Schuster, 1978.

Miller, Janet L. *Creating Spaces and Finding Voices: Teachers Collaborating for Empowerment.* Albany: State University of New York Press, 1990.

Mishler, Elliot. *Research Interviewing: Context and Narrative.* London: Cambridge University Press, 1986.

Mitchell, W. J. T., ed. *On Narrative.* Chicago: University of Chicago Press, 1981.

―――. *The Politics of Interpretation.* Chicago: University of Chicago Press, 1986.

Moraga, Cherrie, and Gloria Anzaldua, eds. *This Bridge Called My Back: Writings by Radical Women of Color.* Latham, N.Y.: Women of Color Press, 1983.

Morgan, Robin, ed. "Introduction." In *Sisterhood Is Powerful: An Anthology of Writings from the Women's Liberation Movement,* pp. xv–xlvi. New York: Vintage, 1970.

Morrison, Toni. *Beloved.* New York: Knopf, 1987.

Myers, Greg. "Reality, Consensus and Reform in the Rhetoric of Composition Teaching." *College English* 48 (1986):154–74.

Newkirk, Thomas. "Direction and Misdirection in Peer Response." *College Composition and Communication* 35 (1984):300–11.

Noddings, Nel, and Carol Witherell, eds. *Stories Lives Tell: Narrative and Dialogue in Education.* New York: Teachers College Press, 1991.

Oakes, Jeannie. *Keeping Track: How Schools Structure Inequality.* New Haven: Yale University Press, 1985.

O'Flaherty, Wendy Doniger. *Other People's Myths.* New York: MacMillan, 1988.

Ohmann, Richard. "Graduate Students, Professionals, Intellectuals." *College English* 52 (1990):247–57.

Ong, Walter. *Orality and Literacy: The Technologizing of the Word.* New York: Methuen, 1982.

Paley, Vivian. *The Boy Who Would Be a Helicopter: The Uses of Storytelling in the Classroom.* Cambridge: Harvard University Press, 1990.

———. *White Teacher.* Cambridge: Harvard University Press, 1989.

Patterson, Orlando. "Rethinking Black History." *African Report* 17 (1989):29–31.

Polakow, Valerie. "Whose Stories Should We Tell? Critical Phenomenology as a Call to Action." *Language Arts* 62: (1985:1–16.

Polanyi, Michael. *Personal Knowledge: Towards a Post-Critical Philosophy.* Chicago: University of Chicago Press, 1962.

Price, Richard. *First-Time: The Historical Vision of an Afro-American People.* Baltimore: Johns Hopkins University Press, 1983.

Punch, Maurice. *The Politics and Ethics of Fieldwork.* London: Sage, 1986.

Rabinow, Paul. *Reflecting on Fieldwork in Morocco.* Berkeley and Los Angeles: University of California Press, 1973.

Reid, Ian. *The Making of Literature.* New York: Routledge, 1990.

Rich, Adrienne. "Notes Toward a Politics of Location," In *Women, Feminist Identity, and Society in the 1980's.* Ed. Myriam Diaz-Diacaretz and Iris Zavata. pp. 7–22. Amsterdam/Philadelphia: John Benjamins, 1985.

Riffatere, Michael. *Fictional Truth.* Baltimore: Johns Hopkins University Press, 1990.

Robinson, Beverly. "Historical Arenas of African-American Storytelling." In *Talk That Talk: An Anthology of African-American Storytelling.* Ed. Linda Goss and Marian Barnes, pp. 211–16. New York: Simon and Schuster, 1989.

Robinson, Jay. *Conversations on the Written Word: Essays on Language and Literacy.* Portsmouth, N.H.: Heinemann, 1990.

Robinson, Jay, and Patricia Stock. "The Politics of Literacy." In *Conversations on the Written Word: Essays on Language and Literacy,* ed. Jay Robinson, pp. 271–317. Portsmouth, N.H.: Heinemann, 1990.

Romano, Tom. *Clearing the Way: Working with Teenage Writers.* Portsmouth, N.H.: Heinemann, 1987.

Rorty, Richard. *Contingency, Irony, and Solidarity.* Cambridge: Cambridge University Press, 1989.

Rose, Mike. *Lives on the Boundary: The Struggles and Achievements of America's Underprepared.* New York: MacMillan, 1989.

Rosen, Betty. *And None of It Was Nonsense: The Power of Storytelling in School.* Portsmouth, N.H.: Heinemann, 1988.

Rosen, Harold. *Stories and Meanings.* London: NATE Publications, 1982.

Said, Edward. "Opponents, Audiences, Constituencies, and Community." In *The Politics of Interpretation,* ed. W. J. T. Mitchell, pp. 7–32. Chicago: University of Chicago Press, 1986.

Schaafsma, David. "Gilbert and Dave's Stories: Narrative and Knowing." *English Journal* 78 (1989):89–91.

———. "Lillie Dancing." *Language Arts* 67 (1990):116–27.

Schaafsma, David, Colleen Fairbanks, and Laura Roop. "Developing Teacher Empowerment: Case Studies of Teacher Research." Unpublished manuscript. University of Michigan, 1989.

Schafer, Roy. *A New Language for Psychoanalysis.* New Haven, Conn.: Yale University Press, 1976.

Scott, Hugh. "Urban School Districts and How We Can Create Effective Education Within Those Schools." Presentation, University of Michigan, October 27, 1989.

Shank, Roger. *Tell Me a Story: A New Look at Real and Artificial Memory.* New York: Scribner's, 1990.

Shapiro, Michael. *Language and Political Understanding: The Politics of Discursive Practices.* London: Yale University Press, 1981.

Shor, Ira., ed. *Critical Teaching and Everyday Life.* Boston: South End Press, 1980.

———. *Freire for the Classroom: A Sourcebook for Liberatory Teaching.* Portsmouth, N.H.: Heinemann, 1987.

Shor, Ira, and Paolo Freire. *A Pedagogy for Liberation: Dialogues on Transformation.* Boston: Bergin and Harvey, 1987.

Shuman, Amy. *Storytelling Rights: The Uses of Oral and Written Texts by Urban Adolescents.* London: Cambridge University Press, 1986.

Silko, Leslie Marmon. *Ceremony.* New York: Knopf, 1978.

———. *Storyteller.* New York: Seaver Books, 1981.

Sizer, Theodore R. *Horace's Compromise: The Dilemma of the American High School.* Boston: Houghton Mifflin, 1985.

Sledd, James. "Anglo-Conformity: Folk Remedy for Lost Hegemony." In *Not Only English: Affirming America's Multilingual Heritage,* ed. Harvey A. Daniels, pp. 85–95. Urbana, Ill.: NCTE, 1990.

Smith, Barbara, ed. *Home Girls: A Black Feminist Anthology.* Latham, N.Y.: Women of Color Press, 1983.

Smitherman, Geneva. *Talkin and Testifyin: The Language of Black America.* Detroit: Wayne State University Press, 1977.

Spivak, Gayatri. *In Other Worlds: Essays in Cultural Politics.* New York: Methuen, 1987.

———. *The Post-Colonial Critic: Interviews, Strategies, Dialogues.* New York: Routledge, 1990.

Spradley, James. *You Owe Yourself a Drunk: An Ethnography of Urban Nomads.* Boston: Little, Brown, 1970.

Stenhouse, Lawrence. *Research as a Basis for Teaching.* London: Heinemann, 1985.

Stock, Patricia Lambert. "The Dialogic Curriculum: Students and Teachers Researching Together." Photocopy, 1991.

———. *The Teacher as Researcher: Rethinking the Discursive Practices of Education.* Ph.D. diss., University of Michigan, 1987.

Stock, Patricia Lambert, ed. *fforum: Essays on Theory and Practice in the Teaching of Writing.* Portsmouth, N.H.: Boynton/Cook, 1983.

Stock, Patricia, and Jay Robinson. "Literacy as Conversation: Classroom Talk as Text Building. In *Conversations on the Written Word: Essays on Language and Literacy,* ed. Jay Robinson, pp. 163–238. Portsmouth, N.H.: Heinemann, 1990.

Taylor, Denny. "Teaching Without Testing: Assessing the Complexity of Children's Literacy Learning." *English Education* 22: (1990):4–74.

Taylor, Denny, and Catherine Dorsey-Gaines. *Growing Up Literate: Learning from Inner-City Families.* Portsmouth, N.H.: Heinemann, 1988.

Thompson, Clara Jane. Interview with author. Detroit, Mich., 24 September 1989.

Todorov, Tzvetan. *The Poetics of Prose.* Trans. Richard Howard. Ithaca, N.Y.: Cornell University Press, 1977.

Trimbur, John. "Collaborative Learning and Teaching Writing." In *Perspectives on Research and Scholarship in Composition.* ed. Ben McClelland and Timothy Donovan, pp. 87–109. New York: Modern Language Association, 1985.

———. "Consensus and Difference in Collaborative Learning." *College English* 51: (1989):234–47.

Tyler, Ralph. *Basic Principles of Curriculum and Instruction.* Chicago: University of Chicago Press, 1949.

U.S. Department of Education. *A Nation at Risk: The Imperative for Educational Reform. A Report to the Nation and the Secretary of Education by the National Commission on Excellence in Education.* Washington, D.C.: GPO, 1984, pp. 24–31.

VanManen, John. *Tales of the Field: On Writing Ethnography.* Chicago: University of Chicago Press, 1949.

VanManen, Max. *Researching Lived Experience: Human Science for an Action Sensitive Pedagogy.* London, Ontario: The Althouse Press, 1990.

Volisinov, V. N. *Marxism and the Philosophy of Language.* Trans. Ladislav Matejka and I. R. Titunik. Cambridge: Harvard University Press, 1986.

Vygotsky, Lev. *Thought and Language.* Ed. and trans. Alex Kozulin. Cambridge: MIT Press, 1986.

Walker, Alice. *The Color Purple.* New York: Random House, 1984.

Wells, Gordon. *The Meaning Makers: Children Learning Language and Using Language to Learn.* Portsmouth, N.H.: Heinemann, 1986.

Wertsch, James. *Vygotsky and the Social Formation of Mind.* Cambridge: Harvard University Press, 1985.

White, Hayden. *The Content of the Form.* Baltimore: Johns Hopkins University Press, 1987.

White, James Boyd. *Heracle's Bow: Essays on the Rhetoric and Poetics of the Law.* Madison: University of Wisconsin Press, 1985.

————. *When Words Lose Their Meanings.* Chicago: University of Chicago Press, 1984.

Widick, B. J. *Detroit: City of Race and Class Violence.* Detroit: Wayne State University Press, 1989.

Wigginton, Eliot, ed. *Foxfire 2.* Garden City, N.Y.: Anchor Books, 1973.

Willinsky, John. *The New Literacy: Redefining Reading and Writing in the Schools.* London: Routledge, 1990.

————. *The Well-Tempered Tongue: The Politics of Standard English in the High School.* New York: Teachers College Press, 1988.

Witherell, Carol, and Nel Noddings, ed. *Stories Lives Tell: Narrative and Dialogue in Education.* New York: Teachers College Press, 1991.

Wittgenstein. *Philosophical Investigations.* Trans. G.E.M. Anscombe. New York: Macmillan, 1958.

Woodson, Carter G. *The Miseducation of the Negro.* Washington, D.C.: Associated Press, 1933.

Yaeger, Patricia. *Honey-Mad Women: Emancipatory Strategies in Women's Writing.* New York: Columbia University Press, 1988.

Yolen, Jane, ed. *Favorite Folktales from Around the World.* New York: Pantheon Books, 1986.

Zeichner, Kenneth. "Alternative Paradigms in Teacher Education." *Journal of Teacher Education* 34 (1983):114–27.

Pittsburgh Series in Composition, Literacy, and Culture

David Bartholmae and Jean Ferguson Carr, Editors

Academic Discourse and Critical Consciousness
Patricia Bizzell

Eating on the Street: Teaching Literacy in a
Multicultural Society
David Schaafsma

Fragments of Rationality: Postmodernity and the
Subject of Composition
Lester Faigley

The Insistence of the Letter
Bill Green, Editor

Knowledge, Culture, and Power: International Perspectives
on Literacy as Policy and Practice
Peter Freebody and Anthony R. Welch, Editors

Literacy Online: The Promise (and Peril) of Reading and
Writing with Computers
Myron C. Tuman, Editor

Pre/Text: The First Decade
Victor Vitanza, Editor

Word Perfect: Literacy in the Computer Age
Myron C. Tuman